CAMBRIDGE IBERIAN AND LATIN AMERICAN STUDIES

GENERAL EDITOR

P. E. RUSSELL, F.B.A.

EMERITUS PROFESSOR OF SPANISH STUDIES
UNIVERSITY OF OXFORD

The theatre of Valle-Inclán

CAMBRIDGE IBERIAN AND LATIN AMERICAN STUDIES

already published

STEVEN BOLDY, *The novels of Julio Cortázar*

ROBERT I. BURNS, *Muslims, Christians and Jews in the crusader kingdom of Valencia*

JOHN EDWARDS, *Christian Córdoba: the city and its region in the late middle ages*

MAURICE HEMINGWAY, *Emilia Pardo Bazán: the making of a novelist*

JUAN LÓPEZ-MORILLAS, *The Krausist movement and ideological change in Spain, 1854–1874*

LINDA MARTZ, *Poverty and welfare in Habsburg Spain: the example of Toledo*

JULIÁN OLIVARES, *The love poetry of Francisco de Quevedo: an aesthetic and existential study*

ANTHONY PAGDEN, *The fall of natural man: the American Indian and the growth of historical relativism*

EVELYN S. PROCTER, *Curia and cortes in León and Castile, 1072–1295*

A. C. DE C. M. SAUNDERS, *A social history of black slaves and freedmen in Portugal, 1441–1555*

HENRY W. SULLIVAN, *Calderón in the German lands and the Low Countries: his reception and influence, 1654–1980*

DIANE F. UREY, *Galdós and the irony of language*

DAVID E. VASSBERG, *Land and society in Golden Age Castile*

future titles will include

HEATH DILLARD, *Medieval women in Castilian town society, 1100–1300*

FRANCISCO RICO, *The picaresque novel and the point of view*

The theatre of Valle-Inclán

JOHN LYON

UNIVERSITY OF BRISTOL

CAMBRIDGE UNIVERSITY PRESS

CAMBRIDGE

LONDON   NEW YORK   NEW ROCHELLE

MELBOURNE   SYDNEY

Published by the Press Syndicate of the University of Cambridge
The Pitt Building, Trumpington Street, Cambridge CB2 1RP
32 East 57th Street, New York, NY 10022, USA
296 Beaconsfield Parade, Middle Park, Melbourne 3206, Australia

First published 1983

Printed in Great Britain at
the University Press, Cambridge

Library of Congress catalogue card number: 83-7368

British Library cataloguing in publication data
Lyon, John
The theatre of Valle-Inclán.–(Cambridge
Iberian and Latin American studies)
1. Valle-Inclán, Ramón María del–Criticism
and interpretation
I. Title
862'.5   PQ6641.A47

ISBN 0 521 24493 5

SE

Contents

Illustrations

(between pages 72 and 73)

1 Montenegro surprised by the unexpected arrival of his wife, in a scene from Adolfo Marsillach's production of *Aguila de blasón* (1966)

2 A gathering of Montenegro's degenerate sons in another scene from the same production

3 José Luis Alonso's 1967 production of *La enamorada del rey*

4 Simeón Julepe and La Encamada in a scene from *La rosa de papel*

5 Max Estrella followed by his grotesque shadow, Don Latino, in José Tamayo's production of *Luces de Bohemia* (1971)

6 Scene 11 of *Luces de Bohemia*

7 Nuria Espert as Mari-Gaila in a scene from Víctor García's interpretation of *Divinas palabras* (1977) at the National Theatre, London

Illustrations nos. 1–6 are reproduced by permission of the Centro Nacional de Documentación Teatral, Madrid, and no. 7 by permission of Chris Davies, London.

Acknowledgements

I would like to express my gratitude to the following people and institutions: to Bristol University Travel Fund for financial assistance; to Dr Alison Sinclair for helpful suggestions and constructive criticism of the typescript; to Rosemary Jenkins and Jean Healis for many hours spent in typing out the manuscript and coping with my illegible writing; to my wife for invaluable assistance with the bibliography and index, revision and correction of the manuscript, constant support and inexhaustible patience; and to my children for being so understanding about their father's incomprehensible 'work'.

For Liz, Kate, Susie
and Lucy Jane

Introduction

The mainstream of Spanish theatre in the first three decades of the twentieth century remained outside the pattern of cultural change that was evident in the novel, poetry and the essay.[1] Works in these genres showed a fundamental questioning of assumptions, values and styles associated with the nineteenth century. European currents of thought and aesthetics were absorbed by novelists and poets and used to challenge and reappraise traditional Spanish attitudes. The theatre, however, in its official practitioners, showed little spirit of reappraisal or reassessment in its attitudes to the values of the previous century and certainly did not, as was the case with the novel, rush headlong into experimentalism. More conservative by nature, it gauged the cultural shift and made certain adjustments. The theatrical response to the once popular melodrama of José Echegaray was significantly more muted than the open and cutting derision heaped upon him from other quarters.[2] Echegaray had enshrined the values of baroque drama – honour, duty, religion, patriotism – in the dramatic forms and strident language of the Romantic theatre. His taste for extreme situations, dramatic confrontations, revelations, obsession with madness, attitude of high moral seriousness with a dash of Ibsen's modern psychology, added up to a recipe for popular success which had lasted for a quarter of a century. From the late 1890s it is possible to detect a reaction against rhetoric in the theatre, but the way in which it manifested itself revealed no serious questioning of the values behind the rhetoric. On one level, the *género chico*, with its comic stereotypes and conformist good humour, grew in popularity and served as a counterblast to the melodrama. Later on, Muñoz Seca cultivated a brand of spoof melodrama, known as the 'astracán', a purely verbal type of farce based on the parody of established genres, but which no more questioned their values than the medieval farces questioned the fundamentals of the faith. The

I

reaction against rhetoric and moral gravity also produced a new vogue for a blander, more sentimental, non-problematical kind of formula play practised with great consistency and professionalism by the Quintero brothers, once referred to by Valle-Inclán as 'Siamese gramophones' (Madrid, p. 343). The most successful intellectual challenge to Echegaray came from Jacinto Benavente, who, with *El nido ajeno* (1894), *Gente conocida* (1896) and *La comida de las fieras* (1898), brought a new note of seriousness without solemnity to the theatre. Benavente's brand of low-key, urbane, semi-philosophical, semi-satirical discussion plays began to win over the public and by the turn of the century he had established himself as the leading playwright of his generation. Benavente managed to reveal the middle class to itself, to create a middle-class public that was prepared, to a limited extent, to look at itself critically. In his relationship with the theatre public over the next fifty years or so – through two world wars and the Russian Revolution – Benavente continued to be only as challenging as was consistent with popularity, firmly entrenched in a rut of provincialism and attacking customs rather than values or assumptions.

The passage of time has revealed Benavente's innovations as a mere ripple on the surface, a tailoring of dramatic technique and social and moral attitudes to suit a particular section of the Spanish public at a particular point in its history. The plays of Ramón del Valle-Inclán, which were virtually ignored as practical theatre in his own day by all but a handful of devotees, present a different picture in retrospect. His reputation as a writer was unchallenged, but few of his con-temporaries would have forecast that, some forty years after his death, that reputation would have rested on his contribution to the art of the theatre. Time has given Valle-Inclán's theatre a curiously modern appearance. Later developments in drama have provided us with the criteria to evaluate a series of plays which at one time were considered literary, undramatic and unstageable. A number of important productions in the 1960s finally laid that theory to rest and went some way towards giving Valle his due recognition in Spain.[3]

Although Valle's contact with the practical theatre in his capacity as author was limited, his experience in other capacities – particularly between 1900 and 1912 – was far from negligible. Fernández Almagro implies that he had connections with the Teatro Artístico before that group staged his first play *Cenizas* in 1899 and had been involved in the productions of Joaquín Dicenta's *Juan José* and

2

Shakespeare's *The Taming of the Shrew*. The latter, according to Almagro, was directed by Valle-Inclán (Fernández Almagro, pp. 61–2). It is known that he collaborated with Manuel Bueno in staging a version of *Fuenteovejuna* with which the Teatro Español opened its season on 27 October 1903. Although the version was criticized because of its somewhat truncated ending, the review in *La Epoca* (28 October 1903) praises the production for its success in capturing the collective atmosphere of the play – a significant observation in view of the direction Valle's own theatre was to take in three or four years' time. About 1904 Valle seems to have deserted the Español in order to follow a young actress, Josefina Blanco (who became his wife in 1907), on her tours of the Madrid theatres and the provinces with the company of the Teatro de la Princesa under the direction of Francisco García Ortega. A letter to Galdós from Aranjuez, dated 5 August 1904, refers to an excursion 'por varios pueblos de Castilla' (Nuez and Schraibman, p. 28). We also learn from this letter that he was engaged in a dramatization of Galdós's *Marianela*, a project which was never completed and eventually handed over to the Quinteros, who finished it in 1916.

Another letter to Galdós, dated 30 October 1906, from Granada, reveals that Valle was then working as artistic director of the Ricardo Calvo company (p. 29). The letter concerns a production of Galdós's play *Alma y vida* which was currently in rehearsal and shows Valle as immersed in the practical problems of the theatre. His movements and degree of involvement with the professional theatre over the next three years are uncertain. Rubia Barcia tells us that, after their marriage in August 1907, the newly-weds rented a large apartment in the Calle Santa Engracia and that Valle's health began to fail (Rubia Barcia, p. 12). It was a time largely devoted to his own writing and he completed two volumes of his *Comedias bárbaras*, his trilogy of novels on the Carlist wars, in addition to *Cuento de abril* and his children's play *La cabeza del dragón*, both of which were produced in the Teatro de la Comedia in 1910. When, after a two years' absence from the stage, Josefina Blanco returned to the García Ortega company for the 1909–10 season, Valle decided to accompany her on the tour to Buenos Aires. Some weeks after arriving in the Argentine capital, Valle and his wife appear to have joined forces with the company of María Guerrero and Fernando Mendoza and completed a tour of Argentina, Uruguay, Bolivia, Chile and Paraguay before returning to Spain in November 1910.

3

Valle remained with the Guerrero–Mendoza company for the next two and a half years, touring round cities in the north of Spain, Valencia, Barcelona, Zaragoza, Bilbao, Pamplona and San Sebastián. *Voces de gesta* was given its first performance by the company in Barcelona on 18 June 1911 and *El Mercantil Valenciano* notes that many Carlists attended the performance.[4] *La Marquesa Rosalinda* was later performed on 5 March 1912 in the Teatro de la Princesa, Madrid, during a short season in the capital which lasted until the end of May. In late June the company returned to Barcelona to give a second performance of *Voces de gesta* in the Teatro Novedades, but decided to drop the play from their repertoire before going on to Pamplona. Whether this decision was prompted by fears of political disturbances, as Almagro suggests, or by certain unspecified personal reasons hinted at by Mendoza in an interview with 'Garcilaso' in the *Diario de Navarra* (9 July 1911), it resulted in a definitive break between Valle-Inclán and the company. This naturally had financial repercussions for Valle and seriously affected his future plans as a playwright, since the Guerrero–Mendoza company had hitherto been a ready-made outlet for his plays, which, as he himself readily admitted, were a minority taste. The row over *Voces* was closely followed by another one over *El embrujado*, this time with Galdós, then artistic director of the Teatro Español. Shortly after retiring to Cambados in Galicia, Valle wrote a letter to Galdós, dated 22 November 1912, suggesting that his 'comedia bárbara', *El embrujado*, might be 'una comedia capaz para el teatro, reduciéndola en alguna parte' (Nuez and Schraibman, pp. 32–3). Galdós's refusal, after protracted delays, to accept the work deeply offended Valle-Inclán. He severed all his connections with the professional theatre and withdrew to a rented farm – La Merced – in Galicia. His correspondence and published interviews after this time reveal considerable bitterness and resentment towards actors, managers and all the commercial aspects of the stage.[5] After seven years of theatrical silence, Valle re-emerged in 1920 with a series of major plays characterized by a more pronounced emphasis on the grotesque. The evidence of press interviews suggests that this new theatrical vision and style may have been conceived for marionette theatres (see Appendix 8), although we have no indication that any of them were performed in this way. After 1920 he took on a new lease of creative life but showed no sign of returning to the commercial theatre and even admitted to no more than a passing interest in professional

4

productions of his own plays after this date.[6] Such time as he devoted to the practical theatre was spent working with independent groups. The most important and longest-surviving of these was the theatre of La Escuela Nueva directed by C. Rivas Cherif. The purpose of this theatre was social as well as artistic and, like the Théâtre National Populaire, was designed to bridge the gap between theatre and working people. According to an article by Rivas Cherif, Valle gave active support to this theatre and Almagro affirms that he had conducted several rehearsals in the spring of 1921.[7] Valle also collaborated with great enthusiasm in the creation of an intimate theatre, baptized 'El Mirlo Blanco', which the Barojas installed in the dining room of their house in Mendizábal, 34. The prologue and epilogue of *Los cuernos de don Friolera* featured in the first programme there on 8 February 1926 and on 8 May of the same year there was a performance of *Ligazón*. Towards the end of 1926, Valle was instrumental in creating the dramatic group 'El Cántaro Roto', which was to operate in the theatre of *Bellas Artes*. However, as E. Díez-Canedo commented, the very name seemed to concede the likelihood of failure (*El Sol*, 21 December 1926). This, in fact, proved to be the case since its first performance – which included a production of *Ligazón* directed by Valle-Inclán himself – was also its last.

Valle's attitude to the theatre was an ambivalent one. On the one hand he claimed that he did not write for the theatre, yet on the other he showed a keen dramatic awareness and formulated ideas which are evidently a rationalization of his own practice in the theatre. His rejection of the theatre stems mainly from his disdain for the ethics of impresarios, the incompetence of actors and the decadence of public taste. He was profoundly dissatisfied with the theatre of his own day, both with its artistic philosophy and with the conditions under which plays were performed. Conversely, few impresarios wanted anything to do with his theatre. Both by choice and of necessity, therefore, Valle had little opportunity to test the practicality of his plays on stage and make adjustments in the light of rehearsals. He wrote against the system, for a theatre of his imagination and, in the main, for the printed text. Alluding to the difficulties involved in producing his plays in a letter to a certain Barrinaga dated 12 November 1913, Valle makes a revealing comment: 'nadie mejor que yo sabe que no son obras de público, y mucho menos de público de provincias. Son obras para una noche en Madrid, y gracias. No digo esto por modestia, todo lo contrario. *Ya llegará nuestro día pero por ahora aun no alborea*' (italics mine) (Landín Carrasco). On the balance of evidence, it seems that Valle disclaimed any connection with the theatre not because he thought his works were unsuitable for the theatre as he conceived it could become, but because the theatre as it existed was unsuitable for his works.

With the benefit of hindsight, it appears that while Benavente was operating his minimal modification of public taste in the commercial theatre, the real revolution was taking place in the work of Valle-Inclán. Yet the question might be asked, what kind of revolution was it and what made Valle's answer to the commercial theatre so different from that of, say, Unamuno or Azorín? It certainly could not be argued that his early theatre in particular was more challenging, intellectually or philosophically, than the works of these men. Nor is it true that the revolution was a purely technical one, a matter of structure and presentation. Valle's eventual triumph does not rest on the quality of his ideas as such nor on technical reform of the stage. It rests rather on his rejection of ideas, of ideology and moralizing, as the basis for drama. What is radically different about Valle-Inclán's theatre is his point of view, the detached, non-didactic, slightly ironic stance in his perception of human affairs, from which everything else – including technique – flows. In his short article, 'Valle-Inclán, dramaturgo', Pérez de Ayala sketches out a very forward-looking assessment of Valle's contribution to the theatre. The perspicacity of these notes is all the more remarkable since they were written exclusively on the basis of the earlier work up to about 1914. Ayala saw that in Valle's vision of the theatre as collective expression – the 'visión íntegra de la vida' – lay the poetic force of his work and that the rejection of ideology, thesis, character psychology are the natural consequences of such a conception. He also saw that his great contribution to the theatre was the invention of a dramatic language capable of reflecting broad cultural identities, a language which avoided both the pedestrian flatness of imitative naturalism and the self-conscious rhetoric of poetic drama.

But Ayala's view covers only the first stage of Valle's development as a dramatist – the process that goes from the conventional psychological and moral conflicts of *Cenizas* to the collective conception of the *Comedias bárbaras* and *Voces de gesta*. Although the 'visión íntegra de la vida' was undoubtedly an ideal to which Valle adhered throughout most of his life as a writer, a distinct shift of emphasis is discernible from the mythical and legendary perspective of his early work, e.g. the novel *Flor de santidad* and the first *Comedias bárbaras*, to the panoramic detachment of later works like *Divinas palabras*, the novels of *El ruedo ibérico* and *Los cuernos de don Friolera*. It is basically a shift from a temporal to a spatial distancing, which became apparent after Valle's visit to the war front in 1916 and the publication of *La media noche*. In the early work the presentation of character and action is archetypal. They are seen as determined by forces beyond individual psychology and historical circumstances. Yet man's relationship to his context could be described as one of 'heroic determinism', in that the individual is enhanced and given meaning by the collective forces working through him. While the conditioning forces are those of nature and tradition, the view of man remains a heroic one. However, by the logic of the same deterministic view of human behaviour, once other collective forces assume control – social or historical myth, the clichés of rhetoric – human actions degenerate into automatic responses and the individual appears belittled, manipulated, grotesque. We see this transition taking place in Valle's theatre from about 1912 and the publication of *La Marquesa Rosalinda*. The point of crisis was possibly the failed tragedy, *El embrujado* (1913), after which farce is used with an increasingly anti-heroic emphasis. The transition is a gradual one and even certain later works – notably *Divinas palabras* and, in a different way, *Luces de Bohemia* – still reveal a dynamic tension between the tragic and the burlesque. As Valle's awareness of and disenchantment with contemporary social and political life in Spain increased, his work took on a more subversive character. He became less content with impassive contemplation and angled his vision to bring out the jarring contrasts between myth and reality in Spanish life. The characteristic humour of the *esperpento* focuses precisely on the discrepancy between man's heroic self-image and his essentially manipulated condition. Detachment, however, is never sacrificed to more immediate satirical ends and, in this final phase of Valle's theatre, all life – and Spanish political life in particular – appears as a distant charade in which the uniformly grotesque portrayal becomes the expression of a new tragic sense of emptiness.

This, in broad outline, is the evolution of Valle-Inclán's theatre which emerges from an analysis of the texts. Admittedly, any suggested development, in view of Valle's custom of adding to or reworking older material (*Luces de Bohemia* and probably *Cara de plata*)

and the doubts surrounding the date of composition of such plays as
La enamorada del rey and *Divinas palabras*,[8] can at best be only tentative.
This book tries to steer a course between the blow-by-blow catalogue
and over-rigid tabulation into 'periods'. I have, however, chosen to
concentrate on text rather than context, and historical and biographical background has been kept to a minimum to allow
maximum space for the interpretation of individual works. A
moderate amount of descriptive material and plot information where
relevant has been included to enable the non-specialist reader with a
knowledge of Spanish to follow the argument.

The first and last chapters try to relate the philosophical and
aesthetic principles behind Valle's theatre to a wider European
context. It must be stressed that the argument in these chapters is
mostly on the level of related principles rather than specific historical
connections. Valle-Inclán has links with two general European
avant-garde literary movements: his roots are in the idealist philosophy of the Symbolist movement towards the end of the last century
and the full flowering of his maturity looks forward to the crisis of
tragic values in literature which came to a head in the theatrical
avant-garde of the 1950s. The first chapter lays the foundations for an
appreciation of a large part of Valle's output, though it must be
remembered that the principles discussed are the philosophical
subsoil from which the works spring and not ideas which are
illustrated explicitly. Once weaned of an early 'decadent' phase,
associated principally with the first short stories, Valle evolved a
Symbolist aesthetic very similar to that of W. B. Yeats. The
culmination of that period of gestation came with the publication of
La lámpara maravillosa in 1916. Some critics have commented
adversely on what they see as the arbitrarily eclectic and half-baked
nature of this work and, undoubtedly, judged as an academic exegesis
of such doctrines as Gnosticism, theosophy, the Cabala, the *quietismo*
of Miguel de Molinos, etc., the book may leave much to be desired
(e.g. M. E. Pérez). Looked at as an expression of an artist's view of the
world, however, all the diverse elements – though perhaps distortions
of the original forms – merge into the unity of Valle's intuitive vision.
That fundamentally detached and mystical view of existence never
really left him, despite the undoubted veering towards social and
political subject matter which took place in the twenties. One of my
main contentions in the later chapters will be that the *esperpento* does
not involve a displacement of the mystical by the social view of life,

8

but comes from a growing sense of incongruity between his increasingly jaundiced vision of contemporary humanity and his transcendental philosophy, which nevertheless remained. These later developments have stimulated comparisons both with the socially orientated theatre of Brecht and the metaphysical theatre of the Absurd which will be examined in the last chapter. There are interesting parallels here, but there are also important distinctions and qualifications to be made and it is with this in mind, as well as the need to see Valle-Inclán as a major European dramatist in a European perspective, that this chapter has been included.

I

Valle-Inclán and Symbolist aesthetics

Valle-Inclán's radical departure from the theatrical practice of his day was more a consequence of his underlying philosophy than of experimentation with form and technique. Technical aspects of his plays such as episodic structure and visual emphasis, the collective orientation and the non-psychological approach to character all stem from his fundamentally mystical perspective on human affairs. They are the consequence of contemplating life from a certain distance. His notions on theatre and his dramatic technique must therefore be placed in the context of his general philosophy and aesthetics.

This outlook did not evolve purely as an isolated response to the uninspiring state of Spain's commercial theatre. It evolved out of a general European climate of change, originally centred on Paris, which, directly or indirectly, helped to shape it. The nature of that climate was described by W. B. Yeats in 1897:

The reaction against the rationalism of the eighteenth century has mingled with a reaction against the materialism of the nineteenth century, and the symbolical movement, which has come to perfection in Germany in Wagner, in England in the Pre-Raphaelites, in France in Villiers de L'Isle-Adam and Mallarmé, and in Belgium in Maeterlinck, and has stirred the imagination of Ibsen and D'Annunzio, is certainly the only movement that is saying new things. (*Essays*, p. 187)

The impact of this general 'symbolist' or 'idealist' reaction around the turn of the century in Spain has only recently begun to be documented in a number of studies.[1] As a result of this work the literary and intellectual movements of *Modernismo* and the Generation of '98, with their common emphasis on spiritual crisis and the need for regeneration and the restoration of transcendent ideals, are emerging as the Hispanic expression of a general disenchantment with nineteenth-century positivism (and the literary naturalism associated with it), scientific rationalism, the mechanistic view of nature and the social view of man.

Although the phenomenon is as old as literature itself, the term 'Symbolism' is generally applied to the poetic movement whose tenets were formulated in the 1880s by Stéphane Mallarmé.[2] It was subsequently associated with many other poets, including Baudelaire, Verlaine and Rimbaud, and later with a number of dramatists, in particular the Belgian, Maurice Maeterlinck. Among the main sources of ideological inspiration were Schopenhauer, whose philosophy of aesthetics provided the theoretical basis for the movement as a whole, Nietzsche, particularly in his seminal work *The Birth of Tragedy* (1872), and, most important of all as far as Symbolist influence on the theatre was concerned, Richard Wagner with his revolutionary theories on the integration of the arts.

The extent of Valle-Inclán's debt to specific Symbolist writers is difficult to determine. It is, however, highly probable that he would have been familiar with Wagner's aesthetics since he himself admits the direct influence of Wagner in the *Comedias bárbaras* and *Voces de gesta* (see letter to C. Rivas Cherif in *España*, 8 March 1924). The works of D'Annunzio were readily available and there is ample evidence that Valle knew them well, possibly in the original (see Bugliani, pp. 66–9).[3] At least some Wagnerian theory may have percolated through novels like *Il fuoco*, and D'Annunzio's own cult of primitive vitality, interest in popular superstition and the tension between pagan and Christian elements probably left their mark on the *Comedias*, *El embrujado* and *Divinas palabras*. There can be little doubt that he was generally aware of the ideas of Nietzsche, although Gonzalo Sobejano claims that these too were mainly absorbed through reading D'Annunzio (*Nietzsche en España*, p. 214). The direct imprint of Maeterlinck's style and content is visible mainly in the early dramatic sketches, *Tragedia de ensueño* and *Comedia de ensueño*, and also in the 1908 revision of his first play, *El yermo de las almas* (see Kirkpatrick). A more oblique technical influence can be appreciated in the rhythmic dialogue of *Aguila de blasón* and *Romance de lobos*. The dramatists of the Irish theatre would almost certainly have been unknown to Valle-Inclán, at least until 1920 when Juan Ramón Jiménez translated a number of Synge's plays. New ideas on design such as those of Gordon Craig were also slow to arrive in the Peninsula. Craig's theories were probably disseminated through a French translation by Geneviève Seligmann-Loire of *The Art of the Theatre* published in 1916 and for all practical purposes little change was felt in the theatre until Martínez Sierra took over the management of the Teatro Eslava in 1917.[4]

However, my purpose in this chapter is not to trace influences but to isolate some of the more important characteristics of the movement as it affected the theatre and relate these to the aesthetic and dramatic theories of Valle-Inclán with a view to indicating general parallels and Valle's participation in a common fund of ideas. Viewed in the context of Symbolist aesthetics, *La lámpara maravillosa* offers many striking parallels with Schopenhauer, Nietzsche's *Birth of Tragedy* and the mysticism of W. B. Yeats. In common with other writers and philosophers linked with the movement, Valle had sought a theoretical basis for his artistic intuitions in an amalgam of esoteric doctrines, Gnosticism and Pythagorean metaphysics in particular (see Smith, chapter 2). As in the philosophy of Schopenhauer, there is a close association between aesthetic and mystical experience. The aesthetic experience is conceived as a mystical insight into a level of reality unattainable by rational or scientific enquiry. Valle's views on dramatic theory, clearly derived from these general principles, also reveal many similarities to those of Wagner, D'Annunzio, Maeterlinck, Craig, Yeats and Synge, all of whom tried to restore a poetic dimension to a stereotyped and commercialized stage.

In 1891 Ferdinand Brunetière wrote:

Là, dans cette complexité, est la puissance, la beauté, la profondeur du symbole. Ce que la comparaison ou l'allégorie distinguent, divisent et séparent pour l'exprimer alternativement, le symbole, au contraire, l'unit, le joint ensemble, et n'en fait qu'une seule et même chose. Il relie l'homme à la nature, et tous les deux à leur principe caché. Ou encore, et tandis que l'allégorie ou la comparaison ne servent qu'à faire briller l'esprit ou l'habileté du poète, le symbole, allant plus loin et plus profondément, nous fait saisir entre le monde et nous quelqu'une de ces affinités secrètes et de ces lois obscures, : . . . Tout symbole est en ce sens une espèce de révélation. (p. 686)

Brunetière's words serve as a useful working definition of the Symbolist attitude to the world as it will be understood in this discussion. The Symbolist vision perceives an essential unity, not only between man and nature, but between every visible aspect of the life of man and a transcendent principle of harmony which can only be expressed symbolically. In Wagner, Maeterlinck, Yeats and Valle-Inclán Symbolism is to be understood not as the conscious use of tangible elements to suggest wider and more abstract meanings (e.g. Chekhov's cherry orchard or the tower in Ibsen's *The Master Builder*), but as the detection of archetypal forms and patterns which reveal the essential unity of being beneath the multifarious accidents of time and space. The distinction between these two types of symbol was made by Maeterlinck:

Je crois qu'il y a deux sortes de symboles: l'un qu'on pourrait appeler le symbole *a priori*; le symbole de propos délibéré; il part d'abstraction et tâche de revêtir d'humanité ces abstractions . . . L'autre espèce de symbole serait plutôt inconscient, aurait lieu à l'insu du poète, souvent malgré lui, et irait, presque toujours, bien au-delà de sa pensée . . . (Huret, p. 123)

Valle-Inclán's theatre, and his art in general, has always been associated with the latter type. When, in *La lámpara*, he says 'La creación estética es el milagro de la alusión y de la alegoría' (p. 136), he is not referring to intellectual constructs at the service of a moral philosophy, but to an intuitive perception of forms and rhythms able to suggest the static harmony beneath the transient and fragmented appearances. *La lámpara* repeatedly emphasizes that the aesthetic experience is the intuition of unity, the perception of links between the individual and the generic, between the ancient and the contemporary. Chronology and change are illusions of the senses which it is the artist's mission to dispel. The senses fragment our image of the world like light in a prism; the artist must see with his memory and his intuition: 'Es preciso haber contemplado emotivamente la misma imagen desde parajes diversos, para que alumbre en la memoria la ideal mirada fuera de posición geométrica y fuera de posición en el tiempo' (p. 113). To Valle-Inclán the symbolism of Ibsen's plays appeared too cerebral and came perilously close to the theatre of ideas which he, in common with Yeats, explicitly rejects (see Appendix 4 and *Essays*, p. 195). For the Symbolist, art was conceived not as exploration or analysis, but as revelation.

The dedicated pursuit of unity and harmony led many writers around the turn of the century into the area of the esoteric and occult sciences, such as theosophy (Yeats and Valle-Inclán), telepathy (Maeterlinck), spiritualism and magnetism (Villiers de L'Isle-Adam). This same aspiration lay at the root of many other artistic tendencies of the period such as the notion of 'correspondences' between the sense impressions and the Pythagorean idea of infinite correspondences of the microcosm and the macrocosm, the interest in myth and collective lore and the desire to unite in synthesis the different branches of the arts. It clearly forms the basis of Wagner's aspirations to the 'total art-work' in which music, movement and poetry would be as one. Nietzsche in *The Birth of Tragedy*, taking, like

THE THEATRE OF VALLE-INCLÁN

Wagner, Greek tragedy as his starting point and aesthetic ideal, defines the essence of that tragedy as 'a recognition that whatever exists is of a piece and that individuation is the root of all evil' (p. 67) and sees in the Dionysiac dithyramb 'the desire to tear asunder the veil of Maya, to sink back into the original oneness of nature' (p. 27). This aesthetic philosophy later cast a powerful spell over a generation of European dramatists who saw it as their mission to restore poetry to the theatre. Gabriele D'Annunzio, despite his reputation for decadence and eroticism, was also deeply influenced by Wagner's visionary energy. More recent criticism has tended to emphasize the Symbolist aspects of his work and, at the conclusion of a conference on 'D'Annunzio and European Symbolism' held in 1973, it was declared that the dominant line to have emerged from all the contributions was of a 'D'Annunzio vissuto dentro la civiltà del simbolismo, che ha assimilato gli elementi del simbolismo, e che ha sentito sopra tutto questa esigenza di unificare l'uomo con le cose in una continuità senza soluzione . . .' (Sansone, p. 421). Maurice Maeterlinck, the dramatist most linked with Symbolist aesthetics, defines the poetic element as the allusion which links the visible to the unseen, the temporal to the eternal. Maeterlinck has sometimes been accused of dealing with the invisible and the eternal to the exclusion of the visible and the temporal. His theory, however, leaves no doubt that his purpose was to reveal the relationship between the two.[5] Gordon Craig, though not a writer of plays, saw himself very much as creator of theatre and displays in his theories and designs a conviction that all life is unified by transcendent patterns and forces which it was the purpose of theatre to reveal. His discussion of the supernatural element in *Macbeth* is saturated with Symbolist thinking and, in particular, with Maeterlinck whom he quotes to add force to his arguments (pp. 268–9). Yeats, too, saw all life as unified by static laws and, for him, as for Valle-Inclán, the artist's mission was to get to the still centre of things. 'The end of art', he claims, 'is the ecstasy awakened by the presence before an ever-changing mind of what is permanent in the world' (*Essays*, p. 287).

One other point should be made in connection with the Symbolist view of a static universe governed by unifying principles. That is the idea that, to perceive this unity and totality, the artist must abandon all ulterior motives. The notion that *disinterest* is an essential prerequisite of artistic contemplation comes up repeatedly in *La lámpara* and in the essays of Yeats.[6] In all probability, Valle-Inclán gleaned this idea from his reading of Schopenhauer who saw the aesthetic experience as something which liberated human beings from what he termed the 'will', that is to say, determinism by the needs, appetites and desires required for the perpetuation of the species. To transcend the 'will' the artist must become the 'pure, will-less, painless, timeless subject of knowledge' as opposed to the 'knowing individual' in order to rise above the conditioning forces of passion, self-interest and utility which normally determine his relationship to others and to the physical world (Gardiner, pp. 192–6). Artistic contemplation for Valle, as for Schopenhauer, was the only way to transcend the instinctive egoism built in by nature for its own survival and break out of the narrow, 'conditioned', individual viewpoint. Pride and self-centredness are what keep us anchored to the needs of the passing moment and prevent us from achieving the necessary detachment.[7]

The idea of 'disinterested contemplation' should not be confused with 'art for art's sake'. The renunciation of ulterior motive in art was seen as a prelude to the perception of a higher level of reality unattainable by the rational intelligence. It was a form of knowledge of the real world, not a means of creating an alternative to reality. Nevertheless, it was attended by a strong reaction against the notion of conscious purpose in art, the theatre of ideas in general and the *pièce à thèse* in particular. Valle-Inclán shared with Yeats and J. M. Synge a powerful dislike of moralizing and argument (even of a balanced kind) in the theatre. The theatre, he asserted, was no place for argument; it persuades by means of illusion and its appeal is essentially emotive and non-rational. It should therefore neither attempt to teach or make an audience think, but should stimulate and release its imagination by emotional suggestion (see Appendix 1). Yeats reveals himself as a true disciple of Schopenhauer when he argues in an essay on Synge that disinterest is the supreme quality in a work of art: 'Only that which does not teach, which does not cry out, which does not persuade, which does not condescend, which does not explain, is irresistible' (*Essays*, p. 341). This quality he sees exemplified in Synge's portrayal of the peasant culture of the West of Ireland. Synge himself confirms this interpretation of his dramatic philosophy in his preface to *The Tinker's Wedding*, claiming that 'The drama, like the symphony, does not teach or prove anything'. Yeats, with all his advocacy for a national role for his theatre movement, was acutely aware of the difference between art and propaganda. In his advice to playwrights intending to submit work to the Abbey Theatre he stressed that art should concern itself with 'realities of emotion that became self-evident when made vivid to the imagination' (quoted by Miller, pp. 134–5). Well before him, in his *Art-work of the Future* (1849), Wagner had affirmed that in drama we learn and know through feeling and that an action can only be explained when it is completely justified by feeling. It was therefore the dramatic poet's task to make an action so intelligible through its emotional necessity that we may dispense with the intellect's assistance in its justification (vol. 1, pp. 77–82; vol. 2, pp. 208–12). Wagner had argued that drama must appeal directly to the emotions at the deepest collective level by non-rational means, i.e. dance, music, poetry. Such had been the appeal of the choral tragedy of Aeschylus. Valle-Inclán also refers to the decline of the intuitive apprehension of unity in the world after the early Greeks and in fact the text of *La lámpara* itself is conceived as a series of 'spiritual exercises' to try and recover this intuitive perception, to raise the artist's vision from rational meditation to contemplation, because 'ante la razón que medita se vela en el misterio la suprema comprensión del mundo' (pp. 62, 93, 14).

The natural corollary of 'disinterested contemplation' was a detached viewpoint which neither urged opinions on the audience nor identified with individuals within the work. With very few exceptions, Valle-Inclán observes a Flaubertian remoteness in all his writing. This was both because he regarded the expression of opinion as a distraction from the object and because identification limits and distorts the overall picture. His theoretical statements are full of references to the need for artistic impassivity, panoramic vision and collective observation.[8] We find similar views expressed by Yeats and D'Annunzio, to the effect that the artist should suppress his own personality and let the collective voices speak through him.[9] D'Annunzio, for instance, writing in connection with his *La figlia di Iorio*, refers to popular culture as manifested in folk song as the repository of ageless wisdom.[10] His artistic function in writing the play, he claims, was to serve as a channel for the folk imagination: 'it seems to me that the work has not been fashioned by my hands at all, but has come from a very distant past, immemorial and national, and that I have been merely observing a kind of vision which has surged up from the past' (Rhodes, p. 107).[11] Whenever Valle-Inclán mentioned imitating the *pueblo* in his art, as he frequently did, he was invariably referring to this quality of disinterested and detached wisdom in the popular imagination.[12]

These views seem to indicate a general agreement with Nietzsche's opinion that 'the subjective artist is simply a bad artist' and that art in every genre demands 'a triumph over subjectivity, deliverance from the self, the silencing of every personal will and desire' (*Birth of Tragedy*, p. 37). The declared or implicit purpose of drama, according to most of the writers under discussion, was to evoke generic feeling, to get beneath and beyond personality, emotional or ideological conflict, to the deep sub-rational levels where human behaviour merged with the general laws of nature. Valle-Inclán declared that the supreme aspiration of the theatre was to 'recoger, reflejar, dar la sensación de vida de un pueblo o de una raza' (see López Núñez). His *Lámpara* constantly echoes Nietzsche's view of the Dionysian basis of the aesthetic experience, that is, the overwhelming sense of man's generic nature taking over and swamping his individuality (pp. 54 and 83; *Birth of Tragedy*, p. 50). Yeats, in his short essay 'Emotion of Multitude', while reaffirming his stance against the theatre of ideas, equates the poetry of drama with its collective quality and its capacity to evoke 'far off multitudinous things' (*Essays*, pp. 215–16). Symbolism in drama seems to have taken root mainly in countries with a strong popular tradition in their literature – like Belgium, Italy, Spain and Ireland. In many of the dramatists linked to this movement we may observe a predilection for rural cultures where both instincts and language remain vital and intact, untrivialized by contact with modern urban life. This can be seen in Valle-Inclán's semi-feudal Galicia, D'Annunzio's superstition-laden and violent Abbruzzi, J. M. Synge's pagan and imaginative peasant culture of the West of Ireland.

It is generally true that these dramatists were concerned – at least in theory – to re-establish the ritual links between the theatre and the community. The problem of eliciting the right kind of spontaneous response from a middle-class audience, accustomed to regarding theatre as a consumer commodity, is one that has dogged the would-be poetic dramatist ever since Wagner. Wagner himself sought a total universal response by the use of myth and legend (vol. 2, pp. 152–94). His 'art-work of the future' was conceived as one which would necessarily appeal to the masses because the myth at its heart was an expression of their own thought, feelings and aspirations, the 'poetry of a life-view in common' (vol. 2, p. 156). Yeats, D'Annunzio, Synge and Valle-Inclán on the whole limited their range to a national or regional sphere, although the significance of the cultural interaction they envisaged was a universal one. Yeats declared that his purpose was to unite art with life, not as William Morris had done, through utility, but by reuniting it with the religious sub-soil of human nature.[13] Valle-Inclán said as much, though in a more improvised manner, in his newspaper interviews and café *tertulias*. The theatre's function was to reflect the collective ethos of a people and to stimulate collective responses. In one way or another, the *Comedias bárbaras*, *Cuento de abril*, *Voces de gesta*, *La Marquesa Rosalinda* and *Divinas palabras* are concerned with cultural identities. The theatre needs a public unified by an organic spirit, which the dramatist should reflect and, in so doing, elicit the collective collaboration of his audience in the experience (see Appendix 2).

Valle-Inclán's emphasis on non-rational means of communication was a direct result of his conception of the theatre as a collective art. In a lecture entitled 'Capacidad del español para la literatura' delivered at the Casino de Madrid in 1932, he claimed that the Spaniard had a greater capacity for the theatre than any other branch of literature because of its direct appeal to the senses through tone and gesture (Madrid, p. 117). As a race, Spaniards are stirred more deeply by ritualistic spectacles than by rational arguments. Valle explains himself fully on this point in a statement reproduced by Francisco Madrid in his book (see Appendix 2). He cites the examples of the bullfight, the representation of Christ's Passion in *Semana Santa* and the survival of liturgical Latin in the Mass, all of which communicate by their direct impact on the emotions. Valle believed that the theatre, which lives by its capacity to communicate collectively, should follow the same path.

One of the more tangible consequences of Symbolist thinking in drama was on stage presentation. The desire to express the essential unity between human life and nature, between the visible and invisible worlds, was reflected in a new emphasis on synthesis between the different elements involved in theatrical production. From about the 1890s onwards, writers, directors and stage designers began to think of the dramatic performance as an orchestrated synthesis of such components as music, poetry, movement, colour and design. Richard Wagner had been the original visionary in this connection with his ideal of the *gesamtkunstwerk* or 'total art-work'. Not all creative spirits in the theatre necessarily shared Wagner's ideal of an integration of all the arts, but many were inspired by the possibilities contained in the principle of synthesis. Craig, for instance, did not have much to say about music, despite the fact that many of his designs look as though they were conceived for grand opera. He concentrated on a combination of 'action, which is the very spirit of acting; words, which are the body of the play; line and colour, which are the very heart of the scene; rhythm, which is the very essence of the dance' (Craig, p. 138). Wagner's influence also made itself felt on another designer, Adolphe Appia, who, like Walter Pater, believed that music was the condition to which all other arts aspired. For Appia, light did for the physical decor what music, in Wagner's view, did for dramatic action, that is, express the inner nature of appearances and bring out the emotional values of a performance (see Simonson, pp. 351-77).

A number of Wagnerian echoes can be detected in Valle's *Lámpara*, as well as in his general attitude to the theory and practice of drama. His observations on dance, for instance, in the chapter 'El milagro musical', are very close to the spirit of *The Art-work of the Future*. The dance, as a fusion of music, movement, rhythm and line, is described as a supreme example of aesthetic synthesis. The impressions, simultaneously conveyed to eyes and ears, are united in the overriding harmony of rhythm (*Lámpara*, p. 60, and Madrid, p. 355). The creation of a dynamic rhythm, in terms of the dialogue and succession of visual images, was an essential element in Valle's theatre. The verse plays – in particular *La Marquesa Rosalinda* – seem to be primarily conceived as ballets in which the rhyme and rhythm of the verse blend creatively with colour and choreography (see the *Preludio* to *La Marquesa Rosalinda*). His grasp of the emotional significance of varying light is also amply demonstrated in the *Comedias bárbaras*, *Divinas palabras* and *Luces de Bohemia*. Alone of his generation of dramatists in Spain, Valle-Inclán saw the need to harmonize the rhythms of dialogue with the visual patterns and movement on stage in order to communicate at a deeper than rational level. Some confirmation of this may be found in an article by an ex-pupil of Valle's at the Escuela Superior de Bellas Artes, which provides some fascinating sidelights on his ideas for staging plays: 'Valle-Inclán quiso que la entonación para esta obra fuese a base de tonos pardos y verdes oscuros; acorde sombrío, monótono, sin tonos brillantes; la nota vibrante sólo estaba conseguida por los agudos gritos de la protagonista' (V. Durán). This was for the author's own production of *El embrujado* in 1916. Clearly in this case costume and setting are not being considered literally, but as projections of the theme or the dominant mood of a scene.

The new passion for synthesis in the theatre naturally tended to concentrate the power into the hands of one man. For most of the nineteenth century the actor had reigned supreme; now a new autocrat took control: the artistic director or *régisseur*. Instead of Kean, Tree, Bernhardt and Terry, the names that dominated the European stage were those of Reinhardt, Craig, Stanislavski and Meyerhold. As the role of the artistic director became more creative and authors became more aware of the theatre as a 'total' art form, a certain amount of overlapping of functions seemed to take place. Producers and designers tried to annex the territory of writers and vice-versa. Gordon Craig, for instance, envisaged the possibility of a self-sufficient, self-reliant art of the theatre independent of the playwright (p. 148). Yeats, Maeterlinck and Valle-Inclán, for their part, all move into the province of producer or designer to some extent. These writers naturally had different priorities – for Yeats the creation of rich, living speech was of paramount importance – but they shared a common goal of unity of impression. Their plays were not merely written, but visualized and staged in their minds, complete with envisaged movements and strikingly composed stage images. We may cite the examples of Yeats's detailed ideas on costume, colour and movement in his *Plays for Dancers* (*Plays and Controversies*, pp. 415–61) or Maeterlinck's bold use of door and window images in his *La Mort de Tintagiles* and *Intérieur*. Valle-Inclán clearly had a stage director's imagination and wrote for the eye as well as the ear, in which he undoubtedly anticipated and, I believe, influenced García Lorca. Ramón Sender's description of how Valle claimed to approach the composition of a play is remarkably similar to Craig's account of how his ideal director should approach the interpretation of a text (Sender, p. 23; Craig, pp. 155 and 157). Both men describe a process which starts from a general perception of colour and tone and works towards specifics by gradual accretion, trying the while to harmonize visual and aural impressions.

A dramatic philosophy whose aim was to get beyond private emotion, rationalism and opinion to the unifying principles of all nature and to instinctive, generic feeling could not fail to have a profound effect on dramatic language. A theatrical language accustomed to presenting individual relationships, character conflict or ideological argument was no use when called upon to present collective character, the links of man and nature or the mystery of the human condition. The basic premise of Wagner's aesthetic theory — and later Yeats's – was that drama should communicate sub-rationally and speak directly to what is most generic and instinctive in our make-up. Both Wagner and Yeats were insistent that contemporary language had become impoverished as a result of a separation between our rational and sensorial responses. To transform this currency debased by naturalism and the theatre of ideas into one that spoke to the emotions, both Wagner and Yeats devised forms of heightened 'tone speech' which was designed to distance language as practical communication and by-pass the intellect, while retaining the free and spontaneous rhythms of living speech (Stein, pp. 69–79; Yeats, *Essays*, pp. 13–27). Wagner's widely publicized investigations into the union of words and tone had an important effect on dramatists who were sympathetic to his ideals, even though they may have disliked his rhetoric. The dramatic language of Maeterlinck, Yeats and Synge, in the use of repeated motifs and rhythmic development, owes something to this influence. In Spain, Wagnerian theory bore most fruit in the early plays of Valle-Inclán, particularly in the orchestrated language of the *Comedias bárbaras*.

Although Valle-Inclán hardly ever refers to instrumental music in his works, he was always aware of the compelling force of music and tone in language. A whole section of *La lámpara*, 'El milagro musical', is devoted to this phenomenon. For Valle, words encapsulated a kind of latent energy which could only be fully released when the form and sound were right.[14] Though he does not always make the point clear, this energy seems to complement rather than replace the rational meaning. The emotive charge released by tone, rhythm, rhyme or assonance illuminates analogies between man and nature or between the actual and the eternal which could not be detected by intellectual clarity alone. As a dramatist, Valle always tried to build the tone into his dialogue. The non-rational elements of sonority, rhythm and tempo are an integral part of the mood or meaning and their importance can hardly be exaggerated. What one character says to another is not dependent primarily on the exigencies of the narrative, the logic of the character or his state of mind, but on the rhythmical pattern of the scene. In other words, the dramatist is less concerned with the individual characteristics of the interlocutors than with the unity formed by their interaction. It is characteristic of the early plays and a particular feature of the *Comedias* that rhythmic and even metrical dialogue, variation of key and pace, repetitions and cadences operate on the imagination with the effect of music. Valle, in fact, wrote his dialogue as a musician composes his score, to create the appropriate tone. The linked speeches – each acting as a springboard for the next – which quicken the tempo and increase the sense of urgency, the lyrical cadence of evocative proper names (e.g. 'María Soledad' in *Aguila de blasón*) which create an incantatory effect like that of a *romance*, the repeated or partially repeated phrases, all create a rhythm which subsumes the intellect and persuades with its sense of inevitability.[15]

But it must not be assumed that this compelling force comes from euphony alone. Like Yeats, Valle does not equate poetry just with 'beautiful language' but with energy, and that energy can only come from a living tradition (see *Plays and Controversies*, pp. 97 and 118–19). In his remarks on the Castilian language (see Appendix 2) Valle insists that theatrical regeneration can only come from a reintegration of theatre with collective national origins and that, to achieve this, dramatists must forge a tone and idiom rooted in the spirit of the language. He points to the folly of attempting to adapt the analytical 'tono francés' to Castilian. French, with its abundance of vowel sounds and lack of pronounced stress, he describes as a language of the middle registers, rich in nuances and suited to the exploration of subtle states of mind. The special aptitudes of French for suggestion, lightness of touch and inference are revealed only by the interaction of finely tuned minds. Hence, as he says elsewhere, French is the real language of dialogue (see Appendix 6). To try and squeeze such qualities from Castilian would be to expect peaches from a lemon tree, since Castilian is a language of emphasis and powerful stress, suited to the expression of strong and naïve emotional extremes, of spontaneous and categorical feeling: a language of 'labriegos, clérigos y jueces'. For Valle, one of the main functions of dramatic dialogue was to express the genius of a language, and the genius of Castilian lay in its definitive and uncompromising modes of expression: 'la sentencia, la imprecación, el denuesto, el grito'. A glance at almost any scene from the *Comedias bárbaras* would suffice to demonstrate his predilection for these forms of expression. The dialogue does not reason, argue, describe, analyse or relate; it alternates between the expression of spontaneous emotion and ageless choral feeling.

This should not be confused with realism. It is important to realize that in both the Galician Spanish of Valle-Inclán and the Gaelic English of Synge we have not an observed copy of linguistic idiosyncrasies but a stylization of reality, shaped to the expression of collective forces. Not the least of these forces was the conditioning power of language on the imagination and attitudes of a people. The view of language that comes over in *La lámpara* is as something which not only encapsulates the history and character of a region but even helps to determine and perpetuate these things. In chapter 5 of 'El milagro musical' he writes: 'El pensamiento toma su forma en las palabras como el agua en la vasija' and, further on, 'Las palabras imponen normas al pensamiento, lo encadenan, lo guían y le muestran caminos imprevistos, al modo de la rima.' This deterministic view of language leads him to a highly original, if somewhat fanciful, explanation of the Russian Revolution as the result of the penetration into Russian culture of the French language, charged with its subconscious inheritance of the French Revolution! Nevertheless, the idea persists throughout most of Valle's work. The power of rhetoric over minds and attitudes is latent in the earlier work and more explicit in such later plays as *Los cuernos de don Friolera*, *Divinas palabras*, *La rosa de papel* and *Sacrilegio*.

Besides dictating a new approach to dramatic language, the Symbolist philosophy – with its emphasis on unity and integration rather than conflict – also entails the adoption of different dramatic structures. Most nineteenth-century drama rests on the assumption that character differentiation and the conflict of passions or ideas are the very essence of dramatic tension. The notion of conflict – between reason and emotion, individual and society, love and duty, etc. – was certainly fundamental to the drama of Echegaray, for instance. Symbolist theatre – in the sense employed here – tries to illuminate areas where the barriers between individual and individual break down, where moral and ideological categories merge into unity and where, as Maeterlinck says in his essay, 'Mystic Morality', the soul of the Sodomite could have 'the transparent smile of the child in his eyes' (*Trésor*, p. 68). In 'Le Tragique quotidien', Maeterlinck challenges the notion that colliding passions are the only basis for drama (*Trésor*, pp. 190–1). Yeats too argues that tragedy tries to reach a level of the human spirit where differences between man and man no longer have any importance (character differentiation was the province of daily life and of comedy) and speaks of a 'passionless' theatre which for individuality and conflict would substitute 'rhythm, balance, pattern, images that remind us of vast passions, the vagueness of past times, all the chimera that haunt the edge of trance'

23

(*Essays*, p. 243). He found this avoidance of conventional conflicts and these rich evocative qualities exemplified to perfection in the dialogue of Synge's tragedies (*Essays*, p. 305). The doctrine is a dangerous one and runs the risk of being stillborn on the stage. Many critics have dismissed Maeterlinck's work as bloodless and untheatrical and Yeats as a lyric poet who failed to adapt his poetic genius to the stage. Even for Synge, generally acknowledged as the most natural dramatist of the group, general acclaim seems to be restricted to *The Playboy of the Western World*, and plays like *Deirdre of the Sorrows*, much admired by Yeats, are rarely produced. To what extent can a view of the world as an essentially static unity be expressed in terms of an art traditionally requiring dynamic tension?

For many years after Valle's death, his plays were thought to be not only untheatrical, because of the various practical problems they presented, but also undramatic, owing to the absence of conventionally structured climaxes or conflicts. Since the early 1960s, a series of important productions, development of theatrical resources and shifts in critical attitudes have established Valle-Inclán as a dramatist entirely conscious of his aims and purposes. Furthermore, these developments have revealed his plays as some of the most vital and dramatic manifestations of Symbolism in the theatre. The manner in which the plays are written stems from the vision of life that informs them and certainly not, as previously supposed, from a capricious and arbitrary desire to mix up genres (Risco, pp. 112–13). Technically, too, Valle had a genuine alternative to offer to the standard practice inherited from Neoclassicism. The letter written to Rivas Cherif (see Appendix 3), though brief, cryptic and inconclusive, says enough to confirm the evidence of the plays themselves. For unities conceived as an external framework, Valle is trying to substitute internal unities of collective tone and atmosphere via rhythm.

Valle's method of construction is in many ways a reversal of that involved in the 'Well-made Play' and its derivatives.[16] In the latter, dialogue and situation are generally geared to a preconceived pattern. Characters are subordinated to plot and plot to theme. Scenes are 'prepared for' and tension is 'built up'. The emotional graph of the spectator rises as he becomes progressively more aware of the play's themes and tendencies. His attention is projected both backwards to what has led up to a situation and forwards to what is to be the outcome. The artistic process thus tends to go from the idea to its physical embodiment in action, characters, dialogue and setting. The physical embodiment of an action in Valle's theatre is very much an integral part of the play's conception, not a secondary consequence subservient to an idea.[17] With Valle-Inclán, the original conception takes on qualities of light, colour and mass from the beginning. The physical setting is not just a place where it is dramatically convenient for the action to unfold, but a presence which cooperates in moulding the dramatic situation. He is quoted as saying that in drama scenery should create the situation (see Appendix 1) and in fact much of the vitality of his dialogue derives from this principle of welding it to the physical elements of a scene. It is a principle, as he repeated on a number of occasions, inspired by his reading of Shakespeare, and he quotes the example of the graveyard scene in *Hamlet*. Action and dialogue draw their life from and depend directly on the immediate situation.[18] Everything is expressed in terms of direct action on stage and hence 'narrative' or 'explanatory' dialogue (to clarify a preconceived plot or theme) is virtually absent.[19] The tension of the dialogue rarely derives from the pressure of an external situation; the action generates its own energy and gathers its own momentum from within.

To sustain this momentum from scene to scene involved establishing a dynamic and rhythmic pattern of images. Valle claimed that French Neoclassical doctrine had confined the natural vitality of the Spanish tradition in an alien straitjacket and he makes frequent pleas for a more visual approach to the theatre. By this he understands a constantly varying stage-picture, possibly achieved by lighting or variations on composite sets, in harmony with the mood and tempo of a play. He quotes the example of *La Celestina* with its varying moods, locations and 'gestural' dialogue intimately linked to these differing surroundings. On another occasion he draws a comparison with the silent cinema and suggests that the theatre would do well to learn from the techniques of this new art. Valle's advocacy of the multiple-scene principle was really a rejection of what he saw as a spurious Neoclassical concept of unity, that is, unity conceived as sameness. What he wished to substitute was a 'superior unidad de ambiente' by a combination of contrasting but related scenes which would also create a sense of rhythmic continuity.

Ramón Sender sees this attempt to harness the aesthetic responses proper to music and the visual arts as a shortcoming:

Podemos caer en trance leyendo a Valle-Inclán o a Rojas, pero no podremos ver sus obras en un escenario y entrar en el mundo secreto de las realidades determinantes para tener la impresión – es el gran placer del teatro – de que sabemos más de las motivaciones y las consecuencias de lo que pasa en la escena que los mismos personajes de la obra e incluso que el autor mismo. Esa colaboración entre el público y el autor es en Valle-Inclán imposible. El autor no quiere nuestra colaboración. Nos pide que nos dejemos hipnotizar. (p. 37)

Clearly the only kind of collaboration between play and public that Sender considers valid is a rational and intellectual one: an invitation to the spectator to interpret what he calls the 'realidad determinante' behind the 'realidad aparente'. Valle-Inclán does not generally issue such invitations nor does he exploit the dramatic irony of letting the audience see and know more than the characters involved in the action. He does not lead an audience to enquire why things are happening or what will be the outcome. Our interest is not solicited for individual problems, psychology or motivation. His method thus precludes the creation of tension by the interaction between character and situation, i.e. how a given character will react in a given situation. And, perhaps most fundamental of all, he does not use plot as a metaphor for theme. That is to say, events and characters are not generally highlighted or invested with symbolic value in order to illuminate the meaning of the total structure.

It does not follow, however, that because an audience is not invited to probe into a subtext, the only alternative is to fall into a trance. Dramatic tension is present in the best of Valle's plays but it is one created by challenging an audience with stimulating incongruities and contradictions. This tension is not at odds with a sense of unity because the contradictions usually imply a relationship. The association of apparently incongruous elements is, as he explains in one of his lectures, a powerful artistic stimulant: 'Pero el mejor camino para llegar a despertar la memoria nerviosa está en la oposición entre dos sentidos; algo que pudiera llamarse "la armonía de los contrarios"' (Madrid, p. 192). He then goes on to quote the example of feeling the sensation of warmth by a fireside while watching the snow fall outside. One feeling enhances the other by contradiction and a sense of interdependence is thereby created. Valle-Inclán exploited this principle of harmony of contrasts in most of his works from the *Sonatas* onwards. In *Sonata de otoño* (1902) the fear of death and mortal sin, both separately and together, add spice to the motif of love. Similar combinations of death, lust and greed create the dramatic chemistry

26

of works like the *Comedias*, *Divinas palabras* and the *Retablo*. A contrast of different cultural identities forms the axis of certain works: lyrical Provence and ascetic Castile in *Cuento de abril*, freewheeling paganism and dogmatic Catholic morality in *La Marquesa Rosalinda*, and again in *Divinas palabras*, the contradiction of pagan and Catholic strains in the culture of Galicia. Such dramatically fertile contradictions were not simply the result of aesthetic experimentation but insights into the component elements of Spanish culture, of whose contradictions Valle was keenly aware. *La Marquesa Rosalinda*, for instance, stylizes the real contradictions between French and traditional Castilian influences that characterized late-eighteenth-century aristocratic society. From *La Marquesa* onwards Valle discovered the dramatic potential of creating a dual response in the audience – at first half-lyrical, half-comic, and later somewhere between the tragic and grotesque. Even in the earlier work the comic had never been far behind the heroic. In *Aguila de blasón* and *Romance de lobos* absurdity mocks at heroic attitudes – though without undermining them – in the juxtaposition of Montenegro with the buffoon Don Galán and the madman Fuso Negro. In the plays of the final phase, the grotesque begins to undermine the heroic and constitutes a new version of the tragic.

The unified and essentially static world-view shared by the Symbolist playwrights, which in many cases proved to be such intractable dramatic material, is not dissimilar to the Renaissance philosophy behind the works of Shakespeare and the Elizabethans. It was no coincidence that Shakespeare was, for most of these writers, the presiding deity that loomed behind their more immediate influences. It is known that Shakespeare's example was constantly before Valle-Inclán[20] and particularly Shakespeare's capacity to combine a sense of the totality of life and of overall stillness with tension and dynamic movement. G. Wilson Knight's definition of this Shakespearean quality is helpful in trying to understand Valle-Inclán's dramatic method:

the germ of composition is an intuitive perception of a certain stillness, an idea or quality. Such an intuition will condition creation. It will not necessarily come before the work is started, but we must suppose there to be a moment of conception during the early stages of composition when the essential nature of the work to be is first apparent . . . This becomes the nucleus, preliminary drafts or ideas are recoloured to tone with it, action and imagery clothe it, grow from it, cluster round it. Or perhaps it is better to say that all actions, events and images that clash with the central intuition are rejected: it comes to the same thing . . . So we shall assume a single central though dynamic stillness at the back of the process, a hub of the turning wheel. (p. 37)

In his best work Valle-Inclán achieved something of this combination of present vitality and timeless distance, of restless movement within stasis and of contradiction and tension within total unity.

The early theatre:
Cenizas and El Marqués de Bradomín

It is possible that Valle's first play *Cenizas* would never have been given the honour of production if he had not lost his arm as the result of a wound received in a fracas with Manuel Bueno.[1] The performance, in the Teatro Lara on 7 December 1899, was organized by the Teatro Artístico, a group consisting of amateurs and professionals and including many of Valle's friends – Benavente and Martínez Sierra amongst them – to raise funds to buy the author an artificial arm. According to Fernández Almagro, although most of the tickets were sold, the play met with an unenthusiastic and mildly sarcastic response, due only in part to a deficient production, and barely survived its single performance (pp. 61–2). To those familiar with Valle-Inclán's mature work, *Cenizas* comes as a surprise, partly because it is so conventional and partly because it is so comprehensively bad. The theme of adultery treated in the play was one to which Valle was to return repeatedly throughout his artistic career. In dramatic conception and technique, however, the play was unlike anything else Valle wrote and provides more examples of artistic and dramatic attitudes that he was later to reject than lines he was to develop.

Cenizas concerns an adulterous relationship between the protagonist, Octavia, and a young painter, Pedro Pondal. We learn later in the play that Octavia had been married against her will to a man much older than herself. She is torn between her illicit love for Pedro, with whom she is living at the time, and her inherited sense of social morality and fears of eternal damnation. The forces of religion and society are embodied in the Jesuit priest Padre Rojas (whose unctuous self-righteousness is reminiscent of Don Inocencio in *Doña Perfecta*) and Octavia's mother, Doña Soledad, who uses Octavia's little daughter as a pawn in the battle for Octavia's salvation. Throughout the play it is intimated that Octavia is dying, although Valle deliberately eludes any factual explanation for this and even the doctor attending the patient is unspecific on the subject. The reason is that we are intended to see Octavia's death as the result of all the pressures which converge upon her. The twin fanaticisms that work so assiduously for her spiritual salvation successfully bring about her physical destruction. In the last act, while Doña Soledad is preying upon her daughter's fears of damnation, Padre Rojas is working on the offstage conversion of Pedro. The final scene in which Octavia dies as Doña Soledad and Padre Rojas burn her love letters points clearly to the author's view of moral and religious intransigence.

González López relates *Cenizas* to the decadent literature of the *fin de siècle* and, in particular, to the plays of Maeterlinck: 'Se expresa en este drama, en oposición a todo el arte realista, el triunfo del sentimiento sobre las circunstancias exteriores, y la exaltación de la hipersensibilidad hasta la morbosidad.'[2] The 'decadent' resolution of *Cenizas*, the exaltation of feeling above morality, argues, in his opinion, against any identification of this play with the nineteenth-century realism of, for example, Galdós. Ruiz Ramón modifies this view somewhat by saying that Valle, rather than exalting instinctive emotions, deliberately drains the theme of adultery of any ethical content: 'El adulterio está absolutamente desideologizado, pues es simple ocasión para crear una atmósfera literaturizada' (vol. 2, p. 102). What emerges most strongly from the play, however, is the condemnation of religious and moral fanaticism. The 'decadent' love relationship is, in fact, remarkably circumspect and we see Pedro and Octavia together relatively little. The protagonists are considerably weaker than the forces that act upon them. Pedro is a callow youth with little authority who spends most of his time being ordered out of his own house. Octavia is swayed one way then the other depending on who is talking to her. Both are manipulated to such an extent by the pressures exerted upon them that they hardly exist as characters. Far from sweeping conventional morality and codes of ethics aside, their love scarcely carries conviction and is slapped down like an insolent child. Valle's antipathy to the moral and religious abstractions that stifle love is evident and the castigation of intolerance is strongly reminiscent of Galdós.

If we turn to the purely dramatic conception and technique of the play, artistic viewpoint, characterization and dialogue are all cast in the mould of nineteenth-century realism. There is no trace of Symbolist influence in Valle-Inclán's first dramatic venture. The structure, for instance, is founded on the conflicts and tensions in certain individuals in confrontation with certain social or religious imperatives. The result is that some characters are seen emotionally from within, whereas others are seen ideologically from without, representing the abstract pressures of religion and society. In the case of the protagonists, Octavia and Pedro, Valle is interested in the inner life of his characters, their emotions, motivations, ethical dilemmas, all the psychological repercussions in their relationship provoked by the external pressures. The individual is at the centre of the picture and the whole drama focuses ultimately on the emotional suffering and tensions of the protagonists. In adapting his work to the theatre, Valle naturally turned to the accepted norms of the theatre of social problems and the successful models of writers like Dumas (*La Dame aux camélias*), Galdós and Ibsen (see Kirkpatrick and García Pavón). It is worth stressing this point because this was an approach which Valle was later to abandon in favour of a more collective idea of drama. However, before 1900, most of his writing reveals this same concentration on individual psychology and personal relationships. The *cuentos* of *Femeninas* and *Epitalamio* are centred around individual relationships and the technique of these early stories has left its mark on *Cenizas*. The action is developed in a succession of duologues, and entrances and exits are patently engineered to leave only two characters confronting each other on stage. Valle is evidently ill at ease in handling three- or four-cornered dialogues, since, even when a third character is allowed to be present, his or her role is temporarily subordinated to the requirements of the principal confrontation.

The *cuento* on which *Cenizas* itself is based, *Octavia Santino*,[3] presents the relationship between Octavia and Pedro Pondal virtually in isolation from its social and moral context. Their love is not an adulterous one and Octavia's confession to the existence of another lover is provoked by her bad conscience towards Pedro, not towards God or society. *Cenizas* introduces a social and religious dimension, which marks the first step in the process of a widening perspective which goes from the early short stories, through *Cenizas* and *El Marqués de Bradomín*, to the collective theatre of the *Comedias bárbaras*. The protagonists of *Cenizas* are conscious of an inner duality in their make-up, a tension between their instinctive, emotional selves and the exigencies of social and religious codes which they both carry within themselves and which act upon them from outside. To this extent it is possible to speak of *Cenizas* as 'bourgeois' theatre, in spite of

31

the fact that Valle resolves his play in favour of an illicit love which stands condemned in the eyes of church and society, since the dilemma itself is limited to the bourgeois sector of society. It is significant that Valle, in attempting to transcend the theatre of the individual, abandoned the urban bourgeois world in favour of a semi-feudal Galicia in which the characters do not suffer from this division between the demands of self and society. The *señores* are a law unto themselves and the *pueblo* are entirely identified with traditional collective attitudes.

Apart from highlighting the inner tensions and divisions of the individual, *Cenizas* is structured, like most nineteenth-century theatre, round a conflict of principle. The dramatic tension derives from a central 'issue' or 'problem' which is posed in moral terms, i.e. in terms of choice. Characterization is tailored to the requirements of the ideological opposition of love and abstract moral codes. Padre Rojas, Doña Soledad, the doctor and Sabel, the maid, are representative characters – religion, bourgeois society, science and the *pueblo* – such as we never meet again in Valle-Inclán's production. The somewhat myopic concentration on the central problem inhibits the free development of action and dialogue which we associate with Valle's later work. The action proceeds along a single line of development in a rather mechanical see-saw movement as Octavia is swayed first one way then the other. In general the dialogue is predictably consecutive and based on the assumption that the characters all listen to one another and reply in a more or less logical manner. The characters talk *about* the situation rather than in it. There is no sense of physical presence either in characters or decor and the language is lacking in the 'gestural' quality of Valle's more mature work. He had not yet discovered how to make his dialogue convey the same richly textured density of atmosphere as his descriptive prose. One of the main dramatic intuitions he was to develop later was precisely this relationship between the character and his personal landscape, his setting. In *Cenizas* the characters are seen only in relation to the moral problem.

Nine years after the appearance of *Cenizas*, Valle published a revised version of the play under the new title *El yermo de las almas: episodios de la vida íntima*. In this he added a prologue to explain the presence of Octavia in Pedro's house, where she had taken refuge after her husband's discovery of her love letters. There is a slight restructuring of the beginning of act I and certain passages are omitted to tighten up the dialogue, but the most significant modifications are in the stage directions. In *Cenizas* indications of gesture, intonation and movement are given briefly in brackets in the conventional way. The stage settings at the beginning of the play and each of the succeeding acts are also brief and functional. In the revised version the settings are greatly expanded and the stage directions in brackets replaced by extensive descriptive *acotaciones* placed at selected points in the action.

These *acotaciones*, written after *Aguila de blasón* and *Romance de lobos*, naturally reflect the new ideas he had evolved in the intervening years. They reveal a much more physical and visual approach, an eye for detail and a feeling of atmosphere. They evoke sights, sounds and smells. The physical details of expression, gesture and appearance are sharply delineated. The emotionally charged pauses and silences in the dialogue are carefully and sensitively pointed. Maeterlinck's influence has clearly left its mark on the scenic descriptions and on the revised passage of dialogue where Valle tries to restore to the play some of the emotional side of the central relationship and sensual quality of the original story.

Furthermore there is an obvious intention in the *acotaciones* to link, in Symbolist fashion, characters and events with an order and tradition beyond their immediate reality by relating them to literary and artistic archetypes. Pedro is compared to Raphael's self-portrait (p. 10) and on another occasion his 'frente orlada de rizos' is compared to that of 'un dios adolescente' (p. 71). Sabel, the maid, 'alza los brazos al cielo como una mujer de la Biblia' (p. 77), Octavia 'parece una de esas santas que en los remotos santuarios duermen bajo el retablo dorado en urnas de cristal' (p. 101) and her daughter stands framed in the doorway 'con la cabellera de oro flotando sobre los hombros, como el arcángel de la Anunciación' (p. 84). In other words there is a conscious effort to relate the characters both to a physical environment and to a literary and artistic tradition, to give them 'background' in the manner of *Flor de santidad* or the *Comedias bárbaras*. The words the characters speak, however, remain substantially the same. The overall dramatic conception of individually orientated 'problem' theatre and of personal relationships remains unchanged. In strictly dramatic terms, in terms of dialogue and possible performance, *El yermo de las almas* remains a conventional 'fourth-wall drama' conceived for a picture-frame stage, in which the springs of action are social, moral and psychological, and no amount of free-ranging *acotaciones* could alter this. In the early *Comedias bárbaras* the heroic archetypal images, evocations of nature and physical background are part of a total conception in which dialogue plays an integral part. In *Yermo* dialogue and *acotaciones* are at odds; Valle has tried to impose a later conception of theatre on to alien material.

Valle-Inclán must have been aware that the failure of *Cenizas* was due in large measure to his own incompatibility with the principles of realist drama. His second dramatic venture, however, enjoyed no better fortune than his first and has since remained in what is perhaps justified oblivion. Yet, in *El Marqués de Bradomín* (produced by the García Ortega company in 1906) the author clearly constructs his play on very different lines and tries to reflect the spirit of the stories on which it is based. The plot is broadly speaking a dramatization of his earlier *Sonata de otoño* (1902) with elements of *Flor de santidad* (1904) worked in. The dying Concha, referred to in the play as La Dama, sends for her former lover, the Marqués de Bradomín, but his arrival only serves to plunge her deeper into mental anguish, torn as she is between her love for the Marqués and her guilt feelings towards God, her husband and two daughters. Several sections of the dialogue are lifted straight out of the previously published material. Act I makes extensive use of the passages relating to the Ciego de Gondar and the other beggars from *Flor de santidad*. Adega herself appears as a rather pathetic and demented figure who begs from door to door. Act II incorporates the scene between the Marqués and Florisel of the *Sonata*, many of the better-known descriptive passages (e.g. p. 124) and a number of the *bons mots* associated with the Marqués, e.g. 'viva la bagatela', 'soy carlista por estética', and his self-description as 'confesor de princesas y teólogo de amor'. Act III reproduces the story of the princess and the jewels from *Flor de santidad*. The descriptive *acotaciones* and indeed the atmosphere of the play as a whole reflect the mood of the *Sonata* – gardens, roses, ancestral trees, abandoned fountains – a landscape which is a projection of the nostalgic, autumnal mood of the love between Concha and the Marqués.

If, as González López claims, *El Marqués de Bradomín* was intended for reading rather than production (p. 69), there seems to be little point in this rehash in dialogue form of material already published. The fact is that it *was* produced, presumably at Valle's own instigation. His intentions can only be a matter for conjecture, but if we regard this work as an attempt to express in theatrical terms the artistic intuitions of the *Sonatas* and *Flor de santidad*, it emerges as an interesting transitional stage between the early individual and the later collective drama. Like *Cenizas*, it portrays an adulterous situation. Concha's dilemma is comparable to that of Octavia, yet, although we witness the expression of Concha's doubts and anguish, the play does not centre round her inner conflict. Nor are the other characters, the Abad for example, ideologically conceived as a function of the 'central issue'. External pressures and inner psychological repercussions such as we find in *Cenizas* are for most of the play given little prominence. Valle tries to eliminate social and moral issues and psychological motivation, since he is principally concerned with dramatizing a 'mood'. He tries, as he did in the *Sonatas*, to elevate the love of Concha and Bradomín above the plane of personal relationships. Rather than two interacting personalities, Bradomín and Concha constitute a duet harmonizing a song to autumnal nostalgia in which the emotions blend with the natural background.[4]

Whereas the lovers of *Cenizas* are representative only of themselves and their passion, Bradomín has behind him a whole cultural and heraldic tradition. Valle is here more concerned with the forces of tradition and heredity working *through* characters than with the psychological dilemmas of individuals.[5] He has therefore begun to move away from the naturalistic and psychological dramatic tradition of the nineteenth century. Further evidence of Valle's departure from individual theatre to one of collective traditions is provided by his introduction of the itinerant beggars from *Flor de santidad*. What seems to have been in his mind was the creation of a more comprehensive picture of Galicia by fusing the aristocratic world of the *Sonatas* with the rural Galicia of *Flor de santidad*. Yet certain features of the individually orientated drama persist, particularly in the last act where Valle makes a significant change from the *Sonata de otoño* in order to resolve the situation he has prepared in the first two acts. It is here we can see *El Marqués de Bradomín* as a work of transition. The original *Sonata*, rather than tracing a relationship between individuals, derives its emotional impact from the interplay of the motifs of love, religion and death. Unlike the *Sonata*, the play makes little capital out of the approaching death and religious torments of Concha. Concha, in fact, does not die at the end of the play and there are very few references to fears of eternal damnation. We are left solely with the theme of adultery and its residual ethical associations.

There appears to be some confusion of purpose here. On the one hand, Valle evidently wishes to minimize the ethical conflict and concentrate on the aesthetic aspects of mood and atmosphere. On the other hand, he needs, at least at this stage in his career as a dramatist, the element of conflict contained in this situation to bring his play to a satisfactory resolution. The first two acts are diffuse, lyrical and rhapsodic in character and preserve the autumnal tone of the *Sonata*. The last act brings us back to moral and psychological conflict. The *Sonata* is resolved without recourse to psychology. Concha dies in an orgasm of erotic surrender and religious torment which fuses the principal motifs of love, religion and death into a kind of 'symphonic' climax. In the play Valle opts for a scene in which La Dama, having visited her sick husband's bedside, feels a resurgence of compassion and duty (p. 149) and is reduced by the anguish of her dilemma to the subterfuge of telling Bradomín that she has had another lover (a device borrowed from the short story *Octavia Santino*). This sub-terfuge, as Concha explains in a previous conversation with her cousin, Isabel, is the only certain way of enforcing a separation between herself and Bradomín. The last act transforms what had been a sentimental rhapsody into a conflict of emotion. It focuses the action on the central issue of adultery and on the psychological tensions of the characters involved. Concha's invention of a former lover is essentially a *psychological* move since it presupposes a certain type of character in Bradomín: the kind of man who could brook no competition in love, for whom love was an exclusive privilege. At this stage, it appears, the exigencies of dramatic form did not allow Valle to dispense with the emotional climax, the bringing into focus of a moral problem, the confrontation of protagonists in conflict. Whether he considered the 'symphonic' climax of the *Sonata* as inappropriate to the theatre at that time or whether he thought it too strong for presentation on the stage, we shall probably never know. The fact is he chose to replace it with a more traditional and conventional dénouement. Later he came to see the application of musical rhythm and tonal contrasts to the problem of dramatic construction as a practical possibility.

It must also be admitted that Valle's attempt to blend back-ground and foreground figures into a collective picture is far from convincing. The beggars, lifted bodily from *Flor de santidad*, do not achieve, as the author would probably have wished, a truly *choral* function. Their dialogue does not echo or comment on the same themes as those of the protagonists, as it does in the early *Comedias bárbaras*. The only relationship that exists between the two levels is that the *señores* are the dispensers of charity. For the rest, the interludes of the beggars are totally disconnected from the main action. There is an abyss between the decadent nostalgic mood of the protagonists and the earthy humour and stoic resignation of the beggars. It might be argued that Valle was deliberately contrasting the closed rarified world of Concha and Bradomín with the realities of the world outside. If so, why is the contrast not sustained? The fact is that in the last two acts the beggars disappear and the action is focused entirely on Concha and Bradomín. Valle had not yet abandoned the drama of emotional character relationships in favour of a theatre based on broad collective themes. He had not yet discovered, as he did in the *Comedias* and particularly in *Divinas palabras*, how to sustain dramatic interest and tension without recourse to individual conflicts which destroy the collective perspective. Dramatically, *El Marqués de Bradomín* is a hybrid, in which the choral folk background of *Flor de santidad*, the refined nostalgia of the *Sonata de otoño* and the introduction of character psychology from the early story *Octavia Santino* are imperfectly welded together.

3

The hero and his chorus:
the *Comedias bárbaras*

In 1907 and 1908 came the first two *Comedias bárbaras: Aguila de blasón*
and *Romance de lobos*.[1] The third, *Cara de plata*, conceived as the
opening volume to the trilogy, was completed fourteen years after and
corresponds stylistically to a much later period of Valle-Inclán's
development.[2] The central character of these plays, Don Juan
Manuel Montenegro, based on Valle's maternal grandfather, had
previously made brief appearances in some of the early stories (e.g.
Rosario), in the *Sonatas* and in *El Marqués de Bradomín*. But in their
overall conception these works break entirely new ground. Ignoring
the limitations of the conventional stage, Valle gives free rein to his
imagination. It is unlikely that the *Comedias* were written with a view
to stage production, at least in his own lifetime, given the theatrical
conditions that prevailed in his day. Even in his wildest dreams, Valle
could not have imagined that practical solutions could be found for
his multiple scenes, movement on horseback, storms at sea, cattle
grazing on the horizon, etc. in any foreseeable future. He discards all
the nineteenth-century conventions and writes for a theatre of his
mind. Yet, whatever the practical difficulties of staging – and these
have not proved as insuperable as previously supposed – the *Comedias*
are essentially dramatic in conception, because their impact lies in
light and shade, in the tension generated by contrasting motifs and in
the rhythm and texture of the spoken word. Not all the details which
Valle wrote into his *acotaciones* can be reproduced on the stage; nor is
this necessary. The essential requirement is that the *dialogue*, not just
the prose of his scenic descriptions, should have the power to
communicate the world of the *Comedias* as Valle-Inclán imagined it.
The capacity of the dialogue to achieve this will be discussed later in
the chapter.

In a letter to C. Rivas Cherif Valle-Inclán wrote:

He asistido al cambio de una sociedad de castas (los hidalgos que conocí de rapaz) y lo que yo vi no lo verá nadie. Soy el historiador de un mundo que acabó conmigo. Ya nadie volverá a ver vinculeros y mayorazgos. Y en este mundo que yo presento de clérigos, mendigos, escribanos, putas y alcahuetes, lo mejor – con todos sus vicios – era los hidalgos, lo desaparecido. (*España*, 16 February 1924)

For the first time Valle reveals his capacity for creating a work of epic scope and characters of heroic stature. The trilogy (it is convenient for the moment to include *Cara de plata* to give a general idea of content) portrays the disintegration of the Galician rural nobility as Valle remembered it in the late nineteenth century. This portrayal is thickly overlaid with medieval literary reminiscences, and the 'barbarous' elements which stimulated Valle's imagination. The central theme is the moral decay of the house of Montenegro exemplified in the sensual appetite and anachronistic pride of the father and in the violence and greed of his sons, who have inherited his arrogance without his nobility. In the sons the ancient aristocratic impetus and will to power have degenerated into robbery, gambling and crime. As Cara de plata says in *Aguila de blasón*, 'El día en que no podamos alzar partidas por un rey, tendremos que alzarlas por nosotros y robar en los montes. Ése será el final de mis hermanos' (*Aguila*, p. 123). *Cara de plata* reveals a Montenegro still spirited and defiant in defence of his *fueros*, arrogantly denying to all comers what had been a traditional right-of-way across his land. This is followed in *Aguila de blasón* and *Romance de lobos* by the struggle between the pride of the father and the rapacious greed of the sons over the inheritance and Montenegro's final gesture of dispossessing himself and his sons in favour of the poor.

Parallel to the theme of the conflict between Montenegro and his sons is a spiritual conflict in the protagonist himself. As in previous plays the theme of adultery is involved. For many years Montenegro's wife, Doña María, has lived apart from her husband as a result of the latter's sexual excesses. In *Cara de plata* and *Aguila de blasón* we see Montenegro living with his ward, Sabelita. Yet the austere figure of Doña María stirs a residual feeling of guilt and religious conscience in Montenegro. Such guilt feelings have little part to play in *Cara de plata* in which Montenegro's defiance of man and God culminates in an act of deliberate sacrilege. In *Aguila*, however, we see the gradual erosion of his personality by feelings of guilt and remorse, with the jester Don

Galán acting as the voice of his conscience. The death of Doña María in *Romance* brings the conflict to a point of crisis, which Montenegro resolves in an act of self-abasement (albeit a heroic one) and universal charity. The ending of *Romance de lobos* thus resolves both the theme of moral degeneration and that of Montenegro's spiritual conflict.

Both of these themes are richly orchestrated by a multitude of minor characters – the servants of the house, the chaplain, the villagers, beggars, etc. – and by allusions to the Galician landscape. But perhaps more important is the *trasmundo* of superstition and collective forces that transcends the purely social vision and interweaves background and foreground figures into a diverse and closely textured tapestry. If *Cenizas* was a bourgeois interior, *Aguila* and *Romance* are comparable to the collective creations of Brueghel the Elder. The central characters and themes are constantly related to their social and mythical background, even to the extent of occasionally being swamped by it (e.g. Sabelita's encounter with La Preñada and El Abuelo in *Aguila*, III, 6). The forces which determine behaviour in the characters are those of tradition, primary instinct, superstition, caste and heredity. Valle is not concerned here with psychological relationships or interacting personalities in a given situation. Even less is he concerned with any conflict of ethical principle. He abandons analysis and moral or ideological interpretation and echoes the voice of a collectivity. The characters are conceived *archetypally* in that they are seen as products of a natural background and a certain cultural tradition. The heroic stature and authority of Don Juan Manuel comes from the weight of feudal tradition behind him. His every word and act, his *risa feudal*, stamp him as the *gran señor*. We see the force of heredity in the violent and arrogant conduct of his sons, although his nobility and generosity are revealed only in Cara de plata. As Don Pedrito rapes Liberata, the miller's wife, 'siente como un numen profético el alma de los viejos versos que oyeron los héroes en las viejas lenguas' (*Aguila*, p. 51) and, in the combat with Oliveros, Don Mauro stands 'fuerte, soberbio, con la cabeza desnuda y las manos rojas de sangre, como el héroe de un combate primitivo en un viejo romance de Castilla' (*Romance*, p. 102). The serfs and household servants of *Aguila* and the beggars of *Romance* form a choral element whose words and attitudes are entirely identified with traditional beliefs, fears and superstitions. Their dialogue frequently has a rhythmic, ritualistic quality like the ebb and flow of the sea: 'Los criados comentan en voz baja, graves, lentos, reunidos a la redonda de la cesta llena de mazorcas, y sus voces supersticiosas parece que van en la oscuridad de un misterio hacia otro misterio' (*Romance*, p. 115). At certain moments in *Romance de lobos* their voices are raised in a collective chant:

LOS MENDIGOS: ¡Era la madre de los pobres! ¡Nunca hubo puerta de más caridad! ¡Dios nuestro Señor la llamó para sí y la tiene en el cielo al lado de la Virgen Santísima! ¡Era la madre de los pobres! (*Romance*, p. 63)

The beggars are distanced and stylized rather than drawn from life and analysed in a social milieu. They represent the archetypal poor, the eternal 'sheep' at the mercy of the 'wolves' of Montenegro's sons, a part of the inevitable order of things rather than an anomalous injustice to be remedied.

In *Aguila* and *Romance* we see an important development in the function of the background. The dreaming, melancholy gardens in *El Marqués de Bradomín* reflect the dominant autumnal mood of the protagonists. Nature is clearly a projection of the characters. In the *Comedias* it is an objective reality which serves to mould the characters and the situation; not a passive backdrop, but an active, determining presence. In *El Marqués* Valle sees the setting in terms of the action and theme; in *Aguila* and *Romance* he begins to reverse the process. He begins to see action and theme in terms of the setting, the light and the atmosphere. 'Porque se parte de un error fundamental', he is quoted as saying some years later, 'y es éste: el creer que la situación crea el escenario. Eso es una falacia, porque al contrario, es el escenario el que crea la situación' (see Appendix 1). If, by *escenario*, we understand not only the physical conditions but the whole cultural tradition, we can see that the characters of the early *Comedias* are figures in a landscape, formed by the landscape and inseparable from the landscape. In *Romance de lobos* the human drama is moulded, enhanced and magnified by the presence of storm, wind and sea. In the scene between Montenegro and Fuso Negro (III, 4), poetic links are forged between the physical properties of the scene and the human emotions:

EL CABALLERO: ¿Tienes hambre, hermano Fuso Negro?
FUSO NEGRO: Los vinculeros y los abades siéntanse a una mesa con siete manteles, y llenan la andorga de pan trigo y chicharrones. Luego a dormir y que amanezca. ¡Jureles asados! . . . ¡Sartenes sin rabos! . . . ¡Una vieja con los ojos encarnados! . . . ¡El loco tiene siempre hambre! . . .

EL CABALLERO: ¡La furia de tus dientes me desvela!

FUSO NEGRO: ¡Es duro como un hueso este rebojo!

EL CABALLERO: ¡Yo hace dos días que no como y todo el hambre dormida se despierta oyéndote roer!

FUSO NEGRO: ¡Parezco un can!

EL CABALLERO: ¿Es el mar o son tus dientes en el mendrugo?

FUSO NEGRO: ¡Cómo broa el mar!

EL CABALLERO: ¡No sé si el mar, si tus dientes hacen ese gran ruido que no me deja descansar y se agranda dentro de mí!

FUSO NEGRO: ¡Es la voz de la cueva!

This scene, needless to say, has little to do with a psychological confrontation. The two characters do not react to each other as individuals, each with his own character and social background. The dying Montenegro, stripped of his worldly goods, crazed with grief and remorse, weak from hunger, is here reduced, like Lear, to the level of 'unaccommodated man'. In Fuso Negro he meets his 'Poor Tom'. The dialogue links their two worlds poetically by fusing images of physical hunger with the gnawing of conscience and awareness of approaching death. What is worth noting about this scene and about *Romance de lobos* in general is the way Montenegro's 'inner' anguish is expressed in terms of the physical montage: the roar of the sea and Fuso's teeth on the crust of bread.

One of Valle's most significant achievements in the early *Comedias bárbaras* is the new interdependence of foreground and background. The link of character and landscape is one aspect of this. Another is the link between the heroic figures and the choral entourage, conspicuously lacking in *El Marqués de Bradomín*. Don Juan Manuel is as inseparable from his host of dependants as he is from his historical tradition and the physical setting. The household servants, feudal tenants and beggars at the door are the necessary orchestration to his heroic stature. Together they form the naturally complementary halves of the feudal world of the *Comedias bárbaras*. Montenegro even makes the confession of his sins of lust and pride into a gesture of heroic self-abasement and calls, with an inborn sense of theatre, for the presence of his servants and the beggars he has introduced into the house, who 'van llegando de la cocina con un rumor lento, ojos de susto, gesto de misterio, y se detienen sobre el umbral de la puerta' (*Romance*, p. 93). At the end of the confession 'El capellán traza una cruz con su diestra sobre la cabeza del viejo linajudo, y el murmullo de los rostros aldeanos y mendigos, resplandeciente de fe, se eleva en una grave onda' (*Romance*, p. 95). The dialogue of the minor characters is integrated with the central action and sometimes provides a direct gloss or choral comment on events. Throughout *Aguila* and *Romance* Valle intersperses scenes of choral orchestration which afford an alternative view of the central characters from below. There is no sense of *desajuste*, as there was in *El Marqués de Bradomín*, between chorus and protagonists, collective and individual attitudes, since the same general motifs of sensuality, greed, superstition, etc., permeate both the actions of the principal characters and the glosses of the choral elements. The subtly indicated sensuality of Liberata la molinera and the peasant avarice of her complaisant husband Pedro Rey serve as collective echoes of Montenegro's lust and the greed of his sons. After the scene of Don Pedrito's rape of Liberata (*Aguila*, II, 4), Valle places a scene depicting a peasant gathering in the mill in which the ribald comments of the 'mozos que tientan a las mozas en el fondo oscuro, sobre el heno oloroso' and 'las manos atrevidas' which 'huronean bajo las faldas' re-echo the sensuality of the previous scene. In the more fragmented structure of *Aguila de blasón*, the scenes of choral comment are almost always separated off into self-contained units. The scene switches, for instance, from Montenegro's dining hall to a below-stairs scene in the kitchen. Micaela la Roja, the ancient retainer, and, in particular, Don Galán serve as linking characters. *Romance de lobos* achieves a more fluid relationship between chorus and protagonists and Valle is able to dispense with the linking function of these two characters.

The choral function of Valle-Inclán's minor characters was noted – though without specific reference to the *Comedias* – by Pérez de Ayala (pp. 144 and 146). The classical Greek chorus served a purpose of commenting on and generalizing the theme (and thereby acting as an intermediary between play and audience) which modern writers of poetic tragedy have tried to revive in various ways.[3] The generalizing role of the chorus has frequently been felt to be a dramatic requirement, part of the essential shorthand of the theatre, though attempts at revival often have a contrived and artificial air about them. The 'choral' characters of the *Comedias* are not conceived primarily as a dramatic contrivance. They are first and foremost a natural product of the context and, unlike the classical chorus, their collective presence is an integral part of the action and mood of the play. Their dramatic role as a unified chorus blends easily with, and is indeed inseparable from, their natural existence as a group of individuals in the semi-feudal world of the *Comedias*. One of Valle's great achievements in these plays is precisely this balance of group feeling and individual (though not psychological) identity in the minor characters. The household servants are delineated with bold, economical outlines: La Roja with her quiet authority of the oldest retainer, Andreíña la sorda, sly and sententious, the pathetic obtuseness and grotesque appearance of La Rebola and the rustic naïvety of El rapaz de las vacas. In attitude and appearance they are sufficiently differentiated to allow Valle-Inclán subtle fluctuations between choral glosses on events that concern them as a group and cross-talk between individuals.

In the choral scenes Valle reverses foreground and background and views the protagonists obliquely and at a distance, from below. The inspiration for this type of dialogue could well have come from the servants' scene in Maeterlinck's *Pelléas et Mélisande* (v, 4). By their very nature these scenes do not develop the narrative line since they serve primarily as a static gloss on events. Yet Valle's innate dramatic feeling for place and rhythm makes them compelling theatre.

Act III, scene 2 of *Romance de lobos* provides an excellent example of how the dialogue gathers power from an acute sense of the physical context. Montenegro, now on the verge of madness, has locked himself in the room where Doña María had died, firmly resolved to starve himself to death. The servants gather in an anteroom and listen anxiously to the sound of his footsteps pacing restlessly up and down. The opening *acotación* establishes the basic components of the scene: the closed door, the rhythmic pattern of footsteps and the responses of the servants. The scene is constructed on the basis of three entrances, Doña Moncha, Montenegro's niece, the Chaplain and finally Artemisa, Montenegro's illegitimate daughter, each of whom approaches the door, knocks, waits and rejoins the group. This pattern of physical movement, with slight variations for each entrance, is matched by a pattern of responses from the assembled servants ranging from tense silence to solemn ritualistic commentary to uneasy banter. Valle composes the scene for eye and ear, integrating the rhythmic pattern of footsteps offstage with the movements and carefully modulated responses of the onstage characters. It is not sufficient to speak merely of the 'creation of atmosphere' since, despite its static nature, the scene has tension and rhythmic structure. The tension derives from what we imagine to be going on behind the closed door (an oblique device that could have been inspired by Maeterlinck's *La Mort de Tintagiles*).[4] The guilt gnawing at

Montenegro's soul and the madness taking possession of his mind are filtered indirectly through the reactions of the waiting characters as they respond to the obsessive footsteps which approach the door, recede and approach again. A principal action is obliquely portrayed through its choral 'echo'. The scene builds rhythmically with each entrance to the climax of Montenegro's violent eruption from the room at the end.

Even at this early stage in Valle's dramatic career, we can glimpse behind the collective conception of *Aguila* and *Romance* a view of philosophical determinism. A letter written to C. Rivas Cherif in 1924 throws some retrospective light on to this aspect of the *Comedias*.

Creo cada día con mayor fuerza que el hombre no se gobierna por sus ideas y su cultura. Imagino un fatalismo del medio, de la herencia y de las taras fisiológicas, siendo la conducta totalmente desprendida de los pensamientos. Y, en cambio, siendo los oscuros pensamientos motrices consecuencia de las fatalidades de medio, herencia y salud. Sólo el orgullo del hombre le hace suponer que es un animal pensante. En esta *Comedia Bárbara* [*sic*] (dividida en tres tomos: *Cara de plata*, *Aguila de blasón*, y *Romance de lobos*) estos conceptos que vengo expresando motivan desde la forma hasta el más ligero episodio. (*España*, 16 February 1924)

In the early *Comedias* we can see the determinism of tradition, environment and of certain collective passions on the characters. These passions – lust, greed and superstition – are seen as present in the *ambiente* rather than as psychological traits of individuals, although they are not so clearly defined as they are in the later *Divinas palabras* and the *Retablo de la lujuria, la avaricia y la muerte*.

A problem arises with what is after all the nucleus of the plays, around which all the rest gathers: the spiritual conflict in Montenegro. If we interpret Montenegro's adultery, penitence and death at the hands of his sons in the light of Christian morality, as moral retribution for his pride, lust and neglect of his wife, we would be faced with an apparent contradiction, since the determinism implicit in the work largely removes the question of moral responsibility and the rights and wrongs of characters' actions. If we think in terms of original sin, individual conscience, a personal God and Redeemer, we would be forced to conclude that Montenegro's voluntary act of penance does not square with a deterministic view. Yet while the outline of events and even certain Christian ideas of guilt, remorse, conscience, etc. expressed by the characters may seem to support the Christian interpretation, the dramatic presentation tells another story. For, in reality, Valle does not present the conflict in ethical terms and does not situate the choice of Good or Evil in the conscience of the protagonist. Don Juan Manuel is rather the battleground for a titanic struggle of absolutes, seen not internally as a problem of conscience but externally in terms of theatrical imagery and montage. Unlike the adulterous situation in *Cenizas*, Don Juan Manuel's condition is not problematic. There are no half shades, hesitations or moments of agonized indecision. This is well expressed by Francisco Ruiz Ramón who describes Montenegro in these terms:

Héroe de un mundo regido por valores absolutos – positivos o negativos – y por pasiones no menos absolutas, en donde no caben los términos medios entre el bien y el mal, entre la humanidad y la animalidad, ni los compromisos de ninguna índole, y en donde los sentimientos son sustituidos por los actos y las impulsiones inmediatas. (vol. 2, p. 106)

His struggle with the Devil is concomitant with his heroic stature. While using a basically Christian vocabulary, Valle, with his esoteric amalgam of Gnosticism, Christianity and aesthetics, saw Good and Evil more as absolute forces in conflict than as alternative choices for the individual conscience. The forces that fight for supremacy in Montenegro are to a great extent embodied in the characters of Doña María and Fuso Negro: Doña María, epitomizing remote, austere spirituality, more powerful in death than in life, and Fuso Negro, irrational, anarchic, the epitome of animality. These ideas, based on a vision of a radical dualism between God and a benighted humanity in the grips of *mundo*, *demonio* and *carne*, were later crystallized in *La lámpara maravillosa* and also form the basis of *Divinas palabras*. Fuso Negro's explanation of original sin in terms of the incubus and the succubus (*Romance*, III, 4) reveals a world in bondage to Satan's powers, in which all to some degree are possessed by the satanic spirit of pride and egocentric passion.

In view of this cosmic and non-individual perspective, the nature of Montenegro's 'conversion' is difficult to establish. Gustavo Umpierre, in an interesting and thought-provoking article, sees Montenegro as a man who, by his alliance with the poor and defenceless, fuses the spirit of Nietzschean vitalism with Christian compassion (*BHS*, 1973). He discerns in the final apocalyptic struggle of the Pobre de San Lázaro and Don Mauro a visual symbol of the two opposing forces that have been fighting for supremacy in Montenegro's soul: egoistic pride and compassion. As they both fall, locked in combat, into the flames of the hearth, they are consumed, purified and transformed into a synthesis. The idea is ingenious although questionable on several counts. First, Valle mentions only the Pobre de San Lázaro as emerging from the flames, transfigured and 'hermoso como un arcángel'. The stage direction implies that Don Mauro has been defeated and killed. Secondly, it is not clear how this symbolic struggle reflects what after all had been an important element in Montenegro's conflict, i.e. lust. Finally, the assertion that Nietzsche's 'will to power' philosophy lies behind the conception of the central protagonist seems a little dubious. Nietzsche emphasizes that the will to power is a creative process of 'self-overcoming' and self-aggrandizement, directed at the ultimate creation of a humanity that would be the originator of its own values in a world deserted by its creator (Nietzsche, *Thus spake Zarathustra*, pp. 136–9). It is in any case a conscious philosophical stance against despair, nihilism and the engulfing tide of mass standards. Montenegro's vitalism is not a philosophical stance or a *willed* response to life; he has little in common with the will-obsessed protagonists of Baroja's novels. It is not something he has to nurture and cultivate within himself, but an instinctive birthright which springs from his traditional relationship with his dependants and with the poor who rely on his charity. Montenegro's strength is thus not a product of his individuality but of the collective tradition and it is mainly in defence of that tradition that he leads the beggars to take possession of the house which he had abandoned to his sons. What impels him to this action is not so much Christian compassion or, as Greenfield suggests (*Anatomía*, p. 95), his guilt feelings towards the widow of one of the seamen whose lives had been lost on his responsibility, but the knowledge that the traditional right of charity had been denied at his door. He leads his army of beggars not in the name of a new revolutionary order but to restore a traditional order and relationship which the selfish passions of lust and greed had caused to decline.[5]

However, it must be stressed that the determinism of *Aguila* and *Romance* is of a very positive nature. The characters are not mindless puppets or *victims* of forces beyond their control. The individual is not submerged or even threatened. On the contrary, he is enhanced by his total identification with the milieu and the collective tradition. The characters of the *Comedias* draw their strength from that tradition and emerge as archetypes beyond the reach of time and change. A passage from a lecture by Valle in 1910 gives a very good picture of his attitude to characterization about this time:

El artista debe mirar el paisaje con 'ojos de altura' para poder abarcar todo
el conjunto y no los detalles mudables. Conservando en el arte ese aire de
observación colectiva que tiene la literatura popular, las cosas adquieren
una belleza de alejamiento.

Por eso hay que pintar a las figuras añadiéndoles aquello que no hayan
sido. Así un mendigo debe parecerse a Job y un guerrero a Aquiles. (Gómez
de la Serna, p. 110)

When Valle spoke these words he was probably thinking of the
Comedias bárbaras and, in particular, of the Pobre de San Lázaro in
Romance de lobos in whose 'voz gangosa y oscura se arrastra como una
larva la tristeza milenaria de su alma de siervo' (*Romance*, p. 47).[6] The
Pobre de San Lázaro, even with his Job-like humility and his 'alma de
siervo', emerges as a heroic character. Indeed the entire vision that
informs the early *Comedias* is unequivocally heroic. Even the grotesque figure of Don Galán enhances rather than diminishes Montenegro. When the individual becomes inadequate to the roles that
tradition thrusts upon him, we have the *esperpento*.

In *Cenizas* the focus of interest was, as in the case of many
nineteenth-century dramas, a conflict between individual and social
values. The source of dramatic tension is, as it were, built into the
subject matter: the subject is the conflict and the conflict provides the
tension. By the interaction of character and situation, the conflict is
developed and finally resolved in the death of the protagonist. Some
form of tension between character and context, whether overt or
implied, is a constant feature of the problematic individual theatre.
In the *Comedias bárbaras* Valle is interested principally in collective
manifestations as exemplified in a heroic figure and his chorus, in
what unites characters to their context and tradition rather than the
reverse. The tension between context and individual is thereby
eliminated. The elements of conflict that do exist in the work (i.e. the
'conscience' struggle in Montenegro or the conflict between father
and sons) are presented in a distanced manner which does not
stimulate ethical tension in either characters or audience. To this
extent we may speak of them as non-problematic conflicts. The
Comedias bárbaras involve a different conception of how man relates to
the world from *Cenizas* and this, accordingly, dictates a whole new
dramatic technique and language, capable of expressing in theatrical
terms the non-rational, non-personal drives and impulses that
motivate the action. Thus the dramatic technique also tends to
become increasingly non-rational and aimed at stimulating sensual

rather than intellectual or critical responses. From psychological tension between character and character or between character and situation, Valle goes to a theatre of direct visual action, multiple scenes and proliferation of background characters; from engineered climaxes to a dynamic succession of cinematographic images and tonal contrasts; from the language of argument and analysis to the *grito* and the *sentencia* (see Appendix 2).

The visual and cinematographic quality of the early *Comedias bárbaras* needs no emphasis. We follow characters on foot or horseback as they travel along; characters in the background for one scene emerge into the foreground for the next; there is abrupt cutting from interior to exterior settings, from the master in the dining hall to the servants in the kitchen. Light plays an integral role – the varying tones of daylight shading into night, interiors dramatically lit by candlelight or a blazing fire – and the gradations of light serve both dramatic atmosphere and continuity. Valle shapes each scene as a self-contained unit with its appropriate lighting, shape and rhythm and puts them together like camera shots. Of course, not all cinematographic techniques make for legitimate and effective theatre. *Aguila de blasón* is undoubtedly a little uncontrolled and self-indulgent in its diversity of scenes and characters. After act III the play becomes excessively fragmented with the cinematic 'tracking' of Sabelita's flight from Montenegro, the dream of Doña María and the body-snatching episode with Farruquiño, Cara de plata and La Pichona. Many of these scenes are excellent in themselves but tend to divide the reader's or spectator's attention between the main action and the subsidiary episodes. *Romance de lobos*, while using the same techniques, is more successful in conveying a sense of unity and relevance between the principals and the background.

The *Comedias* are organically much more complex than the earlier plays. The dialogue is given a greater degree of density and capacity for suggestion by the interplay of conflicting ingredients and the intertwining of diverse and incongruous strands. It is able to stimulate the imagination in different directions simultaneously. *Cenizas*, by contrast, is thin and one-dimensional. *El Marqués de Bradomín* tries to diversify the mood but fails to establish any connection between the different elements. The play, in fact, does not do what the *Sonata* does extremely well, which is to bring out the ironic counterpoise, the self-mocking irony of the Marqués. *Aguila de blasón* reveals a Valle-Inclán already confident in the technique of tonal counterpoint. In this respect, the creation of Don Galán marks a significant step in his career as a dramatist.

Apart from providing medieval colour, with reminiscences of the court jester and the licensed fool, Don Galán has an essential dramatic function in his relationship with Montenegro. We often see them together when Montenegro is in his darkest moods and the master's anger or brooding is deliberately offset by Don Galán's drunken clowning (e.g. *Aguila*, II, 7). The grotesque is allowed to undermine and comment on the heroic. Yet behind this contrast lies the hint of identification. Montenegro himself calls Don Galán 'una voz de mi conciencia' and tells Doña María 'Don Galán con sus burlas y sus insolencias edifica mi alma, como Don Manuelito edifica la tuya, con sus sermones' (p. 83). Such moments of thematic explicitness are rare in Valle-Inclán and should be respected, but, as Sumner Greenfield suggests, it might be more accurate to see Don Galán as the voice of Montenegro's *subconscious* since what he receives from Don Galán is more a reflection of himself than the moral promptings of conscience (*Anatomía*, p. 69). This implicit relationship is externalized in a powerful image in *Aguila*, IV, 8. A drunken Don Galán invites his master to pray with him for the rest of Sabelita's soul since they believe her to be dead. As they kneel together Montenegro sees their reflection in the mirror.

Don Galán se arrodilla y hace la señal de la cruz con esa torpeza indecisa y sonámbula que tienen los movimientos de los borrachos. La imagen del bufón aparece en el fondo de un espejo, y el Caballero la contempla en el fondo de esa lejanía nebulosa y verdeante como en la quimera de un sueño. Lentamente el cristal de sus ojos se empaña como el nebuloso cristal del espejo. (p. 156)

Montenegro contemplates Don Galán with the mixture of disdain and affectionate sadness of one who recognizes the farce inherent in his own life and the pathetic animality of the human being beneath the pride and the social status. The element of farce in Montenegro's situation comes out strongly in the final scene of *Aguila* when he goes through the charade of hiding his new concubine, Liberata, under the table when they are surprised by the entrance of Doña María who 'permanece muda y altiva ante la farsa carnavelsca del marido que esconde a la manceba debajo de la mesa' (p. 183). The boisterous interplay of threats, jokes, blows and grotesque histrionics between Montenegro and Don Galán has an almost ritualistic quality. Both are playing a part and each knows what the other expects.

Montenegro's laughter at Don Galán, the 'risa soberana y cruel', is ultimately directed at himself. The role of Don Galán is largely taken over in *Romance de lobos* by Fuso Negro. Don Galán is fundamentally a very sympathetic and human character and one who is a natural part of the feudal setting. *Romance* is a play in which the conflict of lust and the spirit in the protagonist is elevated to a more universal plane. Valle therefore required a character who was more 'free' and 'uninvolved'. The mysterious and satanic creation of Fuso Negro is conceived on a more absolute scale.

Dramatic tension in the *Comedias bárbaras* comes from the juxtaposition of disparate and sometimes incongruous tones and ingredients. The scenes of greatest dramatic density are those in which the dialogue is able to reflect these different suggestions and cross-currents. This certainly does not apply equally to all scenes. The first few episodes of *Aguila de blasón*, dealing with the masked intruders into Montenegro's house, are, despite the wealth of physical action, dramatically very thin. The dialogue is keyed almost exclusively to the physical movement of the scene and is totally lacking in background suggestion. In fact we are not far from melodrama. In the next few scenes of act II, at first quiet and reflective by contrast, the cross-currents of superstition, peasant greed, lust and sensuality begin to move in the dialogue.

The most common technique of highlighting these tensions is by juxtaposition in consecutive episodes. For example, the entrances of the austerely spiritual Doña María are often timed to interrupt scenes bordering on slapstick comedy. In *Aguila* (III, 7), her appearance produces an abrupt change of tone when she interrupts the drunken antics of Montenegro and Don Galán. She also enters after the farcical scene in which Montenegro deals with the Escribano and Alguacil who come to investigate the attempted robbery (*Aguila*, III, 2). Conversely, the strange nightmare quality of the scene of Doña María's 'Niño Jesús' fantasy, reflecting her disturbed conscience, is followed by the broad comedy 'de clásica trapisonda' in Montenegro's bed chamber when Liberata and Don Galán debate whether she should get into his bed or not (analysed by Sumner Greenfield in *Anatomía*, pp. 81–2). In *Romance* the scene of Montenegro's sons squabbling over the spoils of their inheritance is placed next to the one describing the laying-out of Doña María's body. The technique is immediately obvious in the plays and it would be pointless to go on listing examples. Less common in the early

Comedias is the interaction of sharply contrasting ingredients within a single episode. The technique is perhaps more characteristic of *Divinas palabras* but there are one or two examples in *Aguila* and *Romance*.

Aguila de blasón IV, 7 is an example of Valle-Inclán's black humour. Don Farruquiño, the sacrilegious seminarist, has persuaded Cara de plata to assist him in digging up a body from the local graveyard in order to sell the skeleton in the Seminary. They bring the body back to La Pichona's cottage where a huge cauldron of water is bubbling in readiness to boil the flesh off the bones. The scene that follows contrasts two activities, that of Farruquiño who sets about boiling the semi-decomposed corpse and hacking the flesh off the bones, and of Cara de plata who makes love to La Pichona in the same room. The corpse tossing and turning in the cauldron and the lovers doing likewise on the bed has the macabre antithetical impact of a medieval 'dance of death', yet with humorous rather than cautionary overtones – the flesh in life and the flesh in death. The visual contrast is underscored by an auditory one: 'Se oye el golpe de las tenazas sobre las costillas de la momia, y los suspiros de la manceba y el rosmar del gato' (p. 150). On another occasion the text refers to the bubbling and sizzling of the cauldron and the creaking of the bed. These juxtaposed elements energize the dialogue. La Pichona's alternations between horror and sensuality serve as the link between the grim application of Farruquiño and the casual jocularity of Cara de plata.

The dramatic vitality of this scene should not make us lose sight of the question of its thematic relevance and justification in the context of the play as a whole. For Sumner Greenfield it reflects what he sees as a fundamental theme of the *Comedias*: 'esa lucha, muy medieval, entre la carne y el espíritu, que se va planteando en Don Juan Manuel y en las dos mujeres cruciales, su mujer y su barragana' (*Anatomía*, p. 80). The objection to this argument is that the spiritual side of the conflict is nowhere to be seen in this episode. The counterpoint here is between a 'gather-ye-rosebuds' carnality and the physical horror of death without the slightest suggestion of any ethical tension. Whereas the theme of lust is certainly fundamental to *Aguila de blasón*, death only emerges as a major theme in *Romance de lobos*. The insertion of this scene in the separate context of *Aguila* (as opposed to the *Comedias* as a whole) is perhaps a little arbitrary. It seems, moreover, to have been written with at least one eye on the reader or audience, to provoke a reaction rather than reflect a reality. If we compare it with similar bold juxtapositions between death and the grotesque elements which make a mockery of death in the final scenes of *Luces de Bohemia*, the difference becomes clear. There the contradictory ingredients give each other mutual support and form a unity because they are anchored in the same perception of reality.

In the second example the conflicting impulses come from within the characters themselves. The ransacking of the Montenegro chapel by Farruquiño and Pedrito in *Romance de lobos* (II, 1) generates a dynamic tension between greed and superstitious fear. This tension starts in a low ironical key as Farruquiño makes a devout genuflexion before setting about the systematic pillaging of the gold and silver ornaments and rises to a peak of hysteria as Pedrito, witnessing this from the chapel gallery, struggles with the incongruous emotions inside him. Greed and terror are juxtaposed in bold primary colours with no psychological half-tones. They are feelings rooted in the collective atmosphere of the play and not in the personal prehistory of the characters. The mounting tension between them, as in the previous example, is developed rhythmically by means of repeated movements and phrases. The frenzied struggle of greed and terror builds to the climax of Pedrito rushing blindly from the chapel gallery and disappearing into the night.

Contrary to the basically Symbolist view of the *Comedias bárbaras* taken so far in this chapter, it should be pointed out that at least two critics have argued in favour of a historical interpretation. Alfredo Matilla Rivas claims that the work must be considered historical drama according to the definition of G. Lukács, since Montenegro constitutes a historical individual whose moral and spiritual transformation reflects a larger social transformation (pp. 53–66). Juan Antonio Hormigón, on the other hand, paying less attention to the spiritual conflict in the protagonist, argues that the real tension is between Montenegro's personal values and the inevitable historical process to which he eventually succumbs (*La cultura*, p. 72). Both these interpretations presuppose the existence of a visible transformational process in the society in which Montenegro moves – a process which is very difficult to see, especially in *Aguila de blasón* and *Romance de lobos*. It could be argued that the attitude of the *chalanes* at the beginning of the later *Cara de plata* is no longer one of feudal acceptance and dependence and reveals a more emancipated and aggressive outlook.

There is some truth in this; on the other hand, *Cara de plata* is in many other respects quite remote from the world of *Aguila* and *Romance* and is perhaps best considered as an independent product of Valle's later period. In any case, one would expect such revolutionary attitudes at the end of the trilogy rather than in the play designed as the opening volume. Oddly, after the revolutionary opening, the social background in *Aguila* and *Romance* reverts to being essentially feudal and static. Montenegro and his sons are not portrayed as caught up in a changing society; we are shown the decadence of the sons in contrast to the nobler qualities of the father but there is little evidence of historical change in the wider social context. The scene of Montenegro's clash with the Escribano and the Alguacil (the only incident quoted by Hormigón) is too isolated an episode to support a general theory of interpretation. For the historical view of the *Comedias* to be tenable there must surely be more evidence either of socio-economic changes which conflict with Montenegro's values or changes of moral attitude in the society which reflect those in the protagonist. It is difficult to support either of these cases, since Valle-Inclán's portrayal of the collectivity, that is, the choral elements of the *Comedias*, concentrates primarily on those aspects which either resist or transcend historical change.

What does emerge from the *Comedias* is the beginnings of a paradox that was to exercise Valle as an artist for most of his career. This is a dual impression of surface movement and fundamental stasis that emanates from the works, the coexistence of sensual immediacy and archetypal distance. In a play like Lorca's *Bodas de sangre* the dialogue reaches down below the surface of character and events to the underlying images of blood, earth and water. But these images live and are nourished at the expense of the characters and their interaction; they devitalize the surface reality of the play. Valle is able to convey the archetypal qualities of character and the presence of unseen forces in the action without losing the edge of present, three-dimensional vitality in the situations.[7]

Pérez de Ayala, with his usual perspicacity, had noted this essentially dramatic paradox in connection with *La lámpara maravillosa*. He had described this work as 'un gran drama metafísico entre el dinamismo absoluto y el estatismo eterno, entre el diablo y Dios' (p. 144). In *La lámpara* Valle elaborates a cosmogony whose antipodes are Time and Movement (associated with the idea of Satan) and Oneness and Quietude (associated with the idea of God).

54

He describes in chapter 5 of 'El quietismo estético' how, through the teaching of Pico della Mirandola, he developed a dual perspective on reality, embracing both the transient reality of things as they strike the senses and the essential reality of things as they relate to the total unity of the world. These ideas were already taking shape in the early *Comedias* and were fully formulated by about 1910. In a lecture given to the Círculo de Bellas Artes of Valencia in 1911, he reaffirms his belief that all art must aspire to a stasis, but also hints that this impression can be achieved through movement:

Pero cualquiera que sea el concepto que un artista pueda tener de la vida . . . su aspiración será siempre la de hacer inmóviles todas las cosas que le rodean. Porque el movimiento es también una aspiración a la quietud. En los círculos dantescos, el torbellino de las almas no es sino ansia proteica de girar eternamente para poder estar en todas partes e igualarse con Dios.

Si ese torbellino fuese tal que llegase a hacer desaparecer la medida de las horas, que llegase a hacerse incontable para nuestros ojos cuando menos, ya habría llegado a la inmovilidad, como ocurre con la rueda de la máquina, que cuando su velocidad es estrema a nuestros ojos, ya finge estar quieta.[8]

This concept of art as the imposition of stasis on the kinetic material of life remained a constant in Valle's work and is fundamental to an understanding of his later plays and novels, when the reconciliation of a fragmented, chaotic reality with a static, unified vision of the world became an agonized struggle. *Aguila* and *Romance* are the first of his major works to show an awareness of this duality and to try (though not in any systematic way) to exploit it dramatically. *Cenizas* did not pose the problem and *El Marqués de Bradomín* aspires only to a lyrical stasis with little attempt to incorporate any of the 'presentness' or physicality of the *Comedias*. *Aguila* and *Romance* do manage to combine a simultaneous effect of timeless distance and immediate sensual impact. The language evokes the gestures, movement and corporeal presence of characters fixed in attitudes determined by the forces of tradition and the environment, outside the flow of time and history. Evidence that Valle himself was aware of the duality is provided by a brief but significant reference in his *Autocrítica*[9] to the inspiration of Dürer in the creation of these works. He alludes to all the figures being 'quietas en un movimiento barroco e estilizado'. Later in the same article he makes a reference to El Greco. It thus seems reasonable to postulate that baroque art, with its sense of petrified and arrested movement, its juxtaposition of the present and the eternal, may have suggested a possible artistic solution to the problem.

Hace usted una observación muy justa cuando señala el funambulismo de la acción, que tiene algo de tramoya de sueño, por donde las larvas pueden dialogar con los vivos. Cierto. A este efecto contribuye lo que pudiéramos llamar angostura del tiempo. Un efecto parecido al del Greco, por la angostura del espacio. Velázquez está todo lleno de espacio. Las figuras pueden cambiar de actitud, esparcirse y hacer lugar a otras forasteras. Pero en el *enterramiento*, sólo El Greco pudo meterlas en tan angosto espacio, y si se desbaratan hará falta un matemático bizantino para rehacer el problema. *Esta angostura de espacio es angostura de tiempo en las Comedias.* Las escenas que parecen arbitrariamente colocadas son las consecuentes en la cronología de los hechos. *Cara de plata* comienza con el alba y acaba a la medianoche. Las otras partes se suceden también sin intervalo. (Italics mine)

Despite the 'epic' potential of the subject matter, the *Comedias* do not range over a wide temporal canvas. The author shows no interest in presenting us with a historical saga. On the contrary, as he says in the *Autocrítica*, the action is deliberately compressed into a narrow temporal framework. And even this does not exist in relation to a past and a future. It does not form part of any historical process, nor is it conceived as a microcosm of a larger historical process. The action of the *Comedias* unfolds in a sort of temporal limbo or 'suspended present' where sunset follows sunrise and sunrise follows sunset but we are never quite sure where we are on a historical time scale. The action is conducted not through passing hours, days, weeks or years, but through the movement of the sun and the changes of light. We are aware of the continuity and dynamic movement of the action, yet do not perceive the passing of time. Although it might be difficult to sustain the literal truth of the claim that there are no time intervals between any of the scenes in *Aguila* and *Romance*, Valle is evidently trying, by placing the action in this abstract pocket of present time, to minimize the notion of temporal development.

Valle mentions in his *Autocrítica* that, in a novel he was writing at the time (probably *Tirano Banderas*), he was experimenting with the same technique of 'filling up time' as El Greco had used in filling up space on his canvases. The method clearly becomes more prominent and more conscious in the later works, *Cara de plata* and *Tirano Banderas* in particular. As a cryptic footnote he adds: 'Algún ruso sabía de esto', and this provides a clue for another possible source of inspiration for the technique: Dostoyevski. A year later, lecturing in Burgos, he makes a more explicit reference to Dostoyevski's technique of compressing the time scale:

Hay escritores que manejan maravillosamente este arte como Dostoevski, a diferencia de Proust. Este diluye todo en el recuerdo, aquél jamás, siempre presenta las cosas ocurriendo. A veces se llega a tanta intensidad en el pensar y en el actuar, que se pierde la norma . . . Y hay una norma pero ocurre desde el principio se suceden las cosas tan a la vez, con tanta intensidad, que pensamos que el tiempo ha pasado veloz y resulta que no ha transcurrido.[10]

He goes on to compare this compression of events in time to El Greco's treatment of objects in space. We are reminded of his comments in the lecture reported in *El Mercantil Valenciano* when, using the example of the rapidly spinning wheel, he observes that through exaggeration of motion one can give the impression of stillness. In view of these observations, there can be little doubt that the artistic purpose of the reduced time-span and of cramming it with intense and largely uninterrupted action was paradoxically similar to an exercise in myth and legend like *Flor de santidad*, that is, to blur the impression of chronology and create a static atmosphere. It is evident that when he wrote the early *Comedias* Valle was intuitively working towards these ideas. However, they were by no means as firmly established in his aesthetic canon as they later became and the next stage of his dramatic evolution shows him embarking on a rather different tack.

4

Culmination of the collective heroic theatre: *Cuento de abril* and *Voces de gesta*

In the *Comedias bárbaras* Valle had set himself the aesthetic problem of presenting collective themes through the medium of a heroic individual and his supporting chorus and of conveying static archetypes through dynamic action. *Cuento de abril* and *Voces de gesta* are both conceived in more general and abstract terms. The characters are given practically no individuality and are tailored to the requirements of the central opposition of cultures, traditions and ways of life that form the basis of these plays. It is possible that Valle had felt that the spiritual torment of the penitent Montenegro was too individual an emotion and not in complete harmony with his conception of collective theatre. It is also possible that he felt that the artistic stasis was insufficiently realized in the portrayal of dynamic action. In addition, the subject matter of the *Comedias* – the passing of a feudal order – seems to invite an historical approach which Valle's artistic convictions (that all art aspired to a stasis) did not allow him to adopt. Although there is no written evidence to suggest that the author had any reservations about his methods in the *Comedias*, *Cuento de abril* and *Voces de gesta* reveal a conscious and abrupt change of emphasis.

The two plays were evidently linked in Valle's mind as attempts to crystallize the spirit of a tradition. Fernández Almagro quotes a statement from an interview with Luis Antón Olmet in *El Debate* which illustrates this point. Speaking of *Voces de gesta*, Valle says: 'Será un libro de leyendas y tradiciones, a la manera de *Cuento de abril*; pero más fuerte, más importante. Recogeré la voz de todo un pueblo. Sólo son grandes los libros que recogen las voces amplias, plebeyas.'[1] *Cuento de abril* is based on a contrast of two cultural traditions – medieval Provence (gentle, lyrical, sensitive) and Castile (ascetic, warlike, aggressive) and *Voces de gesta* is a homily to Carlist traditionalism presented not as a political doctrine but as a cult, a force which animates an entire people. Both plays are marked by a more consciously 'poetic' approach in which the verse and archaic language attempt to capture a legendary and mythical tone. Most of the detail associated with the *Comedias* is omitted. The number of characters is considerably reduced and the figures are less individualized and differentiated. In *Cuento de abril* the Princesa de Imberal is given an accompaniment of 'un coro de azafatas' of unspecified number and the Infante de Castilla 'hasta seis peones de ballesta' whose contributions to the dialogue remain strictly anonymous. The mercenaries of El Rey Pagano in *Voces* are also nameless and are designated only by the weapons they carry: *una pica, una lanza, una bisarma*. The gestural, muscular language of the *Comedias* is replaced by abstract rhetoric; interacting dialogue and variety of pace by a uniformly heightened form of diction and a uniformly slow pace of action. In fact, the physical, pictorial emphasis of the *Comedias* gives way to a linguistic one. They are dramatic poems rather than theatre.

Cuento and *Voces* are currently regarded as the weakest and most dated part of Valle's dramatic output. In his recent book on Valle-Inclán's theatre, Sumner Greenfield gives them little more than a page of cursory comment (*Anatomía*, pp. 112–13). Yet they are not simply stop-gaps or pot-boilers, since Valle himself clearly attached a great deal of importance to them and *Voces*, at least, was highly regarded by those who saw it performed in his own day. Coming after the *Comedias bárbaras*, the change of style may appear a retrograde step from a dramatic point of view, yet these works represent a perfectly conscious development in Valle's constant and dedicated search for literary expression. It is indeed strange that he should have eliminated the very elements that gave the *Comedias* their vitality. Nonetheless, it is probable that this sacrifice was made on the altar of greater classical purity of expression: pure poetic theatre in the case of *Cuento* and pure tragic theatre in the case of *Voces*, in which the particularities of plot, character and setting are subordinated to a monolithic, collective simplicity. Valle's intentions were to broaden the basis of his theatre. To this end he eliminates the central heroic figure. To this end too he sacrifices the dynamic flow and open-ended structure of the *Comedias*. In a much more explicit way than anything he had previously attempted in the theatre, both these plays are attempts to express popular culture and tradition in their essence. Valle's view of tradition has nothing to do with the reactionary attitude of those who merely defend their own convenience or self-interest and rationalize it in political terms. For him it was the living and permanent essence of a race. His traditionalism has been admirably summed up in an excellent article by J. A. Maravall as follows:

> Su estética, su filosofía, su política, se relacionan con la visión estática de una sociedad arcaica. La realidad no está hecha, para él, en forma de cadena, cuyos eslabones se suceden y avanzan, sino de 'círculos concéntricos al modo que los engendra la piedra en la laguna'. Su movimiento es pura apariencia. Las cosas siguen donde y como estaban. Esto es lo que estéticamente hay que buscar: 'la suprema inmovilidad de las cosas'; y a lo que su filosofía aspira: 'el conocimiento de todas las cosas por aquella condición que no muda en ellas'. Esa inmovilidad, en el orden social, se llama tradición. (p. 233)

To some extent *Cuento de abril* is rooted in what Rubén Darío called 'la pendejada de la época', that is, the stock *modernista* imagery of a medieval Provence of princesses and troubadours, by which poets expressed their revulsion against the more crass manifestations of naturalism. The play is given greater weight and objectivity by the fact that it contrasts the idealized vision of Provence with the harsh asceticism of Castile. It is not just a subjective fantasy, although an account of the trivial and somewhat tenuous plot might lead one to believe otherwise.

The troubadour, Pedro Vidal, is hopelessly in love with his unattainable mistress, the Princesa de Imberal. The princess is betrothed to a Castilian prince whose arrival is declared to be imminent in the first act. The vain and frivolous princess, in connivance with her ladies-in-waiting, tempts the unfortunate poet into revealing his love. He is persuaded that the princess is under the influence of a love potion, places a chaste kiss upon her lips as she is sleeping and is exiled for his audacity. Later the troubadour, living the life of a hermit and dressed only in a wolfskin, is mistaken for a wolf by the Castilian Infante's hunting party and is savaged by the dogs. The princess is shocked by the Infante's callous attitude to his victim and regrets her former cruelty. The troubadour is readmitted to the palace and the Infante, scandalized by the pagan licence and lack of hierarchy of the Provençal court and convinced of the incompatibility of the two cultures, leaves in a huff for Castile, bent on continuing the holy war against the infidel.

This fairy-tale plot is used simply to highlight the contrast between two lifestyles or, more specifically, between two attitudes to love: the pagan idea of love as natural harmony and the Catholic idea of love as a violent flame wafted by the consciousness of sin, death and the Devil. It would perhaps be misleading to speak of a conflict between these two attitudes, since the degree of dramatic interaction is negligible. It is a contrast which shows itself mainly in imagery and style of speech. The Provençal ideal is associated with the language of courtly love, of madrigals, sonnets, flowers, the moon and the beauty of nature, and Castilian passion is expressed in images of war and the hunt, spears and arrows. The subsidiary characters are arranged in pairs of opposites around the central figure of the princess: the lyrical troubadour and the iron-clad warrior prince, the chorus of nubile *azafatas* and the rude and cumbersome *ballesteros*. As in most of Valle's plays, the tension comes from the expressive texture of the dialogue more than the narrative structure. The development of the plot, such as it is, conveys very little dramatic impact. There is perhaps only one dramatic moment in the play, when the princess returns the troubadour's kiss, an action which brings all the Infante's prejudice and antipathy to the boil. The dramatic axis, however, is the counterpoint of tone, style and content presented by the two different cultures and their representatives.

In the *Comedias bárbaras*, the action is imagined first of all in physical, pictorial terms and the dialogue derives from the vividly perceived physical situation. In *Cuento de abril* the physical situation has little bearing on the dialogue which tends to be static and to express generalized attitudes rather than reactions to present situations. Instead of gestural action–dialogue we have a lyrical or descriptive dialogue which paints pictures in the mind. The only two sets of the play, the garden of acts I and III and the oak grove of act II, are little more than functional backdrops, painted cloths with no relevance to the characters or dialogue – a far cry from the active role of the landscape in the *Comedias*. Similarly, if we compare these settings with the whimsical decor of *La Marquesa Rosalinda* we can appreciate the difference between 'active' and 'passive' scenery in Valle's plays. *Cuento*, with its stylistic emphasis, evokes all its images in the poetry. Particularly impressive is the austere picture of Castile we receive from the Infante's descriptions (e.g. p. 119).

Pérez de Ayala observes that the poetic quality of *Cuento de abril* lies in its grasp of collective cultural identities, its 'visión íntegra de la vida' (pp. 140–1).[2] The impression of Castile comes over as a more genuine distillation of experience; behind the Infante's words we sense a social and historical perspective, a feeling of people living and working in a certain landscape. The portrayal of Provençal culture with its love-lorn pages and knights, its madrigals and jousts, is necessarily derived from literature. Ayala goes on to say that *Cuento de abril* presents the two lifestyles in *objective contrast*, which is more difficult to accept. The contrast of these two attitudes is clearly a loaded one in favour of the pagan, the poetic and the Provençal, yet not too loaded. It is presented without excessive sentimentality on the one part or excessive caricature on the other. The dialogue maintains both viewpoints in a balanced and largely unironical counterpoint. Only occasionally does Valle permit himself a sly touch of irony in the *acotaciones* such as when the armour-clad Infante stomps incongruously through the *modernista* garden and shakes the petals off the roses (p. 140). Ultimately, with the Infante's departure, we are left in no doubt where to place our sympathies. Philistinism was a defect that Valle found difficult to condone. The princess sends him off with these words:

> Eres un guerrero que bárbaro y desnudo
> no supiese más música
> que el golpe de la maza en el escudo. (p. 147)

However, the ostensibly objective framework in which Valle sets his apology for lyrical fantasy prevents it from being mere mannered preciosity.

Some two years later Valle wrote *Voces de gesta*, a work which the author himself evidently considered an important and ambitious undertaking, yet which has been consigned to the attic by posterity. Speaking of the *estreno* in Barcelona, he said: 'La obra gustó: es trágica y la acción sacude fuertemente lo que hay de temperamento emocional en el público . . . En nuestro hazañoso historial, y más que nada en la gloriosa tradición, hay sobrados elementos para reconstruir el pasado glorioso del arte nacional' (see Campos). Moreover, unlike the majority of Valle's works that reached the stage, the play was successful. It was received with great enthusiasm on its opening night on 18 June 1911 and the author took a bow after act II (*La Vanguardia*, 19 June 1911). We have the testimony of 'Garcilaso', writing in the *Diario de Navarra* to protest against the exclusion of *Voces* from the current repertoire of the visiting company, that the play had enjoyed considerable success wherever it had been performed.[3] After the Madrid performances in May 1912, it was given a second run in Barcelona in early July of the same year by popular request. The reasons for this success are not hard to find since the play is a

reasonably overt apology for Carlist traditionalism and was used by
Carlist supporters as a rallying point. In the same interview quoted
above Valle confirms his intentions in writing the play and notes that
it aroused antagonism in certain quarters: 'Tal vez por sustentar estas
ideas, porque soy tradicionalista y hago fe de mis creencias, no fuese
simpática *Voces de gesta* en ciertas esferas. Hay casos grandes, donde
hasta los aciertos literarios del modesto amante del ideal
tradicionalista-monárquico, pueden llegar a desvelar.'

Juan Antonio Hormigón makes some interesting comments on this
play which he defines as 'un auto sacramental de exaltación
tradicionalista' (*La Cultura*, p. 155). He sees the struggle between Rey
Carlino and the Rey Pagano as representing that of the legitimate
monarchy against the liberal (usurping) monarchy throughout
Spanish nineteenth-century history. This struggle is seen in absolute
'manichean' terms of Good and Evil (hence the definition of 'auto
sacramental'), the Good being associated with the idea of a static,
rural social order and the Evil with the notion of 'progress' and
capitalism. Hormigón draws special attention to the fact that *Voces*
marks the first appearance of political elements in Valle's work,
however abstract and naïve the treatment of the subject (pp. 40–6).
Valle himself states explicitly that the play was written to express his
faith in the traditionalist ideal and to that extent it must be considered
politically motivated. But Hormigón's thesis exaggerates the political
and dramatic importance of the Rey Carlino–Rey Pagano struggle.
It is not like *Cuento de abril* which does present two ideologies and two
cultures in opposition. The mercenaries of the usurping Rey Pagano
represent no kind of contrary *ideology*. There is no evidence in the text
to suggest that they are associated with the idea of progress or
capitalism or with the town as opposed to the country. In their two
appearances (end of act I and middle of act II) they are associated
solely with rape and destruction. Valle-Inclán may well have thought
of them as representing the forces of the usurping monarchy, but the
play contains no political or historical allusions to substantiate this.
Moreover, in purely dramatic terms the play does not turn on the
element of conflict or opposition. We are concerned mainly with the
voice of tradition that speaks through the followers of Rey Carlino
and which emerges triumphant in the midst of military defeat. The
enemy, like the firing squad in Goya's *3 de mayo*, is a faceless,
dehumanized anti-force and we are invited to look mainly at the faces
of the victims.

Voces de gesta is an amalgam of the spirit of primitive Castile and the

Carlist traditionalism of the Basque province and Navarre. The action actually takes place in a legendary Castile, but the strongholds of Carlism are suggested in repeated allusions to the *fueros*, the *roble foral* and in the character of El Versolari. In the first act a mood of defeatism reigns amongst the shepherds and goatherds of Monte Araal. The kingdom has been invaded by a foreign monarch (referred to as the Rey Pagano) and their legitimate king, Carlino, lives in the hills like a hunted animal, trying to raise factions in his support. The patriarch Tibaldo is seen carving a horn that will summon support for the exiled king, and his granddaughter, Ginebra, refuses to marry her suitor, Oliveros, until Rey Carlino is restored to the throne. At the end of the act Rey Carlino appears, is given food by Ginebra and Oliveros, but is forced to flee as the enemy soldiers approach. When Ginebra refuses to tell the soldiers which way he went, they put out her eyes and play dice for her. The second act opens ten years later with Monte Araal under the domination of the Rey Pagano. The blind Ginebra now has a small son by the Captain who violated her. This same Captain arrives in the company of other soldiers in search of concubines who will give them sons to replenish the ranks of their army. The Captain, angered by the boy's arrogance, kills him and Ginebra, guided by the hand of another peasant woman, cuts off the head of the Captain as he lies asleep in a drunken stupor.

At the beginning of act III, Ginebra has been wandering for ten years in search of Rey Carlino, carrying the Captain's head as an offering to the cause. Under the *roble foral*, the shepherds – turned warriors of the king – are lamenting the loss of a battle, while in the background an old man is digging a grave. Throughout this final act, the tree and the grave are juxtaposed images of hope and despair. Then the wounded Rey Carlino is carried in on a shield by the remnants of his defeated army. When Ginebra presents her offering, the king sees his enemy's skull only as consolation in the hour of his own death:

> En mi vencimiento serás compañera,
> en mi desventura me confortarás,
> y al ser de enemigo, muda calavera,
> a mi alma con voces de espanto hablarás.

Ginebra, however, sees it as a symbol of vengeance and a call to action:

> Voces de venganza son las que ha de darte,

64

> no voces de espanto sobre un folio abierto,
> como al ermitaño que el tiempo reparte
> en meditaciones y cavar el huerto. (p. 89)

Ginebra's example revives the king's spirits. He ends by renouncing his royalty and identifying himself entirely with his people:

> Deja que al olvido arroje mi nombre
> y si muero Rey, que renazca hombre. (p. 90)

The play ends with a resounding hymn to the *roble foral* as the symbol of tradition.

The foregoing summary of the action should make it clear that the play's axis is the relationship of Rey Carlino to his people rather than a conflict of political forces (e.g. traditionalist versus liberal). Valle's main purpose was to stress the popular character of Carlist traditionalism, its nature as a cult and a living force rather than as a political doctrine. Much depends on the interpretation of the king himself. The text provides sufficient evidence for an interpretation of the king as a somewhat incomplete character, probably to underline the point that his historical strength lies in his people. For most of the play he is a lost soul, an errant shadow, a man on the run. His behaviour is characterized more by epic lamentation than by moral strength or the capacity to inspire. According to J. B. Avalle-Arce, Valle is lamenting the decline of the heroic cause of Carlism and the 'ausencia de los mejores' (*Appraisal*, pp. 361–73). He argues that the name Carlino is in itself indicative of degeneration, particularly in view of the names of his two ancestors.

> GINEBRA: ¡Del Rey Carlo Magno de barba florida,
>   del otro rey Carlos de barba bellida
>   se acabó la raza!
> TIBALDO: ¿Pues el Rey Carlino?
> GINEBRA: Tanto le persigue su negro destino
>   que vive en el monte como otro cabrero. (p. 22)

Carlo Magno, Carlos, Carlino: a descending order of merit seems to be implied. Valle's point is that the real force of an idea lies in the collective tradition, represented in the play by the blind Ginebra. Ginebra's offering is at first taken by the king as an omen of his own death, then merely as a consolation in defeat. It is only through Ginebra's single-minded devotion that Carlino is reminded of his responsibility to history. No criticism of the monarchist ideal is implied here. Valle is simply stressing the reciprocal nature of the relationship between a king and his people. Ginebra and Rey Carlino are complementary figures. The king is sustained only by his people, yet the people need the ideal of the king to sustain them.

The comments on the dramatic technique of *Cuento de abril* also apply to *Voces de gesta*. Emphasis on the verse rather than on dramatic action, elimination of dynamism and interaction, rhetorical dialogue and statuesque characterization. As the title suggests we are left with the 'Voices'. It is not without significance that Valle referred to *Voces* as 'un libreto Wagneriano' (*España*, 8 March 1924). He subscribes to Wagner's views on collective myth as the source of poetic inspiration and on the primacy of emotive stimulus over rational communication. He tries to give the plot of *Voces* the distanced, naïve and massive quality of myth. Almost nothing is particularized, the setting, the period, the historical issues at stake. More than a play, *Voces* is a canto: Wagner without the music. To convey the impression of legendary distance Valle introduces a feature which is unique in his work: the emotive use of passing time. Twenty years elapse during the course of the action which contrasts sharply with the compression of time in the *Comedias bárbaras*. The passing of the years is underlined at the beginning of the second and third acts, principally through El Versolari who serves as a chorus-cum-chronicler, with references to the changing times, the rustic implements converted into instruments of war, the neglected fields, the growing-up of Ginebra's son, the ageing of the characters.

As in *Cuento de abril* visual and physical elements are described in the dialogue, not presented in terms of action. But, in addition to this absence of dramatic action, *Voces de gesta* lacks interest of texture, the element of contrast or counterpoint which – with difficulty – had sustained *Cuento de abril*. The tone is one of unrelieved solemnity. In his desire to distil the pure heroic and tragic essence of his theme, Valle falls into declamation and monotony. There is no humour, no ironic counterpoise, both features which were to become a hallmark of his later work. Coming, as it did, after the trilogy of novels on the Carlist wars and at the height of his involvement with the traditionalist ideology, *Voces de gesta* marks the finale of the epic–heroic phase of Valle's output. From about 1912 onwards there was to be a shift from the epic–heroic to a more cynical, parodic view of the world, a gradual encroachment of self-deflating humour which culminates in the cartoon-like antics of the *esperpentos*.

5

The transitional phase: *La Marquesa Rosalinda* and *El embrujado*

Before *Cuento de abril* and *Voces de gesta*, which mark Valle's final attempts to write 'straight' collective drama in either the lyrical or the heroic vein, he had produced the *Farsa infantil de la cabeza del dragón* (1909) which, in many ways, could be said to anticipate the parodic and satiric humour he was to develop in his later *farsas* and *esperpentos*. This children's fairy tale in fact contains a number of satirical allusions and puppet techniques which have induced some critics to interpret it as a pre-*esperpento* (see Speratti-Piñero). Certainly many of the allusions to Spanish political and social life would be lost on an audience of children. The satire of traditional protocol in the figure of the Maestro de Ceremonias, the parody of *honor* in the blustering Espandián, the comparison of the ecstatic posture of the palace storks with that of the admirers of Wagner's music, the reference to the dragon's head being 'pesada como una tesis doctoral', the bufón's intention to abandon the kingdom 'para dar conferencias en las Indias', the blatant anachronism of the latter's allusion to a new law requiring all old people and cripples to be run down by motor cars on the public highways – all these contemporary references give the *farsa* the air of a modern English pantomime in which most of the jokes are directed at the adults in the audience. The stylization of movement heralds the balletic exits and entrances of *La Marquesa Rosalinda*: 'Aparece otra vez el Duende entre las almenas, y en lo alto de las torres puntiagudas, las cigüeñas cambian de pata. El Duende saluda con una pirueta' (p. 93). The gardens of El Rey Micromicón's palace contain all the standard *modernista* fixtures: roses, marble staircases, peacocks, the lake with 'dos cisnes unánimes' and the 'laberinto de mirtos'. The pages, court officials and ladies-in-waiting have the stiff and fragile air of porcelain figurines: 'accionan con el aire pueril de los muñecos que tienen el movimiento regido por un cimbel. Saben hacer cortesías y sonreír con los ojos quietos, redondos y brillantes

67

como las cuentas de un collar' (p. 119). The deliberate preciosity of these *modernista* elements is offset by the boisterous interventions of the braggadocio, Espandián, and the exquisite sentiments of the Prince Charming figure, Verdemar, are pleasantly balanced by descents into the vernacular. One can detect in *La cabeza del dragón* an ambivalence of tone later to be more consciously exploited in *La Marquesa Rosalinda*.

Pérez de Ayala's interpretation of this play as the revolt of unconstrained fantasy against the determinism of the universe seems a little weighty for a piece that was intended for children (p. 142). It presupposes in the first place that Valle-Inclán felt the need to escape from an all too oppressive world governed by inexorable laws. The play itself lends little support to this particular argument and, in any case, *La guerra carlista*, on which he was working about that time, and the later *Voces de gesta*, show conclusively that Valle's universe, though perhaps deterministic, was nevertheless still a heroic one from which he had no desire to escape. The farcical, satirical or puppet-like elements of *La cabeza del dragón* carry none of the moral and philosophical overtones with which they are used in later plays. At the most it can be said that some of the serious possibilities of farce may have been revealed to the author as a result of writing the play, but the work in itself is essentially a light and amusing entertainment.

The first real signs of a change of attitude came with *La Marquesa Rosalinda* (1912). Here the juxtaposition of farce and lyricism is significant because it implies deliberate self-parody. It is a play which subtly and systematically undermines its own conventional arti-ficiality and deflates its own rhetoric. The mild scepticism of the play is, however, directed at the superannuated aspects of *Modernismo* and does not touch on any fundamental attitudes of the author. In fact, the juxtaposition of lyrical and grotesque elements seems to have been undertaken largely as a literary experiment. The intrusion of humour and the grotesque into the *modernista* fantasy do not argue any anti-tragic view of existence or any conscious questioning of tragic values. The basic categories of the comic and the tragic remain separate and undisturbed. It is therefore not entirely surprising that Valle should have made another attempt to write pure tragedy in *El embrujado* (1913), subtitled *Tragedia de tierras de Salnés*, in which he tried to capture the tragic essence of Galicia. The contrast between the style and content of *La Marquesa Rosalinda* and *El embrujado* is absolute. The first exhibits a lively display of conscious frivolity and breezy self-parody and the second strains heavy-handedly after dark and tragic effects. This polarization of styles shows Valle in a period of vacillation and conflicting values, sometimes seeking new possibilities of expression, sometimes returning to dried-up sources of inspiration, as yet uncertain of the direction to follow. The period between 1912 and the First World War was one of transition, quiet reflection and artistic stocktaking in his Galician retreat of El Pazo de la Merced, culminating in his visit to the French front and his chronicles from the theatre of war for the newspaper *El Imparcial*, later published as *La media noche*.[1] In this period we do not yet see the hardening of whimsical humour and parody into the systematic anti-tragic use of the grotesque, but we do see the undoubted decline of the heroic vision. *La media noche* is of special interest in this respect because it places Valle squarely before a subject of his own historical present and its self-confessed artistic failure stems largely from the inability of Valle's old vision of life to cope with this material.

'LA MARQUESA ROSALINDA'

Thematically, *La Marquesa Rosalinda* invites comparison with *Cuento de abril*. The emphasis is on national or regional, i.e. collective, expression and it involves a contrast of cultures: the dogmatic religious tradition of Castile with all its obscurantism and the 'pagan' cultural tradition associated with France and Italy. The *cuento abrileño* had been a naïve and simple confrontation of values between the Castilian and Provençal courts set in the context of a medieval fantasy. *La Marquesa Rosalinda* is a much more ambiguous and ironic vision of the ideological cross-currents of the Spanish eighteenth century in the stylized setting of the palace gardens at Aranjuez. Behind the fantasy lie the conflicting values produced by the confluence of different cultures in eighteenth-century Spain, as we read in the prelude:

> Con las espumas del champaña
> y la malicia de sus crónicas,
> Francia proyecta sobre España
> las grandes narices borbónicas.

> Versalles pone sus empaques,
> Aranjuez, sus albas rientes,
> y un grotesco de miriñaques,
> don Francisco Goya y Lucientes. (Preludio, p. 12)

By comparison with the lyrical seriousness of *Cuento* and the epic solemnity of *Voces*, *La Marquesa* impresses with its air of polished nonchalance and calculated levity. It is, as Valle declares in the Preludio, a work of deliberate artificiality:

> Y sollocen otros poetas
> sobre los cuernos de la lira,
> con el ritmo de las piruetas
> yo rimo mi bella mentira.

The play was conceived as a pastiche of diverse pictorial and musical elements associated with eighteenth-century court life. 'Yo he querido dar', he is reported as saying in a press interview, 'la sensación de vitrina que contiene objetos del siglo XVIII . . . lo ficticio: lo de los objetos . . . no la vida, sino las figulinas' (see 'Duende'). *La Marquesa* presents a world of porcelain figurines, ornate fans, enamelled snuff boxes, clavichords and pavanes. Within this framework of elegant artificiality, Valle combines and contrasts pagan, cosmopolitan elements (features of the *commedia dell'arte*, sensual Neoclassical *Modernismo* in the style of Rubén Darío)[2] with traditional aspects of Spanish literature and social life (parody of the Golden Age *comedia*, picaresque literature, the obscurantist religiosity of the Dueña). In a very perceptive chapter on *La Marquesa Rosalinda*, Sumner Greenfield defines the essence of the play in a phrase quoted from the *Decoración* to act III: 'una sonata ambigua de aventura galante y de convento' (see *Anatomía*, pp. 119–24). The phrase neatly sums up the contrast of cultures but, perhaps more important, suggests their partial fusion. As we shall see, it is the element of ambivalence (as opposed to simple antithesis and counterpoint in *Cuento de abril*) that mainly interests Valle in the play. The interplay of pagan and religious ingredients is expressed in the action between the two central characters, the Marquesa herself and Arlequín.

Rosalinda is portrayed as the typical 'afrancesada', an example of semi-emancipated womanhood whose professed 'pagan' attitudes frequently conflict with the fundamental prejudices of her nature. She protests against traditional Spanish attitudes to morality (pp. 29–30) and yet asks the nuns for a special prayer against toothache and the dangers of lightning in the open country (p. 63). As a woman no longer in the full bloom of youth, married to a decrepit marquis, jealous of her daughter whom, according to the Dueña, she sends to a convent in order to avoid odious comparisons, the Marquesa is ripe for illicit love. Arlequín's freewheeling, hedonistic style has all the attractions of forbidden fruit for her. However, as soon as Arlequín begins to court her with his pagan imagery, the Marquesa instantly retreats into traditional Spanish attitudes:

ARLEQUÍN: ¿Las blancas manos tejen guirnalda
            a la bicorne frente de Pan?
            ¡Graciosas ninfas, que llevais falda
            por el decreto de un chambelán!
ROSALINDA: Si ahora nos cubren blondas y sedas,
            no lo mandaron los chambelanes . . .
            Pero aquí llevan en las olmedas
            hoja de parra los egipanes. (p. 38)

Arlequín subtly points out the inconsistency between her words and her attitudes:

¡Señoras mías, como creeros,
si en vuestros labios teneis abejas
griegas, y esconde sus flechas Eros
entre los nardos de vuestras rejas! (p. 42)

At first, the Marquesa flirts outrageously, convinced that her aged husband, reared in the tradition of the French court, will coolly dismiss her infidelity with a Voltairian epigram on the nature of women. The Marquis's disdain for the 'disparates y maridos del teatro español' proves, however, to be less than skin deep, and, although he does not adopt the role of Calderonian hero, he employs the services of two hired ruffians to dispose of Arlequín. Thus threatened, the Marquesa and Arlequín arrange a hasty elopement, but the plans are frustrated by the vigilant Dueña who reports to the authorities that Arlequín has bewitched her mistress with his demoniacal powers. Arlequín is escorted to prison and Rosalinda is despatched to a nunnery. In the last act Rosalinda and Arlequín meet again, but in very different circumstances. Contact with the religious life has changed the Marquesa's outlook and Arlequín's pagan cult of the senses no longer has any appeal for her. She is resolved to return to the peace and tranquillity of the cloister. Despite the evident satire of religious attitudes in the Dueña, there is no trace of irony in the eulogy of the contemplative life that Valle puts into the Marquesa's mouth at the end:

¡Qué santa vida la vida aquella!
Sólo suspiro por el convento
con sus rosales y sus campanas.
¡El coro en blando recogimiento
y las fugaces misas tempranas! (p. 128)

The 'sonata ambigua' is left poised at the point of balance. Valle's antipathy for the obscurantist and inquisitorial aspects of the Castilian tradition is balanced by his admiration for its spiritual strength.

The ambivalence of content is paralleled by a stylistic ambivalence expressed in the play's subtitle: *farsa sentimental y grotesca*. The treatment of the theme in *Cuento de abril* leaves an audience in no doubt where Valle's sympathies lie. The play is an apology for lyrical fantasy and the free-ranging imagination. Such humour as the play possesses is at the expense of the cumbersome, heavy-footed Infante. By contrast, the humour of *La Marquesa Rosalinda* consists in the author's dual perspective, in part identified with the 'bella mentira' he has created and in part pricking the bubble of its fantasy world. Constant intervention of well-judged farce and deliberate bathos offsets the preciosity of sentimental lyricism, well-kempt gardens and overblown rhetoric. There is no special pleading; the inter-play of styles is an end in itself. Action, characters and sentiments are held at the delicate point of balance between sentimental preciosity and ironic humour, between belief and disbelief.

The mood thus ranges from refined lyricism to broad slapstick. Interwoven with the central action between Rosalinda and Arlequín is a tenuous 'subplot' enacted by the traditional *commedia dell'arte* characters. Arlequín is the traditional lover of Colombina whose husband, Pierrot, is the traditional cuckold. Colombina's hysterical jealousy and Pierrot's doleful protests punctuate the aristocratic mood of the main action at strategic points with farcical episodes. The subplot sets up a grotesque counterpoint to the Rosalinda–Arlequín relationship. The stylistic contrast is established right from the beginning. The peace of the idealized eighteenth-century garden, with its 'recortado mirto' reflected in the fountain, the notes of a clavichord playing a pavane and the venerable Abate absorbed in the composition of a sonnet to Galatea, is rudely shattered by the group of Colombina, Pierrot and Polichinela who 'entran bailando asidos de las manos', scandalizing the worthy cleric. After the courtly elegance of Arlequín's elaborate compliments to the Marquesa and the flirtatious coyness of the latter, we are plunged straight into a 'domestic' squabble between Arlequín and Colombina, closely followed by a scene in which Pierrot, having failed to touch Arlequín for money, announces that they must therefore fight a duel over his wife. The poetic farewell scene between Rosalinda and Arlequín is

1 Montenegro surprised by the unexpected arrival of his wife, Doña María, in a scene from Adolfo Marsillach's richly atmospheric production of *Aguila de blasón* (1966). Two recorded tapes operating almost continuously provided background and continuity.

2 A gathering of Montenegro's degenerate sons in another scene from the same production.

3 José Luis Alonso's 1967 production of *La enamorada del rey* (in the same programme as *La cabeza del Bautista* and *La rosa de papel*) was its first performance. The director established the puppet convention in the audience's mind from the beginning, introducing a Narrator (shown here) who spoke Valle-Inclán's expressive stage directions.

4 Simeón Julepe and La Encamada in a scene from *La rosa de papel*. This play was produced as boldly expressionist melodrama in which the use of masks for choral characters and strongly contrasted lighting blends with the extravagant rhetorical attitudes.

5 Max Estrella followed by his grotesque shadow, Don Latino, in José Tamayo's production of *Luces de Bohemia* (1971), described by the director as the finest yet most difficult text he had ever worked with.

6 Scene 11 of *Luces de Bohemia* in which a mother laments the death of her child, killed by a stray bullet. The silhouetted stage image matches the stylized nature of the dialogue in this particular scene.

7 Nuria Espert as Mari-Gaila enjoying her new-found freedom of the open road in a scene from Víctor García's spectacular though idiosyncratic interpretation of *Divinas palabras* (1977) at the National Theatre, London.

interrupted by the appearance of the grotesque Pierrot demanding satisfaction for his honour. The slapstick duel they fight with wooden swords cuts right across the genuinely lyrical mood established by the previous dialogue. Valle-Inclán takes us to the very edge of belief and then abruptly applies the brakes.

The point–counterpoint of aristocratic sentiments and *commedia dell'arte* farce is a juxtaposition of one literary convention against another, with corresponding shifts in style. Valle also satirizes the artificiality of the play's convention by allowing the intrusion of the real world from time to time. There are many examples of deliberate bathos and descents into prosaic realities. For instance, the scene in which Doña Estrella laments her imminent departure for the convent to the down-to-earth Dueña:

> DOÑA ESTRELLA: El ruiseñor entre el follaje
> me dice adiós, un poco triste,
> deseándome buen viaje.
> LA DUEÑA: ¡Como solías darle alpiste! (p. 23)

The deflation of Colombina's romantic illusions by Arlequín's nihilistic cynicism:

> COLOMBINA: ¡Toda la vida guardaré
> el recuerdo de nuestra historia!
> ¡Toda la vida te amaré!
> ARLEQUÍN: Mucho fías a la memoria. (p. 88)

Examples of bathos even appear in the Marquesa's own speech:

> He llorado esta tarde como una Magdalena,
> y empañaron las lágrimas el brillo de mis ojos
> que agonizan, sepultos en dos círculos rojos.
> Apenas puedo entreabrirlos con la jaqueca,
> y me he puesto en las sienes dos parches de manteca. (p. 92)

Yet the irony is essentially affectionate and the comic hyperbole and bathos never completely undermine the sentiment. They check it or correct it but do not destroy it. The general tone of the play suggests a half-nostalgic farewell to the dream world of *Modernismo*, with which, in *El Marqués de Bradomín* for example, Valle had been completely identified. It has been suggested by José F. Montesinos that the work was written about 1910, a date which roughly coincided with the decline of this literary fashion in Spain and after which Darío himself graduated to a more human and personal form of expression in *Cantos de vida y esperanza*. Valle's delicately poised feelings in the play are typified by the dialogues between the Marquesa and her unromantic confidante, Amaranta. In act II Rosalinda tells Amaranta of her husband's changed attitude and of his plans to avenge himself by means of hired assassins. The danger merely gives added stimulus to the Marquesa's imagination and the common-sense warnings of Amaranta fail to undermine the illusion. The effect is like that of Sancho Panza on Don Quixote: the cold douches of realism about the dangers that threaten her and the possible hardships that lie in store for her in the mummers' caravan simply inspire her to new heights of poetic fantasy:

AMARANTA: Marquesa Rosalinda, que le hurtas al bufete
de Colombina, el naipe pringado en colorete,
qué meriendas tan ricas de pan y de cebolla,
harás con la Farándula, si el carro no se atolla
en medio de una senda.

ROSALINDA: No te pongas prosaica.
Cuando cruzó el desierto con hambre y sed, la hebraica
tribu, la luna ahilaba en la noche serena,
benéfico maná sobre la ardiente arena.

AMARANTA: ¿Y esperas que del Cielo te llegue la merienda
en el pico de una paloma de leyenda?

ROSALINDA: Amaranta burlona, si la estrella de amor
nos alumbra la senda, un divino sabor
de miel encontraremos en la hogaza centena
que parta el mesonero al servirnos la cena. (pp. 68–9)

Here, particularly, we can see Valle's dual perspective at work. In a very real sense he is feeling with the Marquesa, yet is ironically aware of the cold realities that beset the dream.

In the final scene the sentimental mood at first predominates but Valle does not allow his 'bella mentira' to end on a note of pathos. The incipient sentimentality of the farewell scene is undercut by a verbal pirouette which reminds us of the artificiality of the whole.

ROSALINDA: ¡Adiós! ¡Por siempre adiós!
ARLEQUÍN: ¡Adiós, señora!
ROSALINDA: ¡Llegó el terrible instante!
ARLEQUÍN: ¡Lindo gesto!
¡No vuelve la cabeza! ¡Es que no llora!
¡Yo tampoco lloro por supuesto! (p. 136)

The idyll ends not with a tear but a shrug. The mood is then further broken by the entrance of Colombina with her usual torrent of recriminations, followed by Polichinela who warns Arlequín of the approach of the *alguaciles*. In a flurry of activity the Farándula takes once more to the road.

Technically, *La Marquesa Rosalinda* makes a significant step towards 'total theatre' in which the rhythms of sounds and physical movements are as important to the overall effect as the dialogue. More specifically it constitutes an attempt to unite the theatre and the dance (consult Amor y Vázquez). Valle's comments on the dance in *La lámpara maravillosa* (p. 60) are clearly the aesthetic criteria behind the creation of *La Marquesa Rosalinda*. The play is conceived in terms of balletic movement and musical accompaniment, often explicitly indicated in the verse *acotaciones* (Colombina, for instance, 'huye de la mano de Polichinela/al ritmo saltante de una tarantela') and always implicit in the rhythms of the verse dialogue.

The movements and sounds of *La Marquesa Rosalinda* echo to a large extent the stylistic duality of the play – refined aristocratic sentiment and grotesquerie – mentioned earlier. The *piruetas* of Arlequín and the *cabriolas* of Polichinela contrast with the *pasos de minué* of El Paje and Doña Estrella. The singing of the nightingale is offset by the croaking of the toad, the aristocratic clavichord by the plebeian barrel organ. Any production of *La Marquesa Rosalinda* would require an extremely physical approach to acting in order to establish visually the distinction between the tumbling and slapstick of the *commedia dell'arte* characters and the eighteenth-century poise and elegance of the courtiers. In many cases, the physical gait of the character is written into the play as an integral part of the balletic conception. Colombina's skipping movements are associated with the rhythm of the barrel organ (p. 91) and the appearances of the Page and Doña Estrella with the steps of the minuet (p. 113). Polichinela, for example, hunch-backed and grotesque, is characterized by his leaps and bounds ('jocundo, grotesco, saltante'). There is a sustained dance sequence at the beginning of act II in which the *meninas* of the court dance round Polichinela like a ring of nymphs encircling a satyr, trying to touch his hump, traditionally reputed to be a source of good luck. The grotesque movements of Polichinela ('que bota danzarín') clumsily trying to elude their attentions are contrasted with the lithe and supple *meninas* who surround him ('haciendo monadas'). The visual contrast here is an essential theatrical element. The character of Arlequín, of course, has a Protean quality and he is master of all situations. He moves easily between the two worlds and is as capable of the well-turned compliment as of the well-turned somersault.

Valle-Inclán rediscovers in this play the dramatic relationship between characters and setting that had been a feature of the *Comedias bárbaras* but had been temporarily abandoned in *Cuento de abril* and *Voces de gesta*. The decor is here far more than a painted backcloth; it is an active participant in the action. In the first place the 'geométrico laberinto' of myrtles and rose bushes provides the perfect stage image for the stylized intrigues of the action. It lends itself to the overhearing of conversations, to prying and peeping and to the sudden appearance of characters from behind convenient hiding places. It is also an active presence in a more general sense. There is hardly a page of *La Marquesa Rosalinda* in which the gardens of Aranjuez, with their laurels, roses, fountains, statuettes of pagan deities, nightingales and swans on ornamental lakes, do not feature in the dialogue. This is because the sights and sounds of the garden so directly reflect the play's spirit of aristocratic fantasy that they naturally form the nucleus around which the dialogue can weave itself. The sounds are especially important because they are frequently used either to echo certain sentiments or to comment ironically on the dialogue. As Sumner Greenfield points out in his chapter on *La Marquesa*, the garden fauna operate as a kind of invisible orchestral accompaniment (*Anatomía*, p. 117). The cricket, the toad, the nightingale are the most frequently heard instruments. A couple of examples should suffice to illustrate this:

> Al borde del camino, su ocarina
> hace sonar el sapo verdinegro,
> y canta el ruiseñor su cavatina
> con las audaces fugas de un alegro. (p. 15)

> Se va el Abate, un comentario
> en rancio Latín mosconea,
> y lo glosa en su estradivario
> el grillo, músico de aldea. (p. 19)

Valle's text suggests a natural background animated rather like that of a Walt Disney cartoon, presided over by a blatantly mechanical moon which coyly observes the action from behind the foliage:

> La luna, enmascarada en el follaje,
> saca un ojo mirando al comediante,

como la dueña que seduce al paje
y deja ver un cuarto de semblante.

The repetition of this refrain at the end of each of the three acts confirms the participating role of the decor and the tone of stylized whimsy that prevails throughout the play.

'EL EMBRUJADO'

There is little doubt that Valle returned to the Galician rural atmosphere and the world of primary passions in *El embrujado* with the intention of writing a tragedy. There is nothing ironic about the play's subtitle, *Tragedia de tierras de Salnés* and both structure and style argue a serious tragic conception. In *El embrujado* we are presented with a view of humanity in which the overriding passions of greed, avarice and, to a lesser extent, lust all but obliterate other human characteristics. Briefly, the situation is as follows. Rosa la Galana uses her charismatic sexual attraction to enslave the helpless and pathetic figure of Anxelo. She entices him to murder the son of a rich landowner, Pedro Bolaño, and then tries to extract money from Bolaño by claiming that her own illegitimate child is in fact Bolaño's grandson. She tries to barter the child in return for some land and a house for herself and Anxelo. The old man's avarice is stronger than his feeling for the child and he rejects her offer. Later, with Bolaño's connivance, one of his servants tries to kidnap the baby, who is killed in the attempt. The death of the innocent child is the tragic outcome of the conflict between Bolaño's avarice and La Galana's greed. The unironic tone becomes clear when one compares *El embrujado* with the other plays of the *Retablo de la avaricia, la lujuria y la muerte* in which it was included in the edition of 1927. In all the other works, written much later, Valle had abandoned the tragic view of human destiny. The characters are the puppets of blind collective forces and the situations are consciously pushed beyond tragedy to grotesque farce. In *El embrujado*, written about 1912, Valle had perhaps begun to lose some of his heroic vision but had not yet formalized an aesthetic of the grotesque. The patriarchal figure of Pedro Bolaño, for instance, has none of the epic stature of Montenegro. He is a business man, a cautious, mean and canny landowner without the heroic qualities of his predecessor. On the other hand, *El embrujado* does not present a systematically distanced and external view of the characters. Bolaño is the victim of his avarice but is conscious of being so. On hearing the

77

voice of his wounded servant, he exclaims: 'Su voz llega hasta mí como un remordimiento. Tiemblo de miedo y de angustia . . . ¡Y de dudas también! . . . ¿Acaso la avaricia me ha endurecido el corazón?' (p. 143). Both Bolaño and even the 'bewitched' Anxelo struggle (albeit ineffectually) against the forces that possess them and it is this small element of self-awareness that distinguishes them from the automata of the other plays of the *Retablo*.

Yet Valle never really believes in his characters' ability to resist the forces that manipulate them and their struggles to do so sometimes border on comic melodrama. There is an example of this in act II when Anxelo, tormented by guilt, wishes to confess to the murder of Bolaño's son and reveal the whole truth about the plot with Rosa Galans. His wife, Mauriña, knows about the liaison with Rosa, the child of their union and the murder, yet is swayed more by greed than moral considerations. The contrast of Anxelo's guilt-ridden fears and superstitions and Mauriña's hard-bitten avarice comes across as a grotesque – and comic – inversion of moral values: a man's wife urging him to return to his former lover for the sake of the family fortunes. El Ciego de Gondar and his Moza also try to persuade him to return to his 'obligation' with Rosa Galans. Anxelo's tormented lamentations are treated with such total incomprehension or ridicule by the other characters that they are made to appear absurd. The speeches, in this act especially, have a declamatory, self-parodying quality which would make it difficult to play them 'straight'. Nevertheless, the general tone of the play does not permit an interpretation of it as *consciously* absurd melodrama with a deliberate anti-tragic purpose, such as we find, say, in *La rosa de papel*. It is almost as if Valle, in the self-conscious pursuit of tragedy, finds himself in the sphere of comedy without realizing it.

Another feature of the play which pushes it in the direction of melodrama is the unaccustomed concentration on plot. Judging by a letter written to Galdós when the latter was artistic director of the Teatro Español, it seems that Valle had made conscious efforts to produce a work conforming to the then acceptable standards of a theatre company (Nuez and Schraibman, pp. 32–3). At the time he had just broken with the Guerrero–Mendoza company and presumably needed the money. *El embrujado* has none of the free dynamic development of the *Comedias bárbaras* or the later *Divinas palabras*. Its conventional three-act structure corresponds to three well-defined sets: the front of Bolaño's house, a riverside ferry and the kitchen of Bolaño's house, all strictly practicable and feasible even by the standards of his own time. The action is likewise more closely keyed to the demands of a central plot: the intended deception by Rosa Galans and Anxelo on Pedro Bolaño. This explains the unusually large proportion of reported narrative and explanatory dialogue (e.g. by El Ciego de Gondar in act I and by Anxelo in act II). It also accounts for the highly artificial succession of entrances (no fewer than seven) in the last act. Valle tries to weave this plot into a collective choral background by using the incidental characters of the *hilanderas*, the *foráneos*, the *abuela* and her niece and El Ciego de Gondar as commentators on the main action. For the most part, however, the chorus is at the service of the plot and functions as a supplier of background information rather than as a dramatic presence (see pp. 84–7). Consequently the dialogue seems thin by comparison with the *Comedias* and lacking in the rich texture and orchestration of those works. The collective feeling is sacrificed to the clarification of cause and effect in the plot. The plot line is a rod that Valle makes for his own back and the small episodes that contribute nothing to this, such as the dialogue with Valerio el pajarito and the by-play between the two blind men in act II, seem all the more pointless because of it.

The concentration upon plot to suit the requirements of conventional theatre also produces another side effect in *El embrujado*. It destroys the interdependence between natural background, dramatic action and character that had been a feature of the *Comedias* and, in a different way, of *La Marquesa Rosalinda*. Dialogue is required to serve plot and is not allowed to flow from the physical context. As a result, the settings of *El embrujado* impinge very little on the dialogue and characters and revert to being mere functional backdrops, places where it is convenient for the action to take place.

Sumner Greenfield attributes Valle's failure in *El embrujado* to exhaustion, i.e. his failure to revive themes (such as that of witchcraft in *Jardín umbrío* and the choral motifs of the early *Comedias*) and a style that no longer had sufficient meaning for him (*Anatomía*, p. 134). It is true that Valle does return to former sources of inspiration, but not simply to resuscitate old material, which he could probably have done quite satisfactorily. What he is trying to do is to present that material as tragedy, which, as we have seen in *Voces de gesta*, was a genre manifestly unsuited to his talents. He was also trying to convey the collective spirit of the *Comedias* whilst restricting himself to the unities of place and action. Both of these attempts go against the grain of Valle's imagination and account for the failure of the play.

El embrujado marks a point of crisis in Valle's development as a dramatist. It seems to have been the cause of a definitive break in his association with the professional theatre. Galdós's refusal to accept the play for the Teatro Español, coming as it did after Valle's rupture with the Guerrero–Mendoza company, was clearly the last straw. Valle never again associated himself for a prolonged period with any professional company. When the subject of the professional theatre was raised in press interviews, Valle's comments were invariably venomous. It also appears that he took very little interest in the later productions of such works as *Farsa y licencia de la reina castiza* and *Divinas palabras*. It was seven years before he wrote another play. *El embrujado* was also Valle's swan song as far as 'pure' tragedy was concerned. After the years of artistic stock-taking which followed, the year 1920 saw the appearance of two *farsas*, a *tragicomedia* and the first of the *esperpentos*, in which the tragic view of life is explicitly rejected.

6

Two late farces: *La enamorada del rey* and *Farsa y licencia de la reina castiza*

After his seven years of theatrical silence, Valle staged a dramatic come-back in 1920 when he published four plays. The striking feature about these works is their great diversity of style and content. *Farsa italiana de la enamorada del rey* is a farce in the gentle style of *La Marquesa Rosalinda*, containing some satirical allusions and social comment, but basically concerned with defending a *modernista* aesthetic. *Farsa y licencia de la reina castiza* is a farce in a very different dimension, a lampoon of Spanish political life set in the reign of Isabel II. *Divinas palabras* introduces us to a new tragicomic vision of Galicia, stripped of all the heroic idealization and medieval patina. Finally, *Luces de Bohemia*, the first of the *esperpentos*, takes a new and deliberately anti-heroic view of the artist in his contemporary urban context.

Valle-Inclán emerged from his period of retreat in the Pazo de la Merced, near Caramiñal, with a more satirical eye for his contemporary surroundings and a more jaundiced view of humanity. The social and psychological reasons for this change of attitude would require a detailed biographical investigation and fall outside the scope of this book. However, for many years it was assumed that Valle's visit to the war front as a reporter for *El Imparcial* in 1916 and his contact with the squalid realities of trench warfare were instrumental in bringing about the cynical new *musa moderna* of *La pipa de Kif* (1919) and *Farsa y licencia*. I have argued elsewhere that the actual text of these reports (later published as *La media noche* in 1917) gives little support to the thesis that experience of the war radically altered his way of looking at the world (Lyon, *BHS*, 1975). The artistic aims and criteria of this work are essentially those which Valle had been elaborating over the previous decade and which had just found their definitive expression in *La lámpara maravillosa*, completed and published before his departure for the front. The purpose – as the Prologue makes clear – was essentially Symbolist in character: to illuminate, through this account of the conflict, certain transcendent laws which govern human behaviour in times of war. The reappraisal of his attitudes seems to have come, not as a result of the actual experience, but as a result of his dissatisfaction with the work that came out of it. In his *Breve Noticia*, Valle – somewhat untypically – admits failure: 'He fracasado en el empeño, mi droga índica en esta occasión me negó su efluvio maravilloso. Estas páginas que ahora salen a la luz no son más que un balbuceo del ideal soñado.' He gives no explanation for this failure, but probably became aware of the contradictions within the work between material and treatment. We see in *La media noche* the first indications of a widening gap between Valle's Symbolist philosophy and manifestations of contemporary life. The mosaic of incidents observed from Valle's stellar vantage-point does little to elucidate the underlying *arquitectura ideal* referred to in chapter 33 (see p. 164 of this book). It is possible that in writing his first book on an entirely contemporary subject, he became aware of the abyss between his philosophy and the material. The *esperpento* was born when he became fully conscious of the overwhelming incongruity between the universal norms, which for him were unchanging and unchangeable, and the unheroic and inadequate nature of modern man. We see the beginnings of this process and the repercussions on Valle's style in the contrast between the two farces published in 1920.

It is difficult to say exactly how *Farsa italiana de la enamorada del rey* fits into Valle-Inclán's development. The late date of its publication (1920) and certain aspects of its theme and treatment seem to link it with the later works, while in other respects form and content point to an earlier date of composition. The tenuous story line concerns Mari-Justina, the innkeeper's daughter, who falls hopelessly in love with the king after catching a brief glimpse of him as he rode past with his hunting party. Her idealization of the hunchbacked and decrepit monarch into a handsome fairy-tale prince and her subsequent disillusionment seem to imply a comment on the relationship between the monarchy and the people. Mari-Justina's creation of an ideal image despite the reality recalls the point made in *Voces de gesta* that the strength of a people lies in the ability of the collective imagination to forge an ideal image of its historical identity. In the *farsa*, however, the point has been deliberately distorted. What had once been the stuff of heroic tragedy is now considered appropriate for farce, for while Valle retains his respect for the *pueblo*, his attitude to the monarchy, and particularly to the court, has changed radically. The king is made physically grotesque ('un viejo chepudo/estevado y narigudo') with a crown too large for his head threatening to fall over his ears and 'entrarle de corbatín'. The principal targets of Valle's satire are the courtiers, Don Facundo, the king's minister, and Don Bártolo, academician and confessor to the queen, caricatures of pomposity, fossilized literary and academic attitudes and ignorance. The meaningful interdependence between traditional monarchy and the people as exemplified in El Rey Carlino and Ginebra no longer exists between Mari-Justina and the Bourbon king of the *farsa*. It is even tempting to see Mari-Justina's idealization of the grotesque reality as a self-parodying allusion to Ginebra's devotion to El Rey Carlino, thus aligning the play as a whole with one of the basic themes of the *esperpentos*, the gap between myth and reality.

The *farsa* is certainly more directly critical of social institutions than *La Marquesa Rosalinda*. It shares with that work the eighteenth-century setting and the purpose of sabotaging the humourless gravity of traditional Castilian attitudes which, as he claims in *La lámpara maravillosa*, had hardened the arteries of Spain after the period of the Catholic monarchs (*Lámpara*, p. 54). Yet, whereas the humour of *La Marquesa* is veiled and ambivalent, *La enamorada* is explicitly satirical. It juxtaposes two lifestyles, the popular and the cultured – echoed visually in the two sets of the inn in the heart of La Mancha and the geometrically ordered gardens of the royal palace – with the clear intention of ridiculing the latter. It uses the techniques and situations of broad farce, for example, the intercepted missive or compromising document. A copy of Maese Lotario's *copla* extolling Mari-Justina's love for the king accidentally falls into the hands of the two ministers. This gives rise to a scene of traditional farce in which Don Bártolo tries to disguise his inability to read by claiming to have forgotten his spectacles. The play also exploits the traditional comic device of the dramatic irony of disguise. The king and Don Facundo arrive at the inn grotesquely disguised as two *labradores* and are treated as such by the *ventera*. Traditionally, too, farce has always traded on the deflation of pomposity and the ridiculing of pretentiousness and *La enamorada* relies extensively on both. The farcical element of *La Marquesa* is largely contained in the conventionalized characters of the *commedia dell'arte*, while *La enamorada* draws more on the satirical targets and techniques of the popular *sainete* of Valle's own day. Parody of the classics – so characteristic of the *sainete* (see Zamora

Vicente, pp. 25–61) – is used in the subplot relating to Maese Lotario's shady past when La Dama del manto throws herself at the king's feet and demands justice. It is not difficult to see in this a parody of Guillén de Castro's *Mocedades del Cid*. As in the *sainete*, there is a good sprinkling of verbal humour, some of which is pure music-hall banter.

MAESE LOTARIO: No se enoje, Don Furibundo.
DON FACUNDO: Don Facundo me llamo. ¡Poco a poco!
MAESE LOTARIO: Será, si es poco a poco, Don Fa-cun-do. (p. 34)

The grotesqueness of some of the characterization, the technique of low farce and the contemporary relevance of the satire seem to lend credence to the view that this innocuous-looking *farsa* may be an *esperpento* in disguise.

And yet *La enamorada* leaves a strongly positive impression. The satire on pedantry and formalism goes hand in hand with a defence of poetic fantasy in the shape of Maese Lotario, the Italian puppeteer. Maese Lotario's art is, like that of the *bululú* in the Prologue to *Los cuernos de don Friolera*, Italian and Neapolitan in origin. The primitive puppet farce, as we see from the Prologue to *Los cuernos*, was one of the principal sources of inspiration for the *esperpento*. Yet Valle's treatment of these two characters is significantly different. In *Los cuernos* he sees in his *bululú*'s crude performances the possible regeneration of the Spanish theatre not, as one might expect, in order to restore contact between the theatre and the people, but because, artistically, he saw them as the most suitable vehicle for reflecting a reality that was an absurd parody of itself. Maese Lotario, on the other hand, attaches little importance to the 'retablo de moros y cristianos' which is his bread and butter. He is a puppeteer of necessity, but he is a lyric poet 'enamorado del rostro de la luna' by vocation. Lotario's whole aesthetic creed is an advocacy of the lyrical imagination and it is with this, rather than with the grotesque humour of the puppet farce, that he combats pedantry and pomposity. It is surely this difference in aesthetic approach that marks Lotario as the creation of an earlier period and clearly divides *La enamorada* from the philosophy of the later plays. It was not until after the appeal to lyricism had been abandoned that Valle began to see the aesthetic possibilities of the 'baser' and more strident literary forms.

La enamorada thus shares with *La Marquesa* the emphasis on literary attitudes and on the poetic imagination as an artistic response to prosaic realities – a far cry, as we shall see, from the more despairing outlook of Max Estrella in *Luces de Bohemia*. Consequently, the whole play turns on the figure of the artist, Maese Lotario. His aesthetic outlook cannot be completely identified with the one implicit in *La Marquesa* where the idea of poetic fantasy is associated with that of the 'bella mentira' without roots in reality. For Lotario it should be grounded in collective popular tradition, as we can see in this exchange, when the literary pundits of the court condemn Lotario's verses for being contaminated by French influence.

DON FACUNDO: ¡Novedades francesas!
DON BARTOLO: ¡Contaminatio verba!
MAESE LOT.: Versos, señores míos, de la propia Minerva hispana.
DON BARTOLO: ¡No blasfemes!
MAESE LOT.: No blasfemo si digo
que son versos al modo de Mío Cid Rodrigo. (p. 51)

The itinerant Italian puppeteer is the instrument that revives the primitive lyrical tradition of Old Castile: his love song brings to life the innocent fantasy of Mari-Justina and symbolically links the people and the court.

Mari-Justina's naïve delusion is seen as a positive striving towards a poetic ideal and is referred to by Maese Lotario as the 'locura ideal de Don Quijote' (p. 83). The reference is far from being a casual one and it is not difficult to find other parallels with the *Quijote*. Mari-Justina's idealization of the king parallels Don Quijote's idealization of Dulcinea. Her head, we are told, has been turned by a diet of heroic *romances*:

Tienen las niñas perdidas el seso
por esos cuentos de enamorados.
Tales romances, en un proceso,
debieran todos de ser quemados. (p. 24)

The character of the *ventera*, who speaks these lines, closely parallels that of the *ama* in her down-to-earth realism and in her desire to burn the pernicious literature that has led her daughter astray. The Caballero del Verde Gabán makes a brief and somewhat inconsequential appearance in act I and remarks on the parallel between Maese Lotario and Maese Pedro of the *Quijote*. The setting of the *venta clásica* at the crossroads on the plains of La Mancha could hardly be more explicit:

El patio de la venta es humanista
y picaresco con sabor de aulas
y sabor popular de los caminos:
tiene un vaho de letras del Quijote. (p. 11)

Sumner Greenfield argues that these clearly intended parallels with the *Quijote* and the presence of the Castilian landscape in the play bring Valle into line with the mainstream of '98 thinking (*Anatomía*, pp. 195–207). He evolves an ingenious theory that the play is an attempt to fuse the aesthetic attitudes of *Modernismo* (in particular, the Darío of *Azul*) with the *quijotismo* and vision of Castile of the '98 writers. The antipathy to the dead wood of Spanish traditionalism, religious dogmatism and academicism was shared by most of the younger writers of Valle's time whatever their aesthetic persuasion and, to this limited extent, the work can be considered *noventayochista* in feeling. But, for the rest, Valle's *quijotismo* and vision of the landscape have little in common with those of Unamuno, Azorín or Machado. The evocation of landscape may have, as Greenfield points out, considerable theatrical force, but it has none of the mythical significance associated with the work of these writers. The hallmark of the '98 attitude to the landscape was that it crystallized an image of historical significance – the heroic past, the decrepit present and the potential future. Valle's settings have no such *intrahistoria* and seem unrelated to the human attitudes in the play, either to Maese Lotario's poetry or to Mari-Justina's delusion. It may well be true that Valle agreed with the '98 position on the question of a submerged tradition of primitive Castile buried beneath the 'literatura jactanciosa' of the Golden Age, but the historical and social dimension is lacking in *La enamorada*.[1]

What emerges most strongly from this *farsa* is its advocacy for a certain type of aesthetic attitude to the circumstances. Mari-Justina's 'quixotic' love is equated with the liberating force of the imagination. The lyrical love song composed by Maese Lotario on her behalf stands in deliberate contrast to the grotesque object of that love song. The reality may be grotesque but the impulse to dream is vindicated. To underline this, the king rounds off the play by appointing the poet as his personal adviser:

> Quiero trocar por normas de poesía
> los chabacanos ritos leguleyos,
> sólo es bueno a reinar la fantasía,
> y está mi reino en manos de plebeyos. (p. 85)

This escape route via the imagination is totally denied in the *Farsa y licencia de la reina castiza* which portrays a world in which fantasy cannot breathe.

In *La enamorada del rey* and the other verse farces (*Cuento de abril* and *La Marquesa Rosalinda*) the rejection of certain attitudes (pedantry, empty traditionalism) had always been accompanied by the implied or explicit defence of others (the dedication to beauty and truth). The presence of the artist–poet (the troubadour, Arlequín, Maese Lotario) is representative to a large extent of Valle himself and underlines the aesthetic preoccupation behind the plays. Faith in the poetic view of reality offsets the grotesque and the absurd.

There is no such duality in *Farsa y licencia de la reina castiza*. The artist–poet has withdrawn from the scene and there is no place for artistic fantasy in the context of total corruption and cynicism, no salvation possible in the dreams of a disinterested poet. From the refined frivolity of the eighteenth-century court Valle goes to the coarse farce of bedchamber politics in the reign of Isabel II. There is a total absence of lyricism and the satire stems from ethical and political rather than aesthetic considerations. *Farsa y licencia* is conceived as a kind of theatrical cartoon strip. It is based on the activities at Isabel's court as reported in such satirical reviews of the period as *Gil Blas*, *La Flaca* and *La Gorda*. Its satirical portrayal of a specific historical and social situation in Spain was a new departure for Valle. And, since the play also seems to imply a more general attack on Spanish political instability, it could also be considered the first play in which the author records an attitude to his own time.

Valle's reference in the *Apostillón* to his 'musa moderna' (which 'enarca la pierna,/se cimbra, se ondula,/se comba, se achula') suggests that he was conscious of the stylistic innovations in the play. The publication of *La pipa de kif* in 1919 was the first real manifestation of the debunking spirit and the first systematic attempt to use the grotesque artistically. *Farsa y licencia* is evidently a transference of this anti-tragic and almost anti-art style to the theatre. Perhaps the best way to describe *Farsa y licencia* is to call it a verbal cartoon. The witty, rhythmic rhyming speech of the dialogue is matched by the agile contortions of the characters in defiance of normal anatomical limitations. The queen's laughter, for instance:

> ríe la comadre feliz y carnal
> y un temblor cachondo le baja del papo
> al anca fondona de yegua real. (p. 175)

The simultaneous entrance of Tragatundas and the Intendente has a cartoon-like quality:

Rechina una puerta:
sale repentino
un viejo ladino
que estaba detrás.
Y enfrente aparece,
torciendo el mostacho,
otro mamarracho
al mismo compás. (pp. 195–6)

Similarly the entrance of the Sopón, suspended from the iron fist of Tragatundas, with eyes bolting, legs bent and his tongue hanging out like a bell clapper, has a striking visual immediacy. As in the cartoon, there is no identification, no pain, no death. This is how Lucero del alba and Jorobeta fall:

Con simultánea zapateta,
como en un drama japonés,
se derrumba el Jorobeta
y el manolo del Avapiés. (p. 233)

And then rise again:

Resucitados por la punta
del chapín de Mari-Morena,
con una mueca cejijunta
saltan los muertos en escena. (p. 236)

We have seen how the heroic elements gradually disappear from Valle's theatre. The same now occurs with the lyrical elements. Such lyrical feeling as had maintained the delicately poised ambivalence of *La Marquesa Rosalinda* is now debunked and turned on its head (see Greenfield, *BHS*, 1962). As if to emphasize this point the opening *acotación* presents us with the picture of the royal palace in the moonlight reflected in the lake – a characteristic *modernista* image which is then shattered by a movement of the water:

Cala la luna los follajes,
albea el palacio real,
que, acrobático en los mirajes
del lago, da un salto mortal.

The same technique is used in later *acotaciones*. The standard Neoclassical decor of *Modernismo* is portrayed in a state of trembling instability, either reflected in water or subject to strange effects of light.

> Candelabros con algarabía
> de reflejos, consolas de panza
> y en los muros bailando una danza
> los retratos de la dinastía. (p. 217)

Valle sometimes links these effects to the behaviour of the characters, as if the palace and gardens were cringing with embarrassment at the grotesque antics of their occupants.

> Con la chistera de soslayo
> y un grito terrible de falsete
> se eclipsa Don Gargarabete
> para no hacer un Dos de Mayo.
>   El palacio entre los ramajes
> del jardín se muestra y recata;
> tiembla, invertida en los mirajes
> de las fuentes, su columnata. (p. 166)

The courtly atmosphere, common to all the *farsas*, is here systematically debased and distorted. The courtly language becomes the clipped slang of the *chulería* and the spirit of the *chulo* has infiltrated the court. All the characters are united in their greed, cynicism, corruption and sharp practice. The basis of the plot is the queen's well-known propensity for writing compromising letters to her various lovers, letters which were later used for blackmailing purposes either by the lovers or by the queen's effeminate consort. In this case the lover is a student who arrives at the palace with two letters from the queen and tries to barter them for the archbishopric of Manila. The queen's minister, el Gran Preboste, refuses. The student then tries to blackmail the consort who, together with other hangers-on, tries to blackmail the Gran Preboste himself. The latter refuses again. Faced with this refusal, the consort and his cronies march on the queen's bedroom to demand the king's conjugal rights. The threat of scandal obliges the Gran Preboste to break his staff of office and resign and

> Se viene al suelo la Monarquía
> como una vieja, de un patatú. (p. 233)

The question of whether Valle wrote this *farsa* in the style of his newly evolved *esperpento* is a difficult one. Many critics believe this to be the case or that the differences are negligible (see Buero Vallejo, p. 45).[2] Certainly, there appears to be very little stylistic difference between *Farsa y licencia* and *Los cuernos de don Friolera*. If anything, the distortion of character, speech and movement is even more systematic and extreme. Moreover, in plot structure, there is a close similarity between the *farsa* and *La hija del capitán* (and, to some extent, *Tirano Banderas*) since both plays show the collapse of a political regime originating in an insignificant incident. Why then did Valle not give this play the label of *esperpento*? The suggestion that the *farsa* does not qualify as an *esperpento* partly because it is written in verse is a piece of technical hair-splitting, since there seems to be no reason why the *esperpento* vision should not be accommodated within a verse form (Greenfield, *Anatomía*, pp. 208–9). The fact that the *farsa* does not deal with a contemporary subject is a more substantial argument, but even here the objection could be raised that, although the particular episode referred to the previous century, the theme of political instability had a definite contemporary application. To arrive at any conclusion one should examine the theme in relation to those of the *esperpentos*, at least the way the idea was originally formulated in *Luces de Bohemia* and *Los cuernos de don Friolera*. In questions of this nature there has been a tendency to concentrate on stylistic features, examples of distortion, 'animalization', puppetry and the like, rather than on theme. At the risk of anticipating later arguments, it must be said that the main thematic emphasis of the earlier *esperpentos* was that the grotesque derives from the adherence to myths in circumstances which have made those myths empty of significance. As Valle repeated on many occasions, the original conception of the *esperpento* was a view of man as totally inadequate to a tragic role or situation. This creates a duality between what is proper to the role, the myth or the archetype and what the man *is* objectively. It is this opposition of myth and reality which is absent from *Farsa y licencia*. We are concerned here with the panorama of universal roguery and intrigue, not with the deflation of myths and pompously grand attitudes. In addition, the *esperpento* has a darker side in that it purports to express a basically tragic situation through the grotesque. It goes beyond satire, which *Farsa y licencia* does not. The *farsa* tends more towards caricature than to a general view of human behaviour. It lacks, in other words, an existential dimension, which is certainly implicit in the earlier *esperpentos*.

7

The dynamic tension: *Divinas palabras*

Divinas palabras develops the line of Galician plays initiated in the early *Comedias bárbaras* and continued in *El embrujado*. This is a play about the rural Galicia of Valle's own time. The villagers, beggars, errant tinkers and fairground fortune-tellers that fill its pages are a basically faithful reflection of Galician rural life and not an image that has passed through the heroic filter of memory. Valle has abandoned his backward-looking feudal nostalgia, the medieval reminiscences and the links with aristocratic tradition. The central heroic figure has gone and the choral elements of the *Comedias* have come into the foreground as a collective protagonist. Not only has the heroic tone disappeared, but the grotesque elements, apparent in the second act of *El embrujado*, have become more pronounced. 'Tragi-comedia' is Valle's own designation of the work and the dynamic tension between harsh (and sometimes tragic) realism and grotesque humour is an important constituent of the play. *Divinas palabras* is a tragi-comic tableau of superstition, lust, greed, death, cruelty and primitive innocence.

On the purely narrative level, *Divinas palabras* is structured around two main threads of action. The first concerns Laureano, the hydrocephalic dwarf in his *carretón*, who is left an orphan on the death of his mother Juana la Reina. As the dwarf is exploited as a fairground freak and regarded as a source of income there is a dispute over his possession between the Gailo family and Marica del Reino. They agree to share the *carretón*. Mari-Gaila begins to earn money by displaying Laureano around the local *ferias* and is soon attracted by the nomadic open-air life of the *feriantes*. This leads into the second thread of action which is the adultery of Mari-Gaila with the tinker Séptimo Miau and the consequent reaction of all the villagers to this. Marica del Reino tells her brother Pedro Gailo of his wife's adultery and urges him to take action. The wretched and pusillanimous Pedro

Gailo goes through a grotesque charade of sharpening the knife that will avenge his honour and ends up by trying to climb into bed with his own daughter. When Laureano dies from an excess of alcohol, Mari-Gaila returns home and leaves the *carretón* outside Marica's house to avoid the funeral expenses. With Laureano still awaiting burial, Mari-Gaila arranges another assignation with Séptimo Miau and is caught by the villagers in the act of adultery. They bring her naked on top of a haycart in front of the church where Pedro Gailo, the sacristan, is hiding. He tries to calm their outraged morality by reading the text from the Bible: 'Let he who be without sin amongst you cast the first stone' to which the reply is a shower of stones and insults. When the same sentiments are repeated in Latin – the *divinas palabras* of the title – the effect is immediate and miraculous and the incensed villagers return quietly to their homes.

The play poses difficult problems of interpretation, owing mainly to the apparent lack of an intellectual viewpoint. It would be difficult to encapsulate the action in any kind of moral or philosophical statement. It is a play which does not readily lend itself to analysis and the pencilled line in the margin marking the 'significant' passages. Critics have also been disconcerted by its moral ambiguity. There is little to orientate an audience's response in any particular direction, no character sufficiently contrasted with the world depicted to provide us with a sense of perspective and an alternative point of reference to assist in the formulation of an attitude. The title itself is problematical. What is the author's intention behind the effect of the Latin words uttered by the sacristan and how does this episode link up thematically with the rest of the play?

Allegorical interpretations have been suggested. In his study of *Divinas palabras* Gustavo Umpierre bases his case on evidence from *La lámpara maravillosa* and on currently popular 'vitalist' philosophies – notably Bergson and Nietzsche – which reacted against a mechanistic conception of the universe. Manuel Bermejo sees the play as an allegory of political events in Spain towards the end of the nineteenth century, involving Cánovas, Sagasta, Alfonso XII and others (pp. 187–228). Of these two (mutually exclusive) theories, Umpierre's seems the more plausible. He sees the action as a three-way struggle between competing ideologies: traditional morality represented by Pedro Gailo, indulgence of the vital instincts in the form of Mari-Gaila and the principle of rational or intellectual enquiry (the satanic *yo*) embodied in Séptimo Miau. Each of these philosophies is ultimately sterile and degenerates into hollow rhetoric, moral degeneration or empty pride. The moral indigence of the characters is revealed in the treatment of their common victim, Laureano, who, far from stimulating a spirit of compassion and Christian charity, provokes only greed in most of the characters. Umpierre claims that Valle is pointing – mainly through the medium of Laureano – to the ethical and spiritual solution of Christianity, without posing the problem of belief in God ('*Divinas palabras*', p. 49).

The strongest part of Umpierre's thesis is the demoniacal associations of Séptimo Miau. Certain parallels between Valle's idea of Satan in *La lámpara maravillosa* and the character of Séptimo Miau (or Lucero as he is called at the beginning of the play) undoubtedly exist. As a criminal on the run he is set apart from the others. The name of Lucero, used only in the first scene, was occasionally used by Calderón for his allegorical representations of the Devil.[1] Frequent allusions are made in the text to Séptimo's pact with the Devil, connected with his claims to forecast future events through his dog Coimbra and his fortune-telling bird. Coimbra greets Juana la Reina with a death howl shortly before her death on the roadside. He is then made to predict that Pedro Gailo will be cuckolded by his wife. Séptimo's fortune-telling activities are clearly linked with the idea of Satan in *La lámpara* where the essence of the Devil is identified as the pretension to divine omniscience.[2] There is a passage in the third act which clearly points to these ideas and even echoes the style and vocabulary of *La lámpara*:

PEDRO GAILO: El Demonio se rebeló por querer ver demasiado.
SÉPTIMO MIAU: El Demonio se rebeló por querer saber.
PEDRO GAILO: Ver y saber son frutos de la misma rama. El Demonio quiso tener un ojo en cada sin fin, ver el pasado y el no logrado.
SÉPTIMO MIAU: Pues se salió con la suya.
PEDRO GAILO: La suya era ser tanto como Dios y cegó ante la hora que nunca pasa. ¡Con las tres miradas ya era Dios! (pp. 123–4)

At the other end of the scale, Pedro Gailo's utterances generally express more traditional religious and moral attitudes. He is known as Pedro Gailo but is Pedro del Reino 'en sus papeles'. The possible allusions to the cock (*gailo* = *gallo*) and to the Kingdom of Heaven (*Reino*) in his name could conceivably refer to Saint Peter. In addition, the fact that he is a sacristan and occasionally associated with jangling keys puts one in mind of the traditional image of the saint. In the case of Mari-Gaila the allusions are to pagan mythology.

When her fortune is told by Séptimo Miau's *pájaro adivino* (II, 2), it reads as follows: 'Venus y Ceres. En esta conjunción se descorren los velos de tu destino. Ceres te ofrece frutos. Venus, licencias. Tu destino es el de la mujer hermosa. Tu trono el de la primavera' (p. 62). Mari-Gaila, with the 'ritmos clásicos' of her movements, is linked with the pagan divinities of love and fruitfulness. When she is brought to the door of the village church at the end of the play, mounted naked on a haycart, Valle is clearly seeing the scene in terms of pagan fertility rites, amply borne out by such phrases in the scene descriptions as 'un triunfo de faunalias', 'los ritmos de la agreste faunalia', 'el carro de la faunalia rueda por el camino, en torno salta la encendida guirnalda de mozos', 'el carro del triunfo venusto'. The final image is one of a pagan goddess surrounded by her retinue of satyrs.

Umpierre makes no clear distinction between his use of words such as 'symbol', 'allegory' and 'allusion'. At times he seems to imply that Valle-Inclán works intuitively by suggestion of archetypes, but mostly he commits himself to a strictly allegorical view of the work, an ideological basis of composition and intellectually ordered correspondences between real and abstract levels.[3] There is indeed enough evidence to suggest that the cosmogony of *La lámpara maravillosa* may be *implicit* in the play, but it is quite another matter to interpret it as an *illustration* of these ideas. It is important to be precise about Valle's understanding of allusion and allegory which, in *La lámpara*, is more that of the mystic than of the intellectual. He starts from the conviction that all earthly manifestations, all human actions in time, endure everlastingly in an eternal present and form the pattern of our ultimate destiny, in the manner of the stone which, on falling into the water, sends out the concentric circles of its ripples. Art for Valle was therefore allusion or allegory in so far as it tried to intuit, through the fragmented perceptions offered to our senses, the essential unity of the world. But that sense of unity was always something to be striven after, difficult to grasp, not a known quantity or an assumption. It is misleading to associate Valle-Inclán with the type of allegory which attempts to *represent* ideas in characters and actions and which proceeds from what, for him, is a self-evident truth or ideological conviction to its artistic embodiment. The important difference between allegory as practised by Calderón, for example, and as understood by Valle-Inclán was that the former starts from the concept and the latter from reality. While, therefore, it is salutary to be reminded of the archetypal suggestions that such characters as

Séptimo Miau, Pedro Gailo and Mari-Gaila may convey, it is a very different and more unlikely proposition to see them as pawns in an ideological chess game. Even more unlikely is the assertion that their interaction leads to the demonstration of a moral thesis. The interpretation of Laureano as the principle of Christian charity maltreated, as the catalyst which reveals the moral degradation of both sedentary and nomadic elements in the play, places Valle firmly in the ranks of the moralists. Valle's emphatic rejection of didacticism and moralizing in the theatre should at least persuade us to treat such conclusions with suspicion.

To interpret the play purely on this intellectual plane inevitably gives a lop-sided impression, since the narrative level is relegated to insignificance. The atmosphere of the play is charged with the sights and sounds and the physical presence of Galician rural life. It is a play about collective passions, attitudes and superstitions at work in a primitive community and any attempt to analyse the total impact of this work must take this essentially realistic (though not naturalistic) level into account. Ultimately, it must be decided whether the play is concerned principally with life or with ideas and *Divinas palabras* is no more concerned with ideas as such than Lorca's *Bodas de sangre* or J. M. Synge's *The Tinker's Wedding*, a play which bears an interesting resemblance to Valle's work. Rather than being dedicated to some abstract moral proposition, Valle presents a view of life which accepts confusion and contradiction without necessarily wishing to rationalize. This view is broadly consistent with certain ideas expressed in *La lámpara maravillosa* in that it portrays humanity in the grip of the World, the Flesh and the Devil, imprisoned in a world of time and the senses (notably the passions of lust and greed), but the play is not written as an argument to sustain these ideas. One essential feature of the work which Umpierre's thesis virtually ignores is its tragi-burlesque quality. It would be totally misleading to accept Pedro Gailo as a representative of traditional moral and religious codes if one did not balance this against the grotesque presentation of the character. As in the Irish plays of Synge, the tragi-comic spirit of *Divinas palabras* derives from the contradictions and incongruities in collective attitudes and particularly the contradictions between pagan feeling and the forms of Catholic morality. This tragi-comic perspective suggests an attitude of ironic detachment on the part of the author, rather than moral and religious commitment.

Other critics have tried to extract a moral point from the play while taking it more or less at its face value as a portrayal of Galician rural life. Sumner Greenfield stresses two principal changes of outlook in *Divinas palabras*: a greater degree of psychological density in the characterization and a more explicit moral attitude to the material (*Anatomía*, pp. 151–2). Professor Greenfield maintains that the play presents 'un panorama de las realidades del mal' of adultery, lust, obscenity, cruelty, hypocrisy, incest and homosexuality, among other vices. If it is true that Valle approaches the existence of evil from an ethical angle, it is important to decide exactly what his moral criteria were. Does he judge the panorama of evil from an orthodox Christian standpoint in which every individual is not only responsible for his own destiny but is capable of making moral decisions, or from the more mystical standpoint of *La lámpara* in which man is denied this freedom? Professor Greenfield's approach to character through individual psychology implies that he reads the play as an examination of individual relationships viewed from a more or less orthodox Christian belief. He sees the behaviour of the characters as a function of their psychological and moral make-up rather than as a function of certain primary collective drives at work in the community. For example, he sees Mari-Gaila's histrionic 'planto' at the death of Juana la Reina as a manifestation of her personal hypocrisy (p. 156). Pedro Gailo is treated as an individual portrayal of cuckold psychology (pp. 159 and 162). He also refers to the 'crueldad espantosa' and 'sadismo' of the scene in which Laureano is given wine and dies (p. 170), words which suggest a conscious enjoyment of evil instead of the instinctive amorality referred to previously. The conduct of the characters towards Laureano is seen as morally reprehensible or, at the very least, as culpable ignorance (p. 171).

While it is undoubtedly true that Valle abandoned the backward-looking, heroic view of the *Comedias bárbaras* in favour of a more objective and less romanticized attitude in *Divinas palabras*, it is more questionable to affirm that he plunged straight into psychological realism and sharply critical moral censure. In fact, much more so than in the *Comedias*, the emphasis falls on the collectivity rather than the individual. If one examines the feelings and emotions expressed by the characters, the causes of conflict between them in the dialogue, one finds that they are strictly limited to primary motivations of greed, lust, awe in the face of death, axioms of popular belief. There is a whole range of emotions and motivation involved in psychological relationships which do not interest Valle in the least: doubt, anxiety, mistrust, self-deception, vanity, guilt; the list is infinite. They are characters with no past – at least, none that impinges significantly on the action – no individual problems, no unique inner life. Their behaviour is governed by the collective context in which they live. Valle is not interested in the inner psychological repercussions of external events nor in the intimate effects of one character upon another nor in any process of change inside a character. It may be argued that they are sharply individualized in terms of external attitudes, gestures, etc., but their essential motives are not theirs alone. Any attitude of moral censoriousness would be largely irrelevant because the characters are denied the possibility of moral elevation by means of individual decision and action.

In very general terms the play is structured around these communal motifs of *avaricia*, *lujuria* and *muerte*, themes which play an important role in the *Comedias bárbaras* and a dominant one in the later *Retablo de la avaricia, la lujuria y la muerte*. The motif of death is present in all three acts: in the first, the death and wake of Juana la Reina, in the second, the death of Laureano and in the third, the corpse of Laureano is put on display to raise money for the burial. Into this backcloth are woven the twin strands of greed and lust. The first act is built up around the death of Juana la Reina and the dispute over the inheritance of Laureano and the *carretón*. Dramatic tension is generated by the juxtaposition of awe and ritual in the presence of death and peasant greed and primitive self-interest. The second act links the motifs of greed and lust by fusing together Mari-Gaila's exploitation of the *carretón* with her assignation and subsequent adultery with Séptimo Miau. The lust motif is then developed in the final act, building to the climax of the collective action of the villagers against the adulteress. It is indicative of the play's collective spirit and intention that the whole village should partake in these closing scenes when Mari-Gaila, caught in adultery, is pursued and brought naked on a haycart in front of the church. The essential point about this final sequence is that, while ostensibly being an expression of moral outrage, it is also an expression of collective lust and sensuality. In tabloid form, we thus have the following balanced arrangement of motifs: (1) death, greed; (2) lust, death, greed; (3) lust, death.

All our considerations of the play so far have omitted one fundamental dimension, which is its nature as a *tragicomedia* and the remarkable flavour that Valle achieves through his blend of in-gredients. Neither of the approaches we have discussed takes into account the rich texture of the dialogue and the essentially dramatic tension of its incongruities. Broadly speaking, this flavour comes from the contradictions between instinctive attitudes and inherited moral and religious formulae, similar to those of the comedies of J. M. Synge. The essential opposition of attitudes is established in the first scene with the clash of Lucero's irreligious moral indifference and Pedro Gailo's conventional piety. The basic contrast is established, as it is in *The Tinker's Wedding*, between pagan and Catholic, sedentary and nomadic elements and, in addition, the ground is prepared for Mari-Gaila's desertion of the life of conventional morality for the free amoral life of the *ferias* and the open road.

It is illuminating to compare *Divinas palabras* with Lorca's *Bodas de sangre*. Both are plays about adultery or the flouting of traditional codified morality by the force of instinct. In *Bodas de sangre*, the mother's pride in her caste, the cult of family honour and the carefully nurtured vendetta against the Félix family clash with the instinctive passion which brings Leonardo and the Novia together. Lorca sees this in terms of an inevitable and tragic conflict of opposites – irreconcilable opposites – man-made codes which pervert the course of nature with tragic consequences. The play is laden with a sense of fatality from the first scene; a 'social' marriage of wealth to wealth and traditional enmity between families can never extinguish the smouldering passions below the surface. In *Divinas palabras* it is the sexual instinct that lures the wife away from a socially and religiously consecrated marriage. The outcome of this could have been a tragic one. Valle could have had the villagers stone Mari-Gaila to death for violating the taboo. Such an ending would have placed the emphasis on the element of *conflict* between instinct and the force of abstract codes. However, Valle's resolution of the action and his whole treatment of the adultery theme reveal a point of view radically different from Lorca's. Rather than seeing instinct and abstract codes as tragically opposed, he sees them as *incongruously juxtaposed*. Pedro Gailo's moral posturing is ludicrous precisely because it is incongruous against the background of collective greed and lust which animate the whole community and Pedro Gailo with it. The scene in which the drunken sacristan prepares to avenge his honour by sharpening a large butcher's knife is unmistakably comic in tone and possibly the first example of the parody of honour in Valle's work. The grotesque melodramatic rhetoric and the fact that the character consciously acts out the role expected of him reminds us of similar

scenes in *Los cuernos de don Friolera* in which the protagonist swears
vengeance on the errant wife (e.g. scene 6). Pedro Gailo rehearses his
speech to the Alcalde Mayor: 'Usía ilustrísima manderá que me
prendan. Esta cabeza es la de mi legítima esposa. Mirando por mi
honra se la rebané toda entera. Usía tendrá puesto en sus textos el
castigo que merezco' (p. 77). We can see the beginnings here of the
theme of man as an essentially inauthentic, role-playing animal,
manipulated by forces beyond his conscious will, which Valle was to
develop in *Los cuernos, La rosa de papel* and *Sacrilegio*. Here he is mainly
interested in contrasting the social, 'codified' attitudes with the
instinctive motive. Pedro's over-blown sentiments about honour and
marital fidelity are deflated by his grotesque attempts to climb into
bed with his daughter, Simoniña. Under the rhetoric there is simply a
case of sexual frustration, just as the pious act of Marica del Reino in
warning him of his dishonour is a case of frustrated greed for
possession of the *carretón*. The fact that the characters are dominated
by these primitive instincts makes a mockery of their pretensions to
more elevated motivations.

Perhaps less obvious than this parody of honour is the parody of
charity in the first act. We are introduced to the dying Juana la Reina
begging for charity on the roadside with the *carretón*. Almost every
character and action seem to deny La Reina's appeal for 'un bien de
caridad para el desgraciado sin luz de razón'. The *chalán* rides straight
past and merely curses them for frightening his cattle, La Tatula is
only concerned with being 'compromised' if Juana dies on the
roadside, Miguelín and Séptimo Miau flatly refuse to help and then
steal the dead woman's savings from the *carretón*. Against this
background of non-charitable attitudes, Mari-Gaila and Pedro Gailo
haggle with Marica del Reino over the custody of Laureano, alleging
that they are doing so out of 'charity' and as a token of respect for the
deceased, while pressing their claims for what will be a source of
income. The manoeuvring for advantage and hard bargaining is
interlarded with the ritualistic *plantos* or 'keening' for the departed
Juana la Reina, lamentations which are themselves a comic blend of
solemn rhetoric and daily trivia. The comic incongruity of this
mixture of peasant acquisitiveness, ritual lamentation, pious sentiment and bathos does not indicate any critical sarcasm on the part of
the author. He is merely reflecting objective contradictions with an
irony that is essentially impartial. To read this scene or the Pedro
Gailo scene mentioned above as examples of 'hypocrisy' is to put the

emphasis where it does not belong. Valle is concerned with collective manifestations, not with subjective emotions or with the question of whether they are feigned or not. Moral judgement which distinguishes between the behaviour of one individual, or one value, and another is simply irrelevant. Greed and ritual piety coexist in the characters with the same innocence as comic profanity and religious solemnity coexist in their lamentations for the departed. The factor which unites and gives dramatic force to all this intermingling of pagan and Catholic feeling in act I is the presence of death. Juana la Reina's mute presence dominates the dialogue and makes it work dramatically. Even the apparently irrelevant digression about the bad water and its effects is given comically dramatic point when placed in the physical context of people gathered round the body. The whole of the wake scene and the disputes over the possession of the *carretón* are thereby invested with a tragi-comic tension, similar to that which reappears in the wake scene of *Luces* and in *La rosa de papel*.

More explicit examples of juxtaposition of Catholic and pagan elements appear in the Trasgo Cabrío scene (II, 8) and towards the end of the play. In a complete departure from realism, Valle introduces the Trasgo Cabrío fantasy – suggestive of rampant sexuality – in a scene intended to be a re-enactment of Mari-Gaila's surrender to Séptimo Miau. Mari-Gaila begins, as she does with Séptimo, by trying to reject the advances of the lecherous he-goat, but ends by succumbing voluptuously. The emblem Valle has chosen to externalize Mari-Gaila's lust is an archetype of pagan mythology and folklore, yet the chant Mari-Gaila uses to exorcize this demon is based on Christian iconography with allusions to the creation of sun and moon, the tablets of Moses, the Gospels, the Magi, death of Christ, descent into purgatory and entry into heaven.

Many critics have evidently been disturbed by the moral ambivalence of much of *Divinas palabras* and, in particular, of the final scenes and have felt obliged to postulate some kind of moral or satirical intention. Artistically, it is surely not necessary for Valle to commit himself morally on his characters and there is little to suggest that he does so. The closing scenes, in fact, underline the fact that Valle is accepting contradictions and incongruities rather than trying to rationalize or resolve them.[4] In the first place the collective hysteria that mounts against Mari-Gaila is in itself ambivalent. The sensuality that lies beneath the expression of outraged morality is evident. The crowd make her take off her clothes and dance naked on the haycart.

The lascivious cries of 'jujurujú!' echo those of the Trasgo Cabrío, which in II, 8 had been the externalization of Mari-Gaila's own lust. The sensuality of the scene is enhanced by the allusions to pagan mythology in the *acotaciones*. Valle presents it as an erotic pagan festival with Mari-Gaila resplendent on her throne like a goddess surrounded by her fauns and satyrs. Yet this pagan tableau arrives almost like a float in Holy Week in front of the church. In fact the whole of this concluding sequence offers a picturesque blend of Catholic formulae and pagan feeling. The sacristan grotesquely assumes the priest's function and approaches the 'carro del triunfo venusto' to perform a pagan ceremony of exorcism with the missal and a lighted candle: 'Con el libro abierto y el bonete torcido, cruza la quintana y llega ante el carro del triunfo venusto. Como para recibirle, salta al camino la mujer desnuda, tapándose el sexo. El sacristán le apaga la luz sobre las manos cruzadas y bate en ellas con el libro' (p. 135). He then quotes the words of Christ spoken to the angry mob about to stone the woman caught in adultery. The words, when read in Spanish, merely provoke the crowd to further indignation and violence: 'Cóleras y soberbias desatan las lenguas. Pasa el soplo encendido de un verbo popular y judaico.' The same sentence when read 'con un saludo de iglesia' and in Latin, the language of the Church, produces an immediate calm. '¡Milagro del latín! Una emoción religiosa y litúrgica conmueve las conciencias y cambia el sangriento resplandor de los rostros.'

This ending has given rise to a number of different interpretations; the principal point at issue is whether or not Valle is being ironical. The evangelical interpretation would be that the words of forgiveness spoken in the language of the Church have the mysterious power to purge the villagers of their base passions and moral ignorance and constitute an authentic religious experience. This does not explain why the same sentiments spoken in a language the people can understand meet only with scorn and derision. Other objections to this theory would be that the 'divine words' are placed in the mouth of the grotesque figure of the sacristan and that the dialogue immediately following the impact of the words is far from spiritually uplifting and refers only to avoiding trouble with the civil authorities. In general, the eleventh-hour *deus ex machina* of a religious revelation would blend unhappily with the rest of the play. Most critics, in fact, have opted for an ironic interpretation. The fact that the villagers react only to the words in a language they cannot understand is seen either as an ironic comment on popular superstition – the *mentalidad milagrera* of the people – or on their gullibility and unquestioning acceptance of the dead formulae and outmoded liturgy of the Church. This theory, however, seems to be contradicted by the essentially unironical and even reverential tone of the *acotaciones* that describe the experience: 'Las viejas almas infantiles respiran un aroma de vida eterna' and 'Mari-Gaila . . . percibe el ritmo de la vida bajo un velo de lágrimas.' This does not seem to be the language of irony. Furthermore, Valle's work in general and, in particular, *La lámpara maravillosa* does not bear out the idea of the author as a scoffing rationalist mocking at folk superstition or as a critic of the established Church. On the contrary, the folk *mentalidad milagrera* is something for which he had the greatest respect, as he did for the beauty and evocative power of the Latin language.

If we consider the action of *Divinas palabras* in the light of Valle's personal blend of Gnosticism, Christianity and aesthetics as expressed in *La lámpara maravillosa* we may deduce an interpretation which is neither a moralizing nor a satirical one. In *Divinas palabras* he shows us a humanity in the grip of *mundo*, *demonio* and *carne*, imprisoned in a world of time, sterile motion and the senses, exiled from the ultimate realities and 'eternal norms' of the universe. It is Valle-Inclán's view of the basic human condition in *La lámpara*. We are not concerned with moral distinctions between individuals; the primary passions of self-interest, lust and greed dominate all the characters collectively. Valle stresses in *La lámpara* that the artist's vision of the 'negra carne del mundo' should transcend all ethical principle and should aspire to the principle of universal love, love of life in all its diversity and contradiction. Art for Valle was about intuitive understanding not moral judgements.

En la gran noche del pecado, cuando los malos espíritus volaban sin tregua en torno de los hombres, el sendero de la belleza ya partía como un zodíaco divino, la bóveda obscura y sin luceros. Es el primer camino que se abrió en las conciencias, *es anterior a toda razón ética*, porque desde el nacer los ojos de las criaturas fueron divinizados en la luz, y el logos generador fue Numen.

Las almas estéticas hacen su camino de perfección por el amor de todo lo creado, limpias de egoísmo alcanzan un reflejo de la mística luz, y como fuerzas elementales, imbuídas de una obscura conciencia cósmica, *presienten en su ritmo, el ritmo del mundo*. Adustas acaso para el amor humano, se redimen por el amor universal, y cada una es un pantáculo que sella la maravillosa diversidad del Todo. (p. 145, italics mine)

And he leaves us with this final thought: 'Peregrino sin destino, hermano, ama todas las cosas en la luz del día, y convertirás la negra carne del mundo en el áureo símbolo de la piedra del sabio.'

Reading the end of *Divinas palabras* in the light of these ideas suggests two things: first, that Valle is not taking any kind of ethical stance to his characters, and secondly, that the fleeting glimpse of the ultimate mysteries in which 'las viejas almas infantiles respiran un aroma de vida eterna' was for Valle a solemn reality. The sound of the Latin words which 'vuelan del cielo de los milagros' stirs the sediment of religious awe and superstition and – momentarily – affords the characters a taste of eternity. Valle is neither mocking superstition nor affirming any divine or supernatural inspiration in the Latin words. They are simply the instrument that awakens their dormant sense of mystery. For Mari-Gaila the ugliness of the world is transformed into beauty as 'la enorme cabeza del idiota, coronada de camelias, se le aparece como una cabeza de ángel'. For a brief moment, the laws of time and space are suspended, the veil is drawn aside, revealing the eternal norms beyond. Valle even uses a form of words similar to those in the passage quoted above to describe Mari-Gaila's fleeting mystical experience of union between the world of the suffering flesh and the totality beyond: 'Mari-Gaila, armoniosa y desnuda, pisando descalza sobre las piedras sepulcrales, percibe el ritmo de la vida bajo un velo de lágrimas.' This is how Valle describes a similar experience in *La lámpara maravillosa*:

Y en aquel momento, como mirase hacia el mar, volví a extasiarme, llenos los ojos de inocencia, y el corazón imantado hacia todas las cosas. Las más espúreas estaban en mí con unidad de amor, allegadas por veredas iguales, que se abrían en círculo como los rayos de una lámpara. Eran de amor todos mis caminos, y todos se juntaban en la luz del alma que se hacía extática. La espina de la zarza y la ponzoña de la sierpe me decían un secreto de armonía, igual que la niña, la rosa y la estrella . . . ¡El alma amaba su cárcel de tierra porque era un don recibido del Señor! (p. 139)

Divinas palabras ends on an affirmative note despite the fact that the view of contemporary Galicia has none of the traditional heroic qualities of its predecessors in the genre. The gap between Valle's diminished view of contemporary man and the Symbolist philosophy has visibly widened, not to a point where that philosophy is no longer tenable but certainly to a point where man appears in contrast to his destiny rather than equal to it. However, this discrepancy does not constitute, as it does in the first *esperpentos*, the guiding principle which shapes the work as a whole. His point of view is still that of the contemplative rather than the subversive. In the final analysis, Valle-Inclán's view of the world in *Divinas palabras* is that of a mystic, a view of humanity imprisoned in its 'cárcel de tierra', exiled from its spiritual home. The main point is that, unlike the moralist's, it is a non-judging view of the world. Nor is there any satirical edge to his presentation of 'la negra carne del mundo'. He portrays the tangled skein of reality in which primitive drives are inextricably mingled with the forms of conventional religion and morality in tragi-comic confusion. Like children, the characters of *Divinas palabras* are cruel, but, like children, they are innocent. The effect of the 'divine words' is to reveal them in this primitive, childlike innocence. The play is a tableau of primitive existence, physical ugliness and base passions, tragi-comic in its contradictions, yet ultimately sanctified by its impenetrable mystery.

8

The metamorphoses of the *esperpento*: *Luces de Bohemia*, *Los cuernos de don Friolera*, *Las galas del difunto* and *La hija del capitán*

Valle is reported as saying in an interview during his visit to Mexico in 1921 that the plays he had labelled as *esperpentos* were intended to be performed by puppets and that their purpose was to bring out the comic aspects of tragic situations (see Appendix 8). He quotes the examples of *Luces de Bohemia* and *Los cuernos de don Friolera* and mentions Vittorio Podrecca's Teatro di Piccoli as an illustration of the style of performance he was aiming at. Podrecca's company was founded in 1913 and made several tours around Europe. Valle is usually said to have been influenced by their visit to Madrid in 1924, but the Mexican interview strongly suggests that his contact with the Teatro di Piccoli must pre-date the creation of the *esperpento*. He repeated his interest in writing for puppets in 1923 in an interview with C. Rivas Cherif: 'El teatro es lo que está peor en España. Ya se podrán hacer cosas, ya. Pero hay que empezar por fusilar a los Quintero. Hay que hacer un teatro de muñecos. Yo escribo ahora siempre pensando en la posibilidad de una representación en que la emoción se dé por la visión plástica' (*La Pluma*, January 1923). We have no evidence that any of the *esperpentos* were performed as puppet plays, however, and his later 'melodrama para marionetas', *La cabeza del Bautista*, judging by contemporary reviews, was presented by real actors.[1] The issue was confused by Valle himself when, in 1930, he declared that his *esperpentos* were not only performable by real actors, but were highly suited to the peculiar talents of the Spanish professional (see Appendix 4). Nevertheless, the likelihood is that most, if not all, of the later plays were conceived for puppet-*style* performance, whether by real actors or not. This was in part the result of Valle's disenchantment with the commercial theatre, but there were other more important aesthetic reasons. In its declared intention to show the comedy inherent in tragic situations, the *esperpento* required the elimination of empathy and identification. The puppet style thus responded to Valle's need to create aesthetic distance. At the same time it afforded a whole new range of dramatic possibilities, visual and linguistic, to express what Valle increasingly came to see as the manipulated condition of humanity.

It is perhaps unwise to attempt too many generalizations before examining the plays themselves. Valle-Inclán's coinage of the word *esperpento* to describe *Luces de Bohemia, Los cuernos de don Friolera, Las galas del difunto* and *La hija del capitán* has, in some ways, produced an inhibiting effect on critics in their approach to these plays. Since the word exists, it imposes the need to define it and this obsession with definition has obscured certain aspects of Valle's evolution as a dramatist. There have been two main consequences of this. First, the fixation of critics with the *esperpento* genre has detracted from those later plays not labelled *esperpento* by the author with the result that the short plays of the *Retablo de la avaricia, la lujuria y la muerte* have not received all the critical attention they deserve. Secondly, there has been a strong tendency to study all the *esperpentos* in the light of a single blanket definition generally based on certain passages from scene 12 of *Luces de Bohemia*. Most of the attention has been concentrated on the *type* of play they are rather than on the individual works, each with its own thematic emphasis and dramatic qualities. Consequently, the similarities (which undoubtedly exist) between these works have been given greater importance than the differences which distinguish them. The result has been to obscure the process of evolution that Valle continued to undergo between 1920 and 1927 when he published his last play, *La hija del capitán*. If we simply look at individual plays and do not overconcern ourselves with definitions, it becomes clear that Valle's outlook did not evolve up to the *esperpento* as conceived around 1920 and then stop. The process is continuous up to and *beyond Luces de Bohemia*. A great deal of work has been done on tracing the origins and growth of the *esperpento* vision before 1920, but very little on the evolution of the *esperpento* idea in both theory and practice after that date. There is, for instance, a significant change of emphasis between the original version of *Luces de Bohemia*, published in 1920, and the definitive version in 1924. Furthermore, Valle's theoretical statements about the nature of the *esperpento* made after about 1924 are not easy to reconcile with the theory as expressed in the first *esperpento*. In this chapter I propose to take the four *esperpentos* in chronological order of their appearance and chart the principal shifts of emphasis between them.

'LUCES DE BOHEMIA'

Although *Farsa y licencia de la reina castiza* may allude, in a general way, to a contemporary situation, *Luces de Bohemia* (1920) is certainly the first play which Valle places in a contemporary setting. All the action of *Luces* takes place in the streets, bars, newspaper offices of Madrid in the period following the First World War. The social and political unrest which form the background to the work is based on conditions, principally in Madrid and Barcelona, between 1917 and 1922: the long smouldering industrial strife, the strikes and demonstrations, clashes with the police, political assassinations, the right-wing backlash in the form of vigilante groups like the *Acción ciudadana*, the impact of Lenin and the Bolshevic revolution, workers' meetings in the *Casa del pueblo*.[2] This violent and politicized atmosphere is a palpable presence throughout the play, created by allusions to police patrols, arrests, prisoners shot 'while attempting to escape' (*ley de fugas*), street clashes resulting in the death of innocent people and damage to property. *Luces* is crammed with topical references to contemporary figures in literature, journalism, politics and bullfighting. Most critics are agreed that many of the characters are roughly based on real-life contemporary counterparts (Torre, pp. 136–42). Max Estrella himself is usually identified with Alejandro Sawa, an eccentric bohemian writer whose theatrical lifestyle is said to have resembled that of the play's protagonist. Other characters for whom real-life counterparts have been suggested include the bookseller, Zaratustra, as Gregorio Pueyo, Don Peregrino Gay as the eccentric traveller and author of *Lazarillo español*, Ciro Bayo, Basilio Soulinake as Ernesto Bark, a Russian émigré and bohemian anarchist, the Ministro de la gobernación as Julio Burell. Dorio de Gadex (pseudonym of a contemporary journalist and poet) and, of course, Rubén Darío appear as themselves. In the latter's case, the addiction to absinthe, the fear of death and the constant use of the epithet 'admirable' are faithfully recorded details of the final phase of Rubén's life. The current literary and intellectual fashions are reflected in the dialogues of the bohemian *Modernistas*, the adoration of Verlaine and the deprecation of Galdós, the vogue of theosophy and Madame Blavatsky, the disdainful attitude towards the Academy and the political establishment.

There is something deliberate and almost aggressive about the topicality of *Luces*, to the extent that the contemporary allusions run the risk of obscuring the more durable aspects of the play. It is as if Valle, hitherto so ahistorical in his approach to literature, had consciously decided to immerse himself in the ephemeral confusion of contemporary history. For a subject such as that of *Luces* represented what must have been a descent into Hell for Valle-Inclán who had always sought for stasis or permanent essence in art through a stylized vision of the past or through myth and legend. His earlier work flees from the contemporary world and implies a total rejection of its values. Contemporary reality – especially urban reality – represented for him transience, flux and confusion. Some of his '98 contemporaries expressed surprise that at a time when Spanish writers and intellectuals were engaged upon a relentless examination of themselves and their society, Valle should be indulging in the 'escapist' literature of the *Sonatas*, *Flor de santidad* and the early *Comedias bárbaras*. Yet, as J. A. Maravall points out, Valle's evocation of the past always reflects an attitude to the present. Behind the idealization of the heroic individualism of Montenegro and his kind is the disdain for the encroaching tide of bourgeois ethics that Valle saw around him. The cult of the heroic world was a gesture of defiance to an institutionalized and commercialized world which Valle realized was taking its place. If we examine Valle's attitude to this contemporary world in *Luces de Bohemia*, we can see that his main antipathy is not against disorder or cruelty as such, but against the institutionalization, commercialization and *aburguesamiento* of life. Pica Lagartos and Zaratustra are the representatives of these commercial ethics. The police have become the mindless tool of state bureaucracy. The forces of order kill innocent children in the defence of private property and 'honrado comercio'. Art has become, in the Minister's words, 'un valor que se cotiza'. Max claims that even the religious sensibility of the Spaniards has been institutionalized, that the great enigmas of life and death have become trivialized. Heaven has become 'un kermés sin obscenidades, a donde, con permiso del párroco, pueden asistir las Hijas de María'. The harshest criticism is thus reserved for the anti-heroic, life-reducing aspects of modern existence which trivialize even what is noble and generous. It is the reverse side of the same coin we see in such works as *Aguila de blasón* where similar attitudes are implied though not directly expressed. Given the right circumstances, a direct expression of these attitudes to his historical present was perhaps a more logical development than might at first appear.

But the main intention of *Luces* was not just an indictment of contemporary bourgeois values, capitalism or commercialism. The central issue is how this state of society modifies Valle's view of certain values and attitudes he had once considered to be heroic. The new dimensions of social commitment, concern for the proletariat, the adoption of anti-capitalist attitudes are certainly important but should not be exaggerated or taken out of context. The focus of this first *esperpento* is the relationship between society and the artist, specifically the metamorphosis of the heroic into the absurd under the influence of a trivialized and grotesque social context.

The vision of man and society formulated in scene 12 of *Luces* is a complete reversal of the heroic view. This vehement rejection of the tragic stance is naturally influenced by the changing historical circumstances in Spain and the western world in general after the First World War, but it really makes sense only if, in addition, we see this as a revision of ideals that Valle once held very dear (see Buero Vallejo, p. 123). The contemporary world has created an atmosphere in which the hero can no longer breathe. Collective social pressures and circumstances have become the controlling agents over the life of the individual. In the first two plays to which Valle gave the subtitle *esperpento*, *Luces* and *Los cuernos de don Friolera*, we are essentially concerned with the anti-hero, i.e. a protagonist distorted or manipulated by the context of the society he lives in. In these plays the forces that manipulate the individual are external, social and historical, rather than the internal instinctive drives that operate in his rural drama. It was from about this time that Valle-Inclán began to take an interest in great collective political movements such as Anarchism and Communism, although the full extent of that interest is only seen in the later novels. He is reported on numerous occasions as saying that the age of the individual is dead and that the broad movements of history operate independently of the individual:

Pero hoy se da una interpretación nueva de los hechos. Se les estima necesarios, fatales. El individuo ya es lo de menos. Sin él, los hechos se darán igual. La Revolución Francesa, sin Danton, sin Robespierre, hubiese sido la misma. El hombre ya no tiene importancia. Ahora el protagonista de la vida es el grupo, la colectividad, el gremio, la multitud. (Madrid, p. 284)[3]

Something of this interest in collective proletarian movements is reflected in scene 6 of *Luces de Bohemia* and, certainly, the philosophy of the individual's impotence is fundamental to the play.

In both *Luces* and *Los cuernos* Valle deals with protagonists who in a former era might have been considered tragic or heroic figures. The 'héroe clásico' or literary archetype that he has in mind for Max Estrella is possibly a little confused. Most of the allusions in the text are to classical antecedents as, for instance, when Max's blindness is related to that of Homer, Hermes and Belisarius. Despite this, the archetype that emerges from the character's behaviour and circumstances is, as Sumner Greenfield points out (*Anatomía*, p. 223), more the Romantic image of the bohemian poet, penniless, blind, syphilitic, living in a garret and dying in the street. Friolera, of course, parodies a clearly defined archetype: the hero of the *drama de honor*. In both cases, it is the surrounding context of contemporary circumstances and prevailing attitudes that renders the heroic archetype grotesque and absurd. In a sense, what we see in the first *esperpentos* is life making a mockery of literature.

Earlier characters such as Montenegro and the Marqués de Bradomín are evidently conceived on a heroic scale. They are perhaps not laws unto themselves in so far as they are formed by their tradition and their setting, yet they are conceived on a plane above the trivialities of organized society. Valle himself, like his early heroic creations, had always asserted his independence of his circumstances and historical situation by a conscious effort of will. As Gómez de la Serna puts it in his biography, 'presumía de fáquir' (p. 103). In *La lámpara maravillosa* he establishes this independence of circumstances as the first norm of his aesthetic discipline: 'Sé como el ruiseñor, que no mira a la tierra desde la rama verde donde canta' (p. 18). Max Estrella is one nightingale that is unable to maintain this sublime indifference to his historical situation and, one suspects, the same could be said of his author. The social and political unrest of the country and his own precarious material circumstances inevitably left their mark and changed his view. The artist could no longer ignore circumstances; he had to come to terms with them.

If we see *Luces de Bohemia* as stemming, in part at least, from a disillusionment with previous artistic creeds, it goes some way towards explaining the appearance of the aged Marqués de Bradomín in scene 14 of the final version. After Max's burial, he appears in the cemetery together with Rubén Darío, meditating on the question of death. The introduction of the Marqués at this point is difficult to explain in terms of the play's own internal logic. Its significance perhaps lies in the fact that both Max Estrella and the Marqués represent aspects of Valle-Inclán's own outlook. More specifically, the Marqués of the *Sonatas* represents the *alter ago* of the *modernista* phase, the one who succeeds in living outside the context of organized society on his own terms and according to his own values. In Max, on the other hand, we see something of the Valle that realized the unattainability and perhaps even the undesirability of this ideal. The former literary ideal of aristocratic detachment – a desiccated skeletal figure who wonders whether it is worth while leaving the cemetery – is brought into the play as an ironical postscript to the disillusioned philosophy of the bohemian battered by life. This juxtaposition of past and present attitudes is undoubtedly a piece of self-indulgence on Valle's part, but it does usefully underline the aspect of personal literary disillusionment in *Luces* and how the pressures of living overcame literary ideals.

Before any detailed analysis of *Luces* can be carried out, the problems arising out of the two versions of the text must be discussed. The original version of the play was published in the review *España* and consisted of only twelve scenes.[4] For the definitive text of the Opera Omnia edition (vol. 19) in 1924, Valle-Inclán, in addition to making minor stylistic changes, incorporated three new scenes, bringing the total to fifteen. These were scene 2 (Zaratustra's bookshop), scene 6 (Max Estrella's dialogue with the Catalan prisoner) and scene 11 (the Mother and dead child in the old Austrian quarter of Madrid). Given the freedom of the play's narrative structure, Valle was able to insert the new scenes at appropriate points with only minimal recasting of the existing scenes. The main significance of the interpolations lies not so much in any new direction given to the action as in the resultant shift of tone and emphasis from the original 1920 text.[5]

All three interpolated scenes have one feature in common: Valle-Inclán – uncharacteristically – is speaking with his own voice through his characters, directly and unequivocally expressing views on religion and politics. The Zaratustra scene, in particular, is a 'discussion' scene in which character interaction is subordinated to ideas. Through Max Estrella and Don Gay, Valle delivers a scathing attack on Spanish religious formalism and lack of genuine religious sensitivity to the fundamental mysteries of life and death. The social commitment of the other two scenes is unique in Valle's theatre. Referring to the current industrial strife in Barcelona in scene 6, he overtly condemns the capitalist organization of society, commercial exploitation of workers and the so-called forces of order that defend it and advocates the abolition of inherited wealth and the revolution of the proletariat. Artistic impassivity is temporarily discarded and the note of social concern and personal indignation is allowed to come through. The twelve scenes of the original version contain only passing allusions to the social situation, the street riots and the condition of the proletariat. The specific case of Barcelona is not mentioned. Apart from a brief episode at the end of the second scene (scene 3 in the final version) in which the Chico de la taberna is injured in a clash between workers and the *Acción ciudadana*, the social disturbances are relegated to a rumble in the background, with allusions to broken glass in the streets and the Mounted Police patrols in various *acotaciones*. It would be difficult to postulate any personal commitment on Valle's part with regard to the social problem on the basis of these brief references and a few remarks passed in the give and take of repartee. The inclusion of the additional scenes transforms what had been a passing allusion into a new dimension of the work. Max Estrella is now seen not only in relation to the bohemian sub-world, the fatuous literary and intellectual fringe, the grotesque 'official' Spain of the Ministry and the police, but also in relation to the proletariat. Evidently, between October 1920 and 1924, Valle-Inclán seems to have been stung into a more immediate involvement with social and political issues and came to see *Luces* in a somewhat different light.[6]

The style of scene 11 is significant in this respect. In contrast to the rest of the work, it is almost expressionistic. Instead of the cut-and-thrust interacting dialogue of most of the other scenes, we have a series of glosses and commentaries addressed directly to an audience. The Mother and her dead child are isolated in the centre of a group of representative social types, the commercial exploiters (the Tabernero and the Empeñista), the voices of civil authority (the Guardia and El Retirado), the proletariat (the Albañil and the Portera), all of whom gloss and comment on the situation while the Mother hurls her cries of pain and anger into the void. The Mother's tragic isolation in the middle of this group reveals an unusually committed, explicit and passionate stance on the part of the author.

Of the minor alterations made in the 1924 edition, one stands out as particularly indicative. This concerns the much-quoted phrase spoken by Max in scene 12 (final version): 'España es una deformación grotesca de la civilización europea,' the original version of which ran: 'España es una deformación grotesca de la civilización heleno-cristiana.' The replacement of 'heleno-cristiana' by 'europea' seems to suggest that by the time Valle came to revise the play he saw Spanish society not only as a distortion of traditional and classical archetypes but also, in its contemporary context, as a travesty of other European models. His point of reference has shifted from the heroic past to the world around him.

Apart from the possible insights they afford into Valle's personal attitude and the increased weight they give to the social dimension of the play, the interpolated scenes also complicate and deepen the character of Max Estrella. In the original version Max is portrayed almost exclusively as an anachronistic literary figure and a forgotten poet. He is grotesquely irrelevant to his time and environment; his values are degraded and made ridiculous in the distorting mirror of his social context. Even his dedication to his art is made absurd by the attitude of those around him whose lip-service to artistic values conceals a fundamental indifference. He realizes that art cannot survive in such a context and that it is ludicrous to strike tragic attitudes. The only way to retain human dignity is to see himself objectively as something irrelevant and absurd and amuse himself with his own tragic farce. The *esperpento* vision which Max arrives at is the artistic answer to his circumstances ('deformemos la expresión en el mismo espejo que nos deforma las caras y toda la vida miserable de España'), a way of preserving artistic dignity and objectivity. At the core of the original version of *Luces* lies the problem of the artist who, unable to retain his heroic vision of reality, is obliged to alter his focus.

Basically, this holds good for the final version, but the interpolated scenes broaden the range of Max's sympathies and shift the emphasis away from his situation as an artist to his problem as a human being. They further underline his divorce from the social context, but this time more specifically from the proletariat. The scene of the Catalan prisoner reveals the similarity of the plight of the artist–intellectual to that of the worker but points out the mutual irrelevance of their separate worlds. Max is seen to weep 'de impotencia y de rabia'. In the scene of the Mother and dead child he stands by as a helpless onlooker and in scene 2 Valle deliberately contrasts the intellectual discussion in the bookshop with the hard realities being enacted in the street outside. Max's divorce from the proletarian situation has a more poignant and tragic quality than his divorce from the rest of his social context precisely because he tries to identify himself with the proletarian cause. The added scenes give the lie to his assertion in scene 4 that he is a 'man of the people'. They even introduce a note of doubt about the justification for writing literature at all in such circumstances. It is a feeling of shame that is uppermost in scene 11 (immediately preceding his formulation of the *esperpento* theory) when Max exclaims: '¡Canallas! ¡Todos! ¡Y los primeros nosotros los poetas!' He can only console himself with the dubious thought that he has played no active part in the tragic charade: 'Me muero de hambre, satisfecho de no haber llevado una triste velilla en la trágica mojiganga.'

The definitive version undoubtedly gives greater emphasis to the tragic side of Max Estrella and probes beneath the flamboyance of the 'hiperbólico andaluz' to his real despair. The earlier text had shown him as a character prone to bombast and exhibitionism, principally concerned with his own poverty and literary oblivion. By revealing more of the genuine emotions of anger and shame beneath the surface, Valle gives us a more human and balanced portrait of his character. The original version was perhaps in danger of trying to show us a Max whose values had been made absurd by his surrounding context without much indication of what those values were in the first place. The final version brings out a tragi-grotesque duality in the character latent though not clearly defined in the original. The additional insights into his genuine convictions modify an audience's view of his deliberate flippancy and histrionics. They are seen for what they really are: a self-defence against despair and a preservation of human dignity.

At least two important principles emerge from the theoretical exposition of the *esperpento* in *Luces* (scene 12) and the Prologue to *Los cuernos de don Friolera*. These are the rejection of tragic emotion in favour of systematic distortion and the maintenance of the artist's impassivity. It is curious that Valle-Inclán should have chosen to revise his play by interpolating material whose nature and treatment clearly run contrary to these criteria. For most of the new material (probably written after *Los cuernos*) is neither distorted nor impassively presented. The internal evidence of the text seems to suggest that Valle was writing deeply held convictions out of his system. Whatever Valle's motives may have been, one would not be justified in condemning the additions simply because they do not conform to the artistic principles established in the earlier version and in *Los cuernos*. It is perhaps a salutary reminder that the idea of the *esperpento* did not remain entirely static in Valle's mind after its original conception.

One can only evaluate the final version on its own terms. The interpolations make a somewhat different play of *Luces de Bohemia*; their tone conflicts with that of the existing scenes to some extent but it conflicts to some aesthetic purpose. While remaining the anti-tragic play that Valle intended, the final version achieves a more dynamic balance of tragic and grotesque elements and sets up a tension between these elements. From their juxtaposition we see more clearly the actual process of the grotesque neutralizing the tragic. That *Luces* is designed as an anti-tragedy can be seen in the fact that the author deliberately kills off his protagonist three scenes before the end. Valle consciously avoids making Max's death into a tragic culmination of the events in the play since he wishes to stress the point that, in the eyes of society, Max's death is as irrelevant as his life. And it is this irrelevance to the society around him that consistently turns Max's tragedy into a farce. The last three scenes are a conscious and *dramatic* use of anti-climax. Valle wishes us to see that Max's grotesque circumstances hound him to the grave and beyond. The absurd context undermines the potential tragedy of his wake, his burial and finally his memory. I say 'undermines', but perhaps 'tries to undermine' would be more exact since, despite the accumulation of anti-tragic details, the tragedy refuses to die. I now propose to take a closer look at the structure of the final version to see how the interaction of tragic and anti-tragic elements operates.

In the early part of the play Max reacts to his situation by striking some of the tragic attitudes that he later rejects as absurd. We see him in despair in the opening scene after his dismissal from the literary journal. He talks of a possible suicide pact for the whole family, protests against his rejection by the world, laments his literary oblivion, feels a masochistic self-pity (insisting that his wife should *re-read* the letter to him announcing his dismissal), indulges in nostalgic escapism and visions of the good times past ('¡Hay que renovar aquellos tiempos!') and immediately plunges back into despair when the vision fades ('¡Estoy muerto! Otra vez de noche'). In the early scenes Max is very much the 'hiperbólico andaluz', shouting his rhetorical resentment against the boycott of the press and the indifference of the Academy. He is 'humorista y lunático', indulging in the futility of drinking to excess and being arrested for disorderly behaviour, flamboyant yet pathetic, separate from those around him yet somehow dependent on them. Up to scene 5 he is assuming attitudes for the benefit of his public. With the exception of Madama

Collet and Claudinita, Max has been surrounded by caricatures, who either cynically exploit him like Latino and Zaratustra or treat him with hollow respect like the *Modernistas*. He has not yet come to the realization that he too has something of the caricature in his make-up.

The scene with the Catalan prisoner thus contrasts sharply with the previous caricaturesque encounters. Max's rhetoric begins to sound hollow when compared with the hard social realities seen through the situation of the Preso. For the first time he comes face to face with a reality that is not distorted and which begins to reveal Max himself as the caricature. His irrelevance to the social situation becomes manifest even to himself:

MAX: Pertenecemos a la misma iglesia.
EL PRESO: Usted lleva chalina.
MAX: ¡El dogal de la más horrible servidumbre! Me lo arrancaré para que hablemos.
EL PRESO: Usted no es proletario.
MAX: Yo soy el dolor de un mal sueño.
EL PRESO: Parece usted hombre de luces. Su hablar es como de otros tiempos. (p. 54)

The encounter with the Catalan prisoner gives Max the first glimpse of how he appears to others, the first insight into his anachronistic irrelevance, and prepares the ground for his later self-deprecating humour. The irrelevance of Max is underlined by the following scene in the newspaper office when the 'angry protest' of the *Modernistas* to Don Filiberto about Max's arrest quickly degenerates into trivial badinage and a parade of wit and pseudo erudition. This scene is very similar in conception to scene 8 in *Los cuernos de don Friolera* in which the high-ranking officials gather to discuss the question of Friolera's honour and proceed to indulge in personal reminiscence (Bermejo, pp. 253–5). The irrelevance of the dialogue is only an apparent one since the banter and repartee is in deliberate contrast to the object of their visit to the editor's office and throws into relief the plight of the central character.

In the final version of *Luces*, scene 8, with the Minister of the Interior, is the pivotal scene of the work and the one in which we see an important shift in Max's attitude. Max goes to demand satisfaction for an offence to his dignity and ends up by accepting a cash payment on a regular basis. The heroic posture cannot survive this indignity and Max is now fully aware that he is tainted by the society he lives in: 'Conste que he venido a pedir un desagravio para mi dignidad y un castigo para unos canallas. Conste que no alcanzo ninguna de las dos cosas, y que me das dinero, y que lo acepto porque soy un canalla' (p. 79)

This scene with the Minister and the one with the Catalan anarchist seem to be conceived as a contrast to one another. Valle's subsequent insertion of the prisoner scene is a striking illustration of how he tries to balance pathos and tragedy with the grotesque. Max's unsuccessful attempt to bridge the gulf between himself and the *pueblo* is offset by his fatal and unwilling compromise with *Authority*. The solemn embraces which conclude both scenes are surely far from coincidental. The tragic Max who embraces the man he calls his spiritual brother in the prison cell is later 'esperpentized' in his grotesque embrace with the Minister.

Máximo Estrella, con los brazos abiertos en cruz, la cabeza erguida, los ojos parados, trágicos en su ciega quietud, avanza como un fantasma. Su Excelencia, tripudo, repintado, mantecoso, responde con un arranque de cómico viejo, en el buen melodrama francés. Se abrazan los dos. Su Excelencia, al separarse, tiene una lágrima detenida en los párpados. Estrecha la mano del bohemio, y deja en ella algunos billetes. (pp. 79–80)

From this point in the work Max plays less to the gallery and directs much of his sardonic humour against himself. He detaches himself from his tragic role and sees himself as a puppet. The impact of the humiliation of the previous scene is evident in the abrasive, nihilistic tone he adopts in the dialogue with Rubén Darío. The realization of his degradation by the environment coincides with the realization of his rapidly approaching death. In scene 9 when Max, like Christ, entertains his disciples to a last supper, he harps constantly on the theme of death:

Muerto yo, el cetro de la poesía pasa a ese negro.
. . . me dedico a la taberna mientras llega la muerte.
¡Tú la temes, yo la cortejo! [la muerte]
¡Vengo aquí para estrecharte por última vez la mano!
¡Eterna la nada!
Para mí no hay nada tras la última mueca.

Max's almost jovial acceptance of his imminent extinction is contrasted with Rubén's fear of even mentioning the subject.

The dialogue with the prostitute Lunares provides a further example of Max's self-destructive humour. Not unnaturally, Lunares

THE THEATRE OF VALLE-INCLÁN

mistakes Max for the kind of poet who sings *coplas de ciego* on the street corners. Valle-Inclán's detestation of this kind of popular literature is amply demonstrated in the Prologue and Epilogue to *Los cuernos*. He regarded them as 'periodismo ramplón' and there is every reason to believe that Max Estrella would share this opinion. Nevertheless, Max pretends to be the kind of poet that Lunares thinks he is:

LA LUNARES: ¿Serías tú, por un casual, el que sacó las coplas de Joselito?
MAX: ¡Ese soy!
LA LUNARES: ¿De verdad?
MAX: De verdad.
LA LUNARES: Dílas . . .
MAX: No las recuerdo.
LA LUNARES: Porque no las sacaste de tu sombrerera. Sin mentira, ¿cuáles son las tuyas?
MAX: Las del Espartero.
LA LUNARES: ¿Y las recuerdas?
MAX: Y las canto como un flamenco.
LA LUNARES: ¡Que no eres capaz!
MAX: ¡Tuviera yo una guitarra!
LA LUNARES: ¿La entiendes?
MAX: Para algo soy ciego. (pp. 96–7)

It is sometimes claimed that this scene shows the degradation or *esperpento* of Max's idea of love, his poetic ideal of beauty reduced to commercialized sex. However that may be, it is also true that much of the dialogue with Lunares is based on her idea of poetry and Max's acceptance of that idea. Max amuses himself with his own degraded poet's image. The man who earlier protested that 'me sobran méritos' and 'soy el primer poeta de España' now pretends to be the author of the despised *coplas del Espartero*.

The self-destructive irony turns to a feeling of guilt and self-accusation in scene 11 in which Valle contrasts the death of a child with the pretexts, rationalization and self-justification of the champions of order and commerce. There is the suggestion that Max's lack of commitment to the social situation is not just grotesque but reprehensible. He describes himself as being imprisoned in a dantesque circle of 'rabia' and 'vergüenza'. The element of 'shame' is new and introduced as a deliberate variant on the 'rabia' and 'impotencia' alluded to at the end of scene 6. The attack on Latino which closes the scene could also be interpreted as an attack upon himself, in so far as Latino, as we shall see in a moment, can be seen as a grotesque reflection of Max himself.

The nihilistic view of death, the self-destructive irony, the acceptance of his own irrelevance are all incorporated in Max's formulation of the artist's response to his circumstances in scene 12 when he denies the validity of traditional tragic attitudes. Valle surrounds Max's death with anti-tragic circumstances – Latino refusing to lend him his overcoat, a dog urinating nearby – and makes Max 'act out' his death scene as if he were playing an elaborate joke. The macabre charade that Max goes through – laying himself out in preparation, ordering the funeral dirge to be sung and finally uttering the utterly untragic last words of 'buenas noches' – is Max's clownish response to a world which has denied him a tragic exit. By making his own death into a charade, he is carrying out his own precept of distorting 'la expresión en el mismo espejo que nos deforma las caras y toda la vida miserable de España'.

The distorting mirror of circumstances continues to present a grotesque reflection of Max after death. Latino steals his wallet containing the money and the lottery ticket. The neighbour who discovers his body is concerned only about being delayed in her work. Max's presence still continues to dominate in the scene of the wake since the coffin containing his remains occupies the centre of the stage. This silent presence and the simple, dignified grief of his wife and daughter are locked in a tragi-comic tug-of-war with a whole series of burlesque and farcical details, characters and incidents. The three *Modernistas* standing against the wall like 'tres fantoches en hilera' are clearly a caricaturesque element, as is the arrival of a drunken Latino and his grotesquely rhetorical sentiments. As Dorio escorts Latino from the room, the latter's tailless dog jumps over the coffin and bends one of the candles. The figure of the Russian anarchist, Basilio Soulinake, is pure farce. His claim that Max is not dead but merely in a state of catalepsy is hotly disputed by the vociferous *portera* and an insane argument ensues. The argument is finally resolved by the appearance of the hearse driver who, to settle the dispute, places a lighted match under Max's thumbnail. One might imagine that with such an accumulation of grotesque circumstances, all tragic feeling would be stifled. Surprisingly this does not happen. The fact that all this burlesque is set against the solemn presence of the pine coffin and the pain of Madame Collet and Claudinita retains the tragi-comic tension. Tragic feeling stubbornly survives despite its explicit denial by the circumstances and, significantly, Valle ends this scene of sustained grotesquerie with a genuine *coup de théâtre* which redresses the balance. The scene ends with a long dramatic silence, while all the characters wait for the match to burn itself out, a silence which is broken by a cry of '¡Mi padre! ¡Mi padre! ¡Mi padre!' from Claudinita.

In the cemetery scene the presence of Max recedes into the background as Valle contrasts two dialogues about Max in particular and death in general. One is constituted by the grave and solemn reflections of Rubén Darío and the Marqués de Bradomín and the other by the more down-to-earth sentiments of two gravediggers who simply make a living by burying people. Max is only of passing interest in these dialogues. He features both as a presence and as an absence and again the basic lack of concern on the part of the speakers and the essential irrelevance of the central character is studied and deliberate.

The final stage of *Luces de Bohemia* is that, with Max dead, Latino takes over. In the last scene Max is only remembered for the money he owes. Latino has won a prize on the lottery with the ticket from Max's wallet. What we witness in this last stage is the triumph of mediocrity. Latino is the material inheritor of Max's spiritual laurels since, besides the money, Latino also undertakes to pocket the proceeds from the publication of Max's works. He is even credited with the invention of the term 'esperpento' by the drunk in Pica Lagartos's tavern, for which he earns the praise of 'cráneo privilegiado' previously accorded to Max Estrella.

The juxtaposition of Max and Latino epitomizes the whole tragi-grotesque duality of *Luces*. Don Latino has never been given a real-life counterpart by the critics. Zamora Vicente convincingly suggests that if Max represents the heroic side of Alejandro Sawa, Latino may represent the other side, the sponger (p. 47). Whether or not we take Max and Latino to be a kind of composite representation of Sawa, the important point is that Latino is conceived as a distorted reflection or grotesque shadow of Max Estrella. Latino is, above all, a fake; a pseudo-intellectual and pseudo-friend. His chief characteristic is a lack of authenticity. He cheats Max out of money (scene 1), he refuses to lend him his overcoat and to take him home (scene 4), he protests love and admiration, yet is too cowardly to defend his friend (scene 5), he is pretentious in his aspirations to intellectual knowledge while being profoundly ignorant and insensitive (scene 9), he sees only play-acting in authentic human grief (scene 11), he steals the dead Max's wallet (scene 12) and neglects to assist Max's family when he wins the lottery prize (scene 15): a truly grotesque character without a redeeming feature and the opposite of Max in everything. Yet he is not just used as a foil in order to enhance the nobility of Max's character. Max's relationship with him is more complex than that. Although Valle is not concerned with the psychological intricacies of the relationship, Max's association with Latino clearly argues a degree of dependence. The reason possibly lies in Max's fear of sham, of inauthenticity. To Max, Latino is a reminder of his own absurdity and potential degradation. He sees the debasement of values so evident in Latino as a distorted mirror image of himself. He despises Latino just as he despises himself a little (particularly when he accepts money from the Minister). His attacks upon Latino are, in part, attacks upon himself. The only thing that prevents Max from fully becoming a Don Latino is the honest acceptance of his own degraded image. He associates with Latino to remind himself that, besides being absurd, he could also lose his authenticity as an artist and as a man.

The fact that Max is aware of what history is doing to him, that he is a character in conflict with his environment and modifies his own attitudes to combat that environment make him a problematic character and thus place him in a different category from, say, Montenegro of the *Comedias bárbaras*. All this would seem to suggest that Valle had turned towards a more *psychological* approach to characterization. Valle, however, had never been at home in the field of psychological drama and had repeatedly stated his lack of interest in the individual. *Luces* is really no exception to this general rule in that, despite the tension between character and context and despite a degree of character evolution in the play, it does not work psychologically. Max's transition from bombast to self-deprecating humour is perhaps not immediately apparent because it is not given full psychological orchestration. For instance, Valle rarely shows one individual operating psychologically on another, nor is there a strong interdependence between character and incident. In the first version the change of attitude hinges entirely on the incident of Max being obliged to accept money from the Minister. The psychological impact of the incident is not reinforced by any further allusion to it in the play. The encounter with the Preso catalán in the final version does something to prepare the ground for psychological change and later references to this character in scenes 11 and 12 help to confirm this. But, in general, the psychology of Max's change of outlook is of little interest to the author. What is of interest and what does work dramatically in *Luces* is the tonal contrasts and the constant pull of the tragic against the anti-tragic. In this respect (i.e. the dependence on contrasting tones), the dramatic technique of *Luces* does not differ fundamentally from that of the *Comedias bárbaras*. The logic of plot and character development is subordinated to emotive impact. There are, in fact, two curious oversights in *Luces* which illustrate this priority in Valle-Inclán. One is that we are told that Max dies of starvation or malnutrition, despite the fact that he has just eaten a plentiful supper with Rubén Darío. The other is a remarkable change of season from Spring to Autumn between scenes 10 and 14. In the first *acotación* to scene 10 we read: 'El perfume primaveral de las lilas embalsama la humedad de la noche.' Yet, by scene 14, which can be no more than a day or two later, the climatic conditions have deteriorated to 'la tarde, fría, el viento, adjusto' and the gravediggers make an explicit reference to 'la caída de la hoja', indicating that we are now in Autumn. Unless we accept the possibility that Max dies in the Spring and is buried in the Autumn, it is evident that, in his desire to give a different emotional tone to each of these scenes, Valle has overlooked the logic of his time span.

We have already seen how the final version of *Luces* does to some extent contradict the principle of consistent artistic distance through systematic distortion. There is another aspect of the play which differs from subsequent developments of the *esperpento*. This is in the treatment of the anti-hero and his relationship to society. In *Luces de Bohemia* we hear a great deal about concave mirrors:

Los héroes clásicos *reflejados en los espejos cóncavos* dan el Esperpento.

Las imágenes más bellas *en un espejo cóncavo* son absurdas.

. . . deformemos la expresión *en el mismo espejo que nos deforma las caras y toda la vida miserable de España*. (Italics mine)

The emphasis here is on the distorting agent. No matter how noble and worthy something may be *in itself*, a grotesque context can change its appearance and even its nature. Tragic or heroic values can only survive when the social context corroborates and endorses those values. When that endorsement is lacking, former heroic values and attitudes become irrelevant and consequently ridiculous. Values cannot exist independently of their social context; they are inevitably shaped by it.

Now if we examine Valle's later comments on the *esperpento* vision made after 1924, it appears that the emphasis has changed:

Y estos seres deformados son los héroes llamados a representar una fábula no deformada. Son enanos y patizambos que juegan una tragedia. (see Appendix 7)

Esta es de la manera [*sic*] que he querido yo crear el tipo de Esperpento, fundándome en la inadaptación de los temas trágicos a los personajes que resultan ridículos ante la misma. No sabemos nada de nada, no conocemos nuestras horas. Estamos perdidos en el terrible pecado del mundo. Los hombres llegan a las grandes situaciones y aparecen entonces en toda su pequeñez. (*El Castellano*, 23 October 1925)

The quotations from *Luces* – and the play as a whole – stress the metamorphosis of the hero by his social circumstances. These later comments stress the *inadequacy* of contemporary man to the tragic roles that life calls upon him to play. I am not suggesting that Valle's idea of the *esperpento* changed in any radical way, simply that there is a shift of emphasis. One can detect in *Luces* a note of regret that Max's heroic image is being transmuted into that of a grotesque and irrelevant clown. In the later *esperpentos* (and the change is already perceptible in *Los cuernos*) the anti-heroes are *in themselves* 'enanos y patizambos'. It must be admitted that, in the Montero Alonso interview (quoted in Appendix 10), Valle declares that both Max Estrella and Don Friolera fail to be tragic because of what they are rather than because of what society has made them. This could well be true of Don Friolera, but I find the text of *Luces* gives us a different view of Max Estrella. There is not so much emphasis on Max's inadequacy to the tragic role as on his distortion by the attitudes that surround him. Valle may well have been applying retrospective criteria to *Luces de Bohemia* which were not in his mind at the time of writing the play.

Anthony Zahareas argues that Valle systematically exploits this discrepancy between heroic role and inadequate actor, between the plane of myths and archetypes and that of commonplace contemporary equivalents, in a coherent and interconnected network of symbols which gives *Luces* 'toda su dimensión interna y su fuerza cohesiva' (*Visión*, p. 101). The allusions to literary archetypes are certainly present and are quite numerous. The comparison with Dante's *Divine Comedy* is suggested by the reference to 'círculo infernal' and Max's comment that 'Nuestra vida es un círculo dantesco. Rabia y vergüenza' in scene 11. The name of Max's travelling companion, Latino, could conceivably be a reference to Dante's counterpart, Virgil, on his journey through Hell and Purgatory. Max Estrella, with his blindness, is associated on several occasions with classical models like Homer, Hermes and Belisarius. There is a general parallel between scene 14 in the cemetery and the gravedigger scene in *Hamlet* and there are possible echoes of Christ and the Last Supper in scene 9. In scene 2, the name of the bookseller, Zaratustra, and the reference to his shop as a 'cueva' are clearly parodies of Nietzsche. It has even been suggested that there may be a hint of Don Quixote and Maritornes in the scene of Max and the prostitute, Lunares. Zahareas and Cardona interpret Max's nocturnal journey through Madrid as a recreation of such myths as the Odyssey, Aeneas and Theseus and the Labyrinth, myths which enact the experience of self-discovery in the internal labyrinth of the soul. However, a mere enumeration of allusions and possible allusions does not establish the existence of a symbolic pattern which is alleged to be an integral part of the play's structure. It is difficult to agree with the contention that there is a systematic correspondence between mythical and contemporary levels or that all the various allusions constitute an overall *pattern*. Each allusion can be explained separately but the mechanism that links them is obscure. Unless they can be convincingly related to the dramatic action and structure of the play, unless they have a *functional* role, they remain as incidental allusions and do not acquire the force of symbols. *Luces* cannot be said to function on two interconnected levels; it functions on a basically realistic level while evoking distant and distorted images of a classical tradition. The very disparate and varied nature of these references seems to suggest that Valle was making allusions as they struck him rather than integrating them into a pattern of correspondences. Had Valle really intended the play to work on two levels simultaneously he would have been more likely to restrict himself to a single archetypal antecedent. The critic would be hard pressed to derive a coherent mythical superstructure from all the disparate references that Valle leaves lying around.

Where Zahareas is more convincing (and he has developed this theme in several articles) is in his analysis of Max Estrella's personal dilemma.

Lo esencial de *Luces*, por tanto, es ver por qué medios un tema inherentemente trágico – la muerte de un poeta – puede asumir la forma de lo grotesco y cómo un títere trágico puede llegar a liberarse de su condición de títere y asumir una dimensión auténtica. En otras palabras, ¿es posible que el hombre sea hombre en una situación calificada por él de 'trágica mojiganga'? (*Visión*, p. 85)

It is surely here that the main dramatic interest of *Luces* lies, rather than in the discrepancy between heroic and contemporary levels. How far is Max a victim of his situation and how far is he able to overcome it? Does he remain a comic anachronism or does he achieve authenticity by virtue of his awareness of his situation? It is this duality (rather than the other one) which gives *Luces* its extra dimension. For *Luces* is the only *esperpento* (and in fact the only *play*) Valle wrote in which there is a problematic central character not entirely conditioned by the forces of his environment. He salvages some authenticity by the only means available to him, by means of artistic distance, by standing outside himself and his social connections and observing himself dispassionately. He accepts his own absurdity, rejects the tragic mantle and amuses himself with his own farce. Max liberates himself by breaking out of the tragic mould; Friolera acts out the tragic role and becomes a puppet.

'LOS CUERNOS DE DON FRIOLERA'

In *Luces de Bohemia* Valle-Inclán expressed the theory of the *esperpento* rather than produced an example of it. It is more a play about a man who comes to see life as an *esperpento* than an example of systematic distortion in either style or characterization. In comparison with the other *esperpentos*, style and characterization deviate but little from naturalism. Nor are the principles of non-identification or the negation of tragedy absolute since Valle manifestly gives full weight to the tragic side of Max Estrella and identifies with his viewpoint on several occasions (see Buero Vallejo, pp. 38–9). Valle did not hit upon a style for the *esperpento* until he wrote *Los cuernos de don Friolera* which appeared in the review *La Pluma* in 1921 (April to August). Here the whole dramatic conception is stylized in a Punch-and-Judy knock-about farce. The puppet convention is consistent in decor, characterization, gesture, movement and language. It is not until *Los cuernos* that Valle produced anything approaching 'systematic distortion' or the 'matemática perfecta', alluded to in *Luces*, in which the 'deformación deja de serlo', when, in other words, the grotesque becomes the absolute, the norm.

Los cuernos is particularly interesting as it is the culmination of a theme which Valle had touched upon in many of his previous works: that of adultery and the Spanish mystique of honour. It appears in his first play, *Cenizas*, in which we see his only straight-faced – and somewhat conventional – treatment of the subject. Illicit love and passion are defended against abstract moral codes and rigid social conventions. The same basic, 'anti-Calderonian' view[7] of the adultery–honour theme appears in *El Marqués de Bradomín*, *La Marquesa Rosalinda* and *Divinas palabras*, though the expression of this view becomes increasingly more comic. In *Los cuernos de don Friolera*, the figure of the honour-obsessed cuckold is given the full *esperpento* treatment. The classical hero who is diminished and made ludicrous by his contemporary context is in this case a *teniente* in the *cuerpo de carabineros* – Don Pascual Astete, generally known as Don Friolera. He is warned by an anonymous note that his wife is deceiving him. The lover is a local barber, Pachequín ('cuarentón cojo y narigudo'), and the Iago of the piece who stirs up all the trouble is Doña Tadea Calderón, a witch-like *beata* whose name requires no further comment. The pressures on Don Friolera are two-fold: social and military, both pushing him in the direction of vengeance, urging him to accept suspicion as fact and appearance as reality. The point about *Los cuernos* is that nothing actually happens as the lover Pachequín rather ruefully points out on more than one occasion (e.g. scene 5). Don Friolera is a manipulated puppet whose actions are determined by collective myths of 'honour' and 'dishonour'. The automatism of Friolera's responses is underlined by the fact that when he eventually shoots at his wife, he misses and kills his daughter. The social imperatives can only go so far as to make him pull the trigger; they cannot guide his aim. *Los cuernos* ends in an irrelevant tragedy which only serves to emphasize the emptiness of the dilemmas, passions, vacillations and posturing that have led up to it.

It is difficult to agree with Buero Vallejo that in *Los cuernos* the grotesque does not annihilate the tragic (pp. 40–1). With *Luces de Bohemia* it was an entirely different question. There the anti-tragic humour *reinforces* the tragic emotion because we have been given an insight into the real anguish of Max Estrella and we know that Max is aware of what is happening to him. In *Los cuernos* there is not the same balance of ingredients. The occasional touches of pathos in Don Friolera are the pathos evoked by a *fantoche*, not a man: 'Don Friolera, en el reflejo amarillo del quinqué, es un fantoche trágico' (scene 4).

His situation may be *potentially* tragic (as almost any comic situation could be), but it does not generate the same dialectical tension as in *Luces*. Rodolfo Cardona, in an attempt to find common characteristics between the two *esperpentos*, claims a similar dramatic chemistry for *Los cuernos* as for *Luces*: 'Estamos ante un mundo desconcertante donde la tragedia y la farsa marchan parejas mientras que la angustia y los desatinos del hombre están constantemente en juego tal y como ya vimos en *Luces de Bohemia*' (*Visión*, p. 123).[8] Any tragic element Friolera may have surely hinges upon the question of how self-aware we consider the character to be. Cardona argues that Friolera *is* a self-aware character like Max Estrella, who, unlike Max, later 'falls into the temptation' of playing to the gallery (*Visión*, p. 124). Most of the evidence for this comes from Friolera's long monologue at the beginning in which he goes through a whole gamut of attitudes. However, these switches of attitude in Friolera's *monólogo de cornudo* do not seem to indicate a dilemma attributable in any serious sense to a genuine awareness of the situation. In the first place, the soliloquy, with all its changes of mood, is a stock feature of the theatre of honour that Valle-Inclán is parodying. Moreover, the monologue comes right at the beginning of the play before any character or situation has been established. It thus stands, as it were, in the void. The fluctuating passions, divided feelings and inner conflicts associated with *dramas de honor* and their nineteenth-century derivatives cannot be related to any existing situation or previous knowledge of the character. They are thus drained of meaning and appear merely comic. The 'inner torment' of the hero, as certainty gives way to doubt and doubts give way to renewed suspicion, to self-pity, to incipient revolt and then to despair, is reduced to the level of vacuous posturing. This long monologue sets the tone for most of what is to follow, since the see-sawing of emotions in the action – Will she? Won't she? Will he? Won't he? – is similarly emptied of significance. The basic rhythm of the action and dialogue consists in this meaningless game of commitment to action and withdrawal, advance and retraction, underlining Valle's theme that the Tragic Dilemma is a rhetorical illusion, a masquerade of meaning.

Friolera cannot be said to 'fall into the temptation' of doing society's will, since that would imply that he had a choice in the first place. Valle shows him striking the attitudes and speaking the lines dictated to him by traditional codes. He acts out a part written for him by society. At the beginning of scene 6 we even see him 'rehearsing' his role as the hero of a *drama de honor*, imagining his last heroic words as he stands fearless before the firing squad. Friolera does what Max refuses to do: see himself as the tragic hero. The acting out of traditional roles applies not only to Don Friolera, but also to Pachequín who sees himself as the romantic *galán* and Doña Loreta who sees herself as the tragically torn 'esposa y madre' or 'esposa mártir'.

In *Los cuernos* we can see how the emphasis of the *esperpento* has changed from the idea of transformation by the distorting mirror of society to the idea of manipulation by the strings of collective social myths. In the case of *Los cuernos* it is perhaps more useful to think in terms of the puppet theatre image than of the concave mirror. In this play Valle has tried to bring his practice of the *esperpento* more into line with his theory. The negation of the tragic, for instance, is made much more unequivocal. There is a more systematic exploitation of the incongruity between actor and role. The characters are inadequate to their tragic roles; they are the 'enanos y patizambos que juegan una tragedia', manipulated puppets strutting and declaiming the rhetoric of Love, Honour and Duty. Valle reminds us of this in one of his *acotaciones*: 'El movimiento de las figuras, aquel entrar y salir con los brazos abiertos, tienen la sugestión de una tragedia de fantoches' (scene 4). The theory in the Prologue to *Los cuernos* and the actual text of the play stress, above all, the principle of non-identification in art. Non-identification is also implicit in the theory of the *esperpento* in *Luces*, although the presentation of some of the characters seems to contradict this. In *Los cuernos* Valle removes any possibility of identification. He leads up to this in the Prologue by making his Don Estrafalario comment on a painting he has found of a laughing Devil. The Devil, he argues, cannot laugh (or cry) at humanity because we only laugh or cry at things with which we identify and the Devil, being of a different substance from humanity, cannot possibly identify with it. This leads Estrafalario into an exposition of his own artistic creed. The artist should remain uninvolved, above laughter and tears. The ideal artistic viewpoint is that of the dead watching the comedy of the living 'desde la otra ribera'. This ideal of non-identification is exemplified in the popular puppet farce which Don Estrafalario and his friend Don Manolito see performed by the blind Fidel in the inn yard.[9]

Stylistically, however, *Los cuernos* perhaps reminds us more of an animated cartoon than a puppet show. Valle sees gestures, movements, features in profile, in geometrical terms. His eye picks out caricaturesque detail: the four hairs on Friolera's head, Pachequín's limp and his pronounced nose, Doña Tadea's 'ojos de pajarraco', Teniente Rovirosa's glass eye that leaps out of its socket when the Teniente gets excited. The movements are mechanical and cartoon-like, as, for example, the repeated appearance of Doña Tadea's head at the garret window. What suggests the cartoon rather than the puppet show is Valle's delight in outline and silhouetted forms, e.g. 'Doña Tadea pasa atisbando. El garabato de su silueta se recorta sobre el destello cegador y moruno de las casas encaladas' (scene 2). The language these characters speak is in the main that of the melodrama of Echegaray. All their feelings are externalized into rhetoric. There is no innuendo or suggestion behind the words, everything is explicit and emotion is parodied *in* the words. It is the language of characters who are watching themselves act out a particular role. As Guerrero Zamora says, 'Los personajes esper-pénticos son fantoches porque se autocontemplan y hacen de esa autocontemplación su única energía, su único objeto, su única sustancia. Así se corresponden forma y fondo en *Los cuernos de don Friolera*' (vol. 1, p. 202).

Of all the *esperpentos*, *Los cuernos* is the most literary. Prologue and Epilogue are concerned chiefly with literary criteria and the central action is also literary in that it is based on classical Spanish drama. Friolera himself is the clearest example of an *héroe clásico* reduced to miniscule contemporary proportions. Much more so than in *Luces*, we find examples of literary parody: the very name of Calderón used for a scandal-mongering *beata*, the parody of the soliloquy in Friolera's initial monologue, the parody of Golden Age foreshadowing tech-niques (Pachequín, in his first appearance, has just been to shave a dead sea-captain), the exchange of tokens between the lovers, the abduction of the heroine in which no 'dishonour' takes place (scene 5). This latter scene alludes more to Echegaray than to Calderón *et al.*, in particular to his *El gran galeoto*, since the lovers claim that they have been thrown together by the collective force of prejudice and public opinion. 'El mundo me la da, pues yo la tomo, como dice el eminente Echegaray!' cries Pachequín, echoing the last line of *El gran galeoto*. There are also a couple of references in scene 5 and the Epilogue to *El nudo gordiano* by Eduardo Sellés, of the school of Echegaray. Nor should it be forgotten that Valle's *esperpento* manner was to some extent a reaction against his own former tragi-heroic view of the world. It would therefore not be too far-fetched to perceive an element of *self*-parody in the Doña Loreta–Pachequín relationship, particularly in scene 5. The dilemma of the married woman torn between her illicit lover and the child of her legal yet unloving marriage had received perfectly serious and conventional treatment in the prologue to *El yermo de las almas* (pp. 23–6), added in 1908 to the rewritten version of *Cenizas*. The same dilemma in Doña Loreta between her duty as an 'esposa y madre' and the love of her 'demonio tentador' is reduced to mere comic incongruity.

However, it would be misleading to regard *Los cuernos* purely as literary parody. This becomes apparent when we compare the play with, say, *La venganza de don Mendo* by Muñoz Seca, one example among many of the classical and Romantic parodies current in the light entertainment genres of Valle's day. *Don Mendo* is pure literary parody in that its humour derives from a mental comparison with the models on which it is based. Valle-Inclán does not keep his models consistently in view and one sometimes feels he could have been much funnier at the expense of his models had he wanted to be. It has been suggested that he consciously parodied *El gran galeoto* in *Los cuernos*, yet the parallels are not particularly close. Not, for instance, as close as in *La venganza de don Mendo* and the drama of Romanticism where it is precisely our recognition of the standard attitudes, situations and expressions that create the humour. Valle uses literary parody, but as a means, not as an end in itself. The humour derives not so much from an audience's recognition of the clichés of honour theatre but from the *automatism* of the responses. The purpose is consistently to create the impression of a vacuous frenzy of passions and movement – life viewed with total detachment, as if from the other bank of the Styx. The humour comes largely from the puppet-like gestures and the rhythmic movement of the dialogue. In any case, Valle is here handling not one, but two literary conventions: the *drama de honor* and the Punch-and-Judy-type farce. He casts the action of the former into the dramatic form of the latter. By doing this he is expressing far more than amusement at the attitudes of honour drama, he is expressing a view of human behaviour. The automatism of the characters reflects an attitude to the world, a view of men as mindless puppets of collective myths and conventions. The code of honour is simply one example of the forces and abstract imperatives that shape human lives and reduce them to the level of the *guignol*.

The danger is that, by alienating the characters to such an extent, the link with the spectators' lives may be destroyed and the serious purpose lost amidst the laughter. Careful direction would be necessary to prevent *Los cuernos* from being pure knockabout farce. Ideally it should show *life* as a knockabout charade and make the audience feel that *their* values and *their* passions are being portrayed in this way. For this reason, were the play to be performed by actual puppets or animated drawings, this necessary link with the audience might be lost. The spectator, while being emotionally detached, must nevertheless be made to feel that these *guignol* antics are the essential comedy of his own existence, contemplated from the totally dispassionate viewpoint of the dead.

Rather than concentrating on the literary model, Valle focuses on the gap between myth and reality, between the grandeur of the sentiments and the smallness of those who express them. He does not go for the easy laughs, as the parodist is often tempted to do. In fact, there are very few jokes or puns, a point on which *Los cuernos* contrasts sharply with *La venganza de don Mendo*. He is expressing through parody a view that tragic attitudes have become devoid of meaning, have degenerated into ludicrous posturing. He uses the parody of melodramatic situations and language as some writers of the Absurdist school use the situations of music-hall sketches and the comedies of the silent cinema. The heroic attitudes and pretentious rhetoric of Honour have become devoid of meaning because of the context of social corruption and debased morality. In *Los cuernos* Valle stresses the incongruity between the myth of *honor* and the moral state of the nation and the times. Don Friolera himself is in the pay of smugglers and takes his percentage for turning a blind eye to contraband. In scene 3 the smugglers comment on the fact that he has raised his price since his promotion from sergeant to lieutenant and, in scene 8, Valle contrasts the grotesquely debased morality of the high-ranking officers with their claim to be the 'guardians' of the honour of the military.

It would not be true to say that *Los cuernos* was simply a satire on the military code of honour, i.e. that which dictated that an officer and a gentleman should slay wife and suspected lover first and ask questions afterwards – in other words, not simply an attack on what Valle would have called 'Calderonian' values. Echegaray by no means accepted these values in *El gran galeoto* and yet Valle seems to classify him under the same general heading. Valle's target is both larger and less precise; it is the power of myth, the whole rhetorical illusion associated with honour, dishonour, shame and duty. The popular puppet farce with its unpretentious common sense and sane good humour was not only a salutary antidote to rhetorical literature, but gave a truer picture of a reality in which such values had become hollow. It was Valle's intuition that true artistic seriousness could only be achieved by abandoning the tone of high moral seriousness. He therefore saw the complete alienation of the puppet farce as the only redemption from a theatre strait-jacketed in outdated moral assumptions. In the Prologue Don Estrafalario says: 'Ese tabanque de muñecos sobre la espalda de un viejo prosero, para mí, es más sugestivo que todo el retórico teatro español.' And in the Epilogue he adds: '¡Sólo pueden regenerarnos los muñecos del Compadre Fidel!'

In order to justify – artistically – the use of the puppet convention and to demonstrate the 'regenerative' potential of puppet characters in literature, Valle-Inclán places two contrasting versions of the Friolera story on either side of the central *esperpento*, one in the Prologue and the other in the Epilogue. In the Prologue, Valle's pair of eccentric travellers, Don Estrafalario and Don Manolito, witness a blind man's puppet show of 'la trigedia de Don Friolera'. This takes place on the Portuguese frontier. In the Epilogue, the same two characters are in jail somewhere on the Andalusian coast 'por haber hecho el mal de ojo a un burro en la Alpujarra' and hear a version of Don Friolera's revenge as a *romance de ciego* sung outside their cell window. The play's structure is thus, as Sumner Greenfield has pointed out, that of a triptych, presenting three versions of the same story (*Anatomía*, p. 254).

First let us consider the two 'outer' versions of Prologue and Epilogue. The *bululú*'s puppet show is presented as a spontaneous expression of the popular imagination, crude, unliterary, but 'full of artistic possibilities'. (Valle made a similar observation about the *astracán* comedies of Muñoz Seca.)[10] The puppeteer does not identify with the marionettes; he simply amuses himself with their antics. The episode of Don Friolera's cuckoldry is related as an inconsequential farce with sane ironic detachment. This 'donoso buen sentido' (associated by Valle with Portugal and the Cantabrian region) is contrasted with the 'honor teatral y africano de Castilla' which Valle sees exemplified not only in classical Spanish drama but also in the popular *romances de ciego*. The *romance* of the Epilogue represents what Valle calls the vile contamination of bad literature on the popular imagination. It adopts *en bloc* the moral values and myths of classical

Spanish literature. Friolera's exploits in the *romance* are seen in a heroic perspective; his cause is just, his resolution unshakeable. Woman is denigrated as a weak and lustful vessel. Friolera's revenge earns him the honour and respect of all. The *romance* version exalts all the myths of honour, courage, patriotism, duty and glory. The puppet version is the *burla*, marionettes imitating the antics of people; the *romance* is the *mito*, about people emulating the actions of gods. Artistically, the first is a vision from above and the second a vision from below.[11] It would be tempting to continue that the middle version represented the third viewpoint which is the vision on the same level. Clearly this is not the case. So what is the relationship of the central *esperpento* to the other two versions? Basically, it is the application of the viewpoint and style of the *bululú*'s version to the heroic and mythical content of the *romance* version: the *mito* seen from the viewpoint of the *burla*. In emulating the actions of gods, in adopting the prescribed heroic roles dictated by tradition and society, the characters merely succeed in reducing themselves to the status of puppets.

'LAS GALAS DEL DIFUNTO'

One of the principal changes that took place in Valle's theatre after 1924 was the adoption of a shorter, more compressed dramatic form. He wrote six more plays: the four short works that, together with *El embrujado*, make up the *Retablo de la avaricia, la lujuria y la muerte* (1927) and two final *esperpentos*, *Las galas del difunto* and *La hija del capitán*.[12] Unlike the *Retablo* plays, the two *esperpentos* conserve the multiple-scene principle, each comprised of seven scenes despite the fact that they are of little more than one-act length. They have, moreover, a recognizable political background and contain specific historical allusions. In 1930 Valle grouped them together with *Los cuernos de don Friolera* under the general title of *Martes de carnaval* because of their common basis of anti-militarist satire. The title is in fact a pun meaning both 'Carnival Tuesday' and 'Carnival Soldiers' based on the double meaning of 'Martes' (Tuesday) and 'Marte' (Mars). The latter sense appears on one or two occasions in *La hija del capitán* in the phrases 'invicto marte' or 'un marte ultramarino' used to describe the general. As far as the political and military background is concerned, the plays follow, as Joaquín Casalduero has pointed out, a chronological sequence (pp. 686–94). *Las galas* refers to the colonial wars in Cuba (1898); *Los cuernos* makes some allusions to the disastrous Moroccan campaign and *La hija del capitán* represents in fairly unequivocal terms the military coup which brought Primo de Rivera to power in 1923. Casalduero also observes that we pass in ascending order of rank from the situation of the private soldier in *Las galas*, to the staff officers in *Los cuernos*, to the general and dictator in *La hija del capitán*.

However, the purely political elements in these plays should not be exaggerated. Of the three, only *La hija* is a genuinely political satire, of a type rarely found in Spanish literature. The other two deal less directly with the political and historical events that form their background. The allusions to the Moroccan campaign in *Los cuernos* are restricted to one scene and have no direct bearing on the action of the play. In *Las galas* the background of the Cuban war is perhaps more important and the references to it in scene 1 were greatly expanded for the definitive *Martes de carnaval* version in 1930.[13] Nevertheless, the principal action is not about these historical events as such. The analyses of Cardona and Zahareas (pp. 191–6) and of González López (pp. 263–7) highlight the political allusions to produce a very one-sided interpretation of the play. The political dimension is undoubtedly important but it is not exclusive; there are other aspects of the play to be considered.

In each of the first two *esperpentos* Valle is clearly alluding through the protagonist to a heroic literary archetype. The same question naturally arises in the case of *Las galas*. Which traditional heroic figure is being alluded to? Juan Bautista Avalle-Arce has argued the case for Don Juan Tenorio (*Hispanófila*, 1959). The story of a repatriated soldier from the Cuban war who steals a suit of clothes from a buried corpse in order to impress a prostitute does not perhaps immediately put one in mind of the traditional Don Juan. In fact, were it not for one or two explicit references to the José Zorrilla version in the text, the parallel might well have escaped the notice of critics altogether. One such reference occurs in the graveyard scene when the other repatriated soldiers invite the protagonist Juanito Ventolera to supper and the latter replies 'parece que representáis el Tenorio'. During the supper the soldiers make a wager that Juanito would not dare to claim the bowler hat and stick from the dead man's wife to go with the suit, echoing the wager that Don Juan makes with Don Luis in the Zorrilla play. Valle also inserts two direct quotations from Zorrilla's text into the scene where Juanito returns to the brothel dressed in his new finery: 'Madre Priora . . . ¿Dónde está esa garza enjaulada?' and '¡Luz de donde el sol la toma, no te mires más para desmayarte!' The references to the brothel keeper as 'Madre Priora' and 'Madre Celeste' instantly cause us to associate the brothel with the convent and La Daifa with Doña Inés. Once embarked on this course other parallels readily fall into place: the chemist Sócrates Galindo (father of La Daifa) with Don Gonzalo the Comendador; the group of repatriated soldiers, El Bizco Maluenda, Franco Ricote and Pedro Maside with Capitán Centellas and his associates. Juanito's appearance in the Boticaria's bedroom dressed in her husband's burial suit may contain an allusion to Don Gonzalo's return from the dead, especially if taken in conjunction with the 'fuertes aldabonazos' on the door which announce his arrival. The allusions are perhaps sufficient to convince us that Valle had the Don Juan figure generally in mind, but it is unlikely that he intended the play as a parody of any specific literary model.

Unlike the literary archetypes behind the characters of Max Estrella and Don Friolera, the Don Juan figure had always been a personal obsession with Valle-Inclán. Díaz Plaja singles out three main representatives of this, Bradomín, Montenegro and Juanito Ventolera, and sees them as corresponding to the three main stages into which he divides Valle's literary vision: *visión erótica*, *visión mítica* and *visión degradadora* respectively. Whether or not one accepts Díaz Plaja's categories, Juanito Ventolera must be seen as a development in Valle's meditations on the Don Juan theme rather than as literary parody. He explains in an interview:

Don Juan es un tema eterno y nacional; pero Don Juan no es esencialmente conquistador de mujeres; se caracteriza también por la impiedad y por el desacato a las leyes y a los hombres. En Don Juan se han de desarrollar tres temas. Primero: falta de respeto a los muertos y a la religión, que es una misma cosa. Segundo: satisfacción de sus pasiones saltando sobre el derecho de los demás. Tercero: conquista de mujeres. Es decir, Demonio, mundo y carne respectivamente.

Don Juan es el Angel Rebelde; es monstruo y no engendra; es eterno y no se reproduce, como todo lo monstruoso y todo lo eterno. Don Juan es el ideal para los hombres; todos los hombres admiran a Don Juan y lo admiran por su trinidad monstruosa. (see Tomás)

In his *Autocrítica* published in the review *España* (8 March 1924), he alludes to his creation of Montenegro in the *Comedias bárbaras*:

He querido renovar lo que tiene de galaico la leyenda de don Juan, que yo divido en tres tiempos: impiedad, matonería y mujeres. Este de las mujeres es el último, el sevillano, la nostalgia del moro sin harén. El matón picajoso es el extremeño, gallo de frontera. El impío es gallego, el originario, como explicaba nuestro caro Said Armesto. El Convidado de Piedra es, por sólo ser bulto de piedra, gallego. Aquí la impiedad es la impiedad gallega; no niega ningún dogma, no descree de Dios: es irreverente con los muertos . . . Este fondo del primer Don Juan – Don Galán en el romance viejo – es lo perseguido con mayor empeño, porque lo tengo por la última decantación del alma gallega.

The Don Juan theme had thus always attracted him because it involved the eternal motifs of death and religion, attitude to society and the sexual instinct. Moreover, it was a theme which summed up many aspects of the national character, the Galician character in particular. It emerges not only in the more explicitly donjuanesque characters of Bradomín and Montenegro, but also with different emphases in such characters as Arlequín (*La Marquesa Rosalinda*) and Séptimo Miau (*Divinas palabras*). All these characters are linked by the rebellious satanic libido and the disregard for the laws and conventions of society and Juanito Ventolera is evidently cast in the same mould – a *gallego* in whom impiousness takes the form of irreverence towards the dead.

The question now arises whether, as Avalle-Arce and Díaz Plaja affirm, Valle intended to portray the *esperpentización* of the Don Juan archetype in Juanito. Was the point of *Las galas* to show this degenerate contemporary equivalent of the arch-rebel as a ridiculous and minuscule figure when he came up against the 'grandes situaciones' of life? Is Juanito Ventolera shown as a distortion of a former heroic pattern? In both *Luces* and *Los cuernos* Valle was stressing the *desajuste* between the heroic model and the contemporary counterpart. Max was made conscious of the incongruity and Friolera grotesquely unaware. In the case of Max Estrella, society is seen as responsible for the diminishing of his image; in the case of Friolera the actor is pathetically inadequate in himself to the role that society assigns him. In Juanito Ventolera the relationship between literary archetype and contemporary counterpart is different. He is neither distorted by the concave mirror of society's values nor is he manipulated like a puppet. Neither the mirror nor the puppet theatre image serves us very well in this case. He is not portrayed as inadequate to any heroic role that society or destiny calls upon him to play. Strictly speaking, Juanito is not offered a heroic 'role' in this sense to accept or reject like Friolera or Max. He is therefore not tempted to adopt false or pretentiously absurd postures. His *donjuanismo* or cynical irreverence for everything is not so much a 'role' as a spontaneous response to the degraded values of the society around him, the only response the underdog can make to the *status quo*. Although it might be too extreme to claim Valle's sympathy or approval for Juanito Ventolera, it seems doubtful that the intention is to ridicule or condemn him. The condemnation is reserved for the social attitudes that make Juanito what he is.

The absence of the 'tragic role' removes a duality which had hitherto been an important feature of the *esperpento*: the duality between the imagined role and the objective reality. There is no significant difference between Juanito as he sees himself and Juanito as we see him. This had not been the case with Don Friolera who sees himself in the role of Calderonian hero caught up in a tragic dilemma while being objectively a victim of manipulation by anachronistic social myths. Much of the grotesque humour derives from this difference of perspective. In *Luces*, Max Estrella is given the insight to see himself as others see him. Nevertheless, the temptation to play the tragic role is still present and the anti-tragic humour of the play is a conscious resistance to this temptation. It is clear from an interview Valle gave on his second visit to Mexico in 1921 that parody of 'literary' tragedy was a central feature in the early *esperpentos* (see Appendix 8). Certainly at this stage the *esperpento* involved the basic dramatic irony between the characters as they saw themselves and the way they were viewed by the audience. Now this irony totally disappears in *Las galas*. The characters themselves no longer believe in the 'myths'. Juanito Ventolera does not strike heroic or donjuanesque attitudes which appear grotesque in the contemporary context. Despite the name 'Ventolera', he is not a petulant or pretentious character. On the contrary, he systematically deprecates his own heroics and deflates La Daifa's expectations of heroic deeds:

Siempre se tira de lejos.

El soldado si supiese su obligación y no fuese un paria, debería tirar sobre sus jefes.

LA DAIFA: ¡Has sido un héroe!
VENTOLERA: ¡Un cabrón!

Avalle-Arce points out that the theatrical nature of Juanito's entrance into the Boticaria's bedroom to claim the bowler hat and stick indicates a conscious assumption of the Don Juan role (*Hispanófila*, p. 34). He appears 'algarero' and 'farsante' and 'hace una reverencia'; he enters the bedroom 'haciendo piernas, mofador y chispón', 'los brazos en jarra' and proceeds to pay Doña Terita some theatrical donjuanesque compliments ('si se digna concederme una mirada de sus bellos ojos'). However, at no time does Juanito take the role seriously and this difference from Don Friolera is crucial. He is merely playing a game. Like most of the other characters in the play, he is an unashamedly self-interested rogue who pretends to be nothing else. In *Las galas* (and in *La hija del capitán*) the emphasis falls not so much on the self-parodying heroic postures as on the anti-heroic cynicism. In consequence of this, the *esperpento* undergoes a change of tone. There is appreciably less ironic bombast and rhetoric and more slang and *chulería*. We have a foretaste of this style in scene 7 of *Los cuernos* in the dialogue between Doña Calixta and the smuggler Curro Cadenas. The literary models move from the drama of Echegaray and his school to the *folletín* and the penny dreadful novelette.

If we examine the relationship between the protagonist and the social context in *Las galas*, we get a different picture from the earlier *esperpentos*. In *Luces* and *Los cuernos* we have an individual reacting to and being conditioned by general attitudes around him. In both cases the play is about the process of metamorphosis or manipulation of the individual by the collectivity. Juanito Ventolera is not changed or manipulated; he is a pariah, vilified or ignored by bourgeois society, who turns rebel. The play does not consist of showing how the ethos of society produces this reaction. We are shown the self-interested values of the society and we are shown Juanito's equally self-interested response. There is no visible process of interaction between Juanito and his environment. There is not even a contrast of values since he is neither better nor worse than those around him. Juanito is not a victim in the same sense as Max Estrella whose rejection of heroic postures is a measure to preserve a degree of authenticity for himself. Juanito cocks a deliberate snook at society and places himself beyond the pale. '¡Hay que ser soberbio y dar la cara contra el mundo entero!', he says, '¡A mí me cae simpático el Diablo!' And on another occasion, '¡El hombre que no se pone fuera de la ley es un cabra!' He responds to self-interest with more self-interest. His rebellion thus makes him indistinguishable from the rest and so the whole idea of an individual *vis-à-vis* a general social ethic now disappears. The *esperpento* gravitates towards a more general type of social satire.

Generally speaking, Valle-Inclán was not much given to the use of dramatic symbolism, in the sense of events which have both structural importance for the action and metaphorical importance for the wider

meaning of the play. *Las galas del difunto* is unusual in that it is
constructed around such a symbolic event: the changing of the
clothes.[14] The macabre joke of exchanging his soldier's uniform for
the suit of bourgeois respectability is Juanito's symbolic acceptance of
the dog-eat-dog ethics of survival. With the burial of his uniform and
his medals he buries the myths of military heroism, sacrifice and
patriotism. By putting on the dead man's suit and appropriating (we
are not told how) the dead man's money, he is adopting the bourgeois
values of commercialism and self-interest.

In *Las galas* Valle condemns the colonial war in Cuba in bitter and
unequivocal terms. It is not entirely clear at what stage Valle
abandoned his heroic attitude to war. The attitude towards the First
World War in *La media noche* (1917) retains a belief in the just cause –
the French were fighting to preserve civilized values against the
barbarous Hun – and in the virtue of war for highlighting certain
primitive human drives which have an air of grandeur about them.
Even in *Los cuernos* the war in Morocco is not condemned in the same
explicit way. But in *Las galas* an abyss has opened up between the
myths of heroic sacrifice, patriotism and loyalty to the flag, etc, and
the realities of callous exploitation and criminal disregard for human
life. To be a hero was to be a dupe of the system. Juanito's response to
this society that calls him a hero and then treats him like a leper is
curiously cold and without anger. It is characterized by ironic
detachment rather than resentment or hatred, a reaction above
laughter and tears, above involvement. One is reminded very much
of the ironic detachment of Max Estrella or of the *bululú* in *Los cuernos*,
except that the attitudes are expressed in deliberately anti-social
actions. It is as if Valle were inviting us to share Juanito's disdain for
the values of the society while preventing us from sympathizing with
his rebellion, which has no dignity, which is, as his name suggests,
simply a piece of bravado, a 'ventolera'. Juanito is both a rebel
against hollow myths and, at the same time, a degraded Don Juan
figure. The justification for his rebellion and the inevitable cheapness
of that rebellion are summed up in the juxtaposition of two scenes:
scene 5, in which the Sacristán and the Rapista claim payment from
the Boticaria for her husband's burial before the body is cold, and
scene 6, when Juanito arrives at her balcony like a down-at-heel Don
Juan to demand the deceased's bowler hat and walking stick. Scene 5,
with its sordid and grotesque haggling over the cost of various items
for the funeral, underlines the commercialized ethos of the society to

which Juanito's anarchic irreverence is a response. But the anarchic irreverence of the response in scene 6 is seen as mere *chulería* when Juanito Ventolera, in a suit too big for him, plays out a grotesque parody of a Don Juan scene in which he terrorizes a woman and an idiot boy, robs and – we are led to believe – rapes the unfortunate widow.[15]

The character of La Daifa perhaps requires a word of explanation since she apparently elicits more sympathy from the reader than any of the other characters. I say 'apparently' because, although she is portrayed as a victim of her father's avarice and of the Cuban war, in which her *novio* is killed, she is not a sentimentalized figure. Valle makes her into a character, hardened by life in the brothel, who is half-tempted to wish her father dead in order to inherit some of his estate ('¡No habrá una peste negra que se lo lleve!'). La Bruja's reference to 'tantas ideas' in the first scene when she is writing the letter to her father suggests that La Daifa has been trying to get money out of the old man for some time and by various devices. Her calculating attitude is revealed by her comment that 'la carta va puesta como para conmover una peña'. At the end the play comes back full circle to its point of departure with the reading of the letter. The dramatic point of reading the letter aloud at the end is to sabotage the pathos of the victim's sentiments contained in the letter. As with Juanito, Valle does not allow his audience the luxury of total sympathy with La Daifa. He allows the novelettish clichés of the letter to cast their sentimental spell and then brutally reveals their emptiness by having one of the prostitutes declare that they were copied from the prostitutes' 'manual' and by having the *Madame* dismiss the whole episode as a 'folletín'.

In *Las galas* we see the darker side of the *esperpento* because even the norms and archetypes have disappeared. The anti-heroic does not stand in contrast to anything; it simply exists as a universal phenomenon. The pessimism of *Las galas* is bleaker than anything Valle had previously written. The spirit of self-interest reigns supreme; in the exploitation and corruption of the military, in the avarice of the Boticario and his refusal to assist his daughter, in the commercialization of sex and even in the commercialization of death. The victims of such a society can only respond by becoming equally self-interested. The grotesque, much more so than in previous *esperpentos*, has become the expression of the tragic.

'LA HIJA DEL CAPITÁN'

Valle's final *esperpento* has all the sharp and bitter humour of a political cartoon. Political and historical events are not just a background to the action as they are in *Los cuernos* and *Las galas*, they *are* the action. *La hija del capitán* is similar to *Farsa y licencia de la reina castiza* in that the chain of events is more important than the characters. Both plays trace the odd repercussions of an event – seemingly trivial in the *farsa* and politically irrelevant in the *esperpento* – which leads to a national crisis and the fall of a regime. It is the absurd logic of the events themselves rather than the human attitudes that make them happen that mostly commands attention. Valle's purpose in following this series of repercussions from its trivial origins to its unpredictable and momentous conclusions is to demonstrate the fundamental instability of the social and political system that allows it to happen.

Of all the *esperpentos*, *La hija* is the one which is based most closely on actual historical events. In fact two episodes are being alluded to, one of which was a notorious murder committed in 1913 by an army captain and his daughter and the other was the military coup d'état which brought Primo de Rivera to power in 1923. Before discussing why Valle should have chosen to fuse two such widely separated incidents, it is necessary to sketch in some of the historical details.[16]

On 4 May 1913 an item appeared in the Madrid newspaper *El Imparcial* about the mysterious disappearance of a certain gambler of the Círculo de Bellas Artes, Rodrigo Jalón. This information was followed up by a journalist named Franciso Serrano Anguita, whose subsequent investigations uncovered the crime which later came to be known as 'el crimen del capitán Sánchez'. Some of the newspaper accounts alleged that there was an incestuous relationship between Captain Sánchez and his daughter and that the murder of Jalón was motivated by jealousy. The body was dismembered and disposed of in various ways. Parts of it were later discovered down a lavatory and, according to more sensational accounts, other portions were served up as food for the lower ranks. The repercussions of the murder were equally picturesque, namely the daughter's attempt to cash a 5,000-peseta gambling chip found in the victim's wallet, the veiled hints that appeared in the press as part of a campaign to blackmail the Captain and, perhaps most important from Valle's point of view, the involvement of the military establishment in a cover-up operation. It was clearly the social reactions to the crime – of the army, the press and the public – that most attracted Valle-Inclán to the subject, rather than the sensational aspects of the crime itself. Those reactions can be summed up in the word 'exploitation', whether for money, for power, or simply as a source of entertainment for bored and idle minds.

The crime of Captain Sánchez is linked in the *esperpento* to Primo de Rivera's take-over of power in 1923 with the alleged connivance of Alfonso XII. Historically, the two events are unconnected, but Valle's purpose was to show the military coup as a *potential* consequence of those former events, as a consequence of a chronically unstable society in which everyone is motivated by opportunist self-interest. The character of General Agustín Miranda in the play closely resembles that attributed to Primo de Rivera. The profound antipathy for the press and politicians, the predilection for gambling and women and a taste for highly emotive patriotic vocabulary are characteristic of both fictional character and historical counterpart. Zahareas and Cardona point out that many of the phrases the General uses in the play are direct quotations from certain *Notas oficiosas* that Primo issued to the press in which he explained the reasons for his political decisions (*Visión*, p. 209). Like Primo, the General is a military governor and his coup receives the backing of the king for reasons which, in the play, are not explained but which would not have escaped Valle's contemporaries. The king, it was rumoured, was anxious to distract attention from a public enquiry currently being held into the military disaster at Anual in Spanish Morocco in which 7,000 troops had been massacred by the Moors. The extent of the king's responsibility in this affair has never been disclosed since the coup obliterated all trace of the investigations a week before the commission was due to publish its findings. Historically, therefore, the Primo coup was preceded by an atmosphere of rumours and speculation about the involvement of high-ranking personages similar to that which followed the crime of Captain Sánchez. In 1913 the rumours were about the involvement of military top brass and, although conditions were perhaps ripe, the potential military coup never materialized. In 1923 the rumours were about the involvement of the king, and the coup, to silence all these suspicions, did in fact take place.

Valle's association of these two episodes and the sacrifice of strict historical accuracy was in the interests of making a general comment on the state of Spanish society. By making the origins of the coup remote and improbable he highlights the farcical and arbitrary nature of the political charade, while remaining true to the spirit of events. It should be emphasized that Valle plays down the sensationalism of the crime itself and concentrates on the way it is exploited by others. In fact, he makes the Captain innocent of the murder that eventually causes the downfall of the government. There is no hint of any incestuous relationship or jealousy motive; instead Valle gives the daughter a lover who is responsible for committing the murder. The more sensational aspects of the crime – the dismembering of the corpse and the serving of it in the soldiers' canteen – are relegated to the status of an earlier episode of the Captain's shady past in the Cuban campaign. He has been accused of killing a rebel sergeant (hence the nickname 'Chuletas de sargento') but has managed to avoid court martial by offering his daughter as a concubine to the military governor. The crime which sets all the wheels of self-interest in motion is deliberately made into something unconnected with the military who take power, a completely unforeseen event, a case of mistaken identity. The lover believes he is killing the General. By doing this, Valle stresses the arbitrariness of events, the disparity between root cause and end result. He also underlines the fact that the military establishment acts in defence of its reputation and not to protect its existence.

Dramatically, *La hija del capitán* depends on a complex and absurd concatenation of events which – untypically for Valle-Inclán – requires a scene of explanatory information at the beginning of the play. We are succinctly informed of Captain Sinibaldo Pérez's dubious antecedents, of his arrangement involving his daughter (La Sini) with General Agustín Miranda and of the arrival of La Sini's former lover, El Golfante, who, disguised as an organ grinder, has finally tracked her down to a house in the outskirts of Madrid where the Captain is running a gambling den. After a card session, one of the gamblers, El Pollo de Cartagena, is stabbed by El Golfante believing him to be the General. Although innocent of the crime, the Captain and the General find themselves with a body on their hands. Both agree that to report the murder would lead to exploitation by the press and decide to hide the body in the basement. La Sini, taking advantage of the fact that she could, if provoked, cause a scandal, removes El Pollo's wallet and escapes from the house in the company of El Golfante. It is later discovered that the wallet contains a gambling chip for 5,000 pesetas, two IOUs signed by the General for 20,000 pesetas each and a letter from the same asking for more time to pay. La Sini and El Golfante consult two characters from the underworld – El Sastre Penela and El Batuco – on the best way to exploit this compromising material. The information is then sold to the editor of the newspaper *El Constitucional* and La Sini cashes the gambling chip in the Bellas Artes casino. There she is recognized from a photograph of herself in the nude that El Pollo had been showing around the club (a photograph evidently sold to him by the General). The thinly veiled allusions that appear in *El Constitucional* (the contents of the wallet, the General's debts to El Pollo, the latter's mysterious disappearance), allied to the knowledge that La Sini had cashed El Pollo's gambling chip and had been identified as General Miranda's mistress, mark the beginning of a blackmail campaign against the General. The military establishment rallies round in support of the General who, in his turn, makes political capital out of the situation by using it as a pretext to seize power while proclaiming himself to be the defender of the nation's sacred institutions and moral standards.

The dramatic rhythm of *La hija del capitán* is one of escalation, in which an absurd crime is turned to personal advantage first by one group then another. It is used first of all by La Sini as a means of escaping from the degrading situation in which the Captain has placed her; the petty crooks of the underworld then cream off their share of the profits; the press then steps in with high-level blackmail and finally the military convert the situation into a self-righteous take-over of the government. There is the implication that the escalation of roguery does not end with the generals. The final scene shows the king making his speech of farewell from the royal train, welcoming the change of government. There is nothing explicit to indicate complicity between the king and the rebel general, but Valle gives us a broad hint at the end of the king's speech. An abrupt change of tone from pompous rhetoric to the argot of rogues and gangsters is perhaps intended to make us associate the king with the latter: '¡El antiguo regimen es un fiambre, y los fiambres no resucitan!' The allusion of the 'fiambre' refers us back to the point of departure of this whole political charade, the body of El Pollo. It is also a forceful reminder of the General's own vocabulary when referring to the 'stiff'.

How far has *La hija del capitán* evolved away from the original definition of the *esperpento*? It is not particularly illuminating to see *La hija del capitán* in terms of a protagonist in relation to a social context. In *La hija*, despite the fact that La Sini is the eponymous heroine, the trend established in *Las galas* continues and the central character suffers a further reduction. As in the case of Juanito Ventolera, there is little moral distinction between La Sini and the rest of the characters. She liberates herself from exploitation by adopting society's methods. She is perhaps even more effective at beating the system at its own game than Juanito. She therefore merges more into the general picture than Juanito and, moreover, her role is a more marginal one. The emphasis shifts further away from individual–society relationships to a social panorama. For *La hija* is a general view of society, not just a political lampoon against the military and Primo de Rivera in particular. The military is not the only section of society that exploits the situation. The social panorama is one of uniform roguery and self-interest, a close network of petty crooks, swindlers, opportunists, blackmailers pervading the whole spectrum from the proletariat to the monarch. The implication is that the nation gets the government it deserves.

The element of literary parody – already of reduced importance in *Las galas* – disappears completely. The concept of a discrepancy between a recognizable literary archetype and his contemporary counterpart or between tragi-heroic roles and inadequate players no longer has any relevance. We no longer observe the characters as diminutive figures playing against a backdrop of gigantic archetypal forerunners. Valle has switched the object of his attack from the 'enanos y patizambos' to the hollowness of the so-called principles themselves. *La hija del capitán* is more about the contrast between public and private faces, between the sacrosanct principles and the corrupt mouths that utter them. In the later *esperpentos* self-delusion or the danger of self-delusion has given way to conscious malice.

Nevertheless, despite the disappearance of the literary element, one basic feature of the *esperpento* remains intact: the contrast of myth and reality. For this reason *Farsa y licencia de la reina castiza*, although it contained many *stylistic* features of the *esperpento*, was not classified as such by the author. *La hija* is an *esperpento* precisely because it is structured round this opposition. The early scenes expose the degenerate reality of the 'príncipe de la milicia' who is to be the recipient of such pious adulation at the end of the play. The image of the General dancing drunkenly with his flies open round the gambling den of Chuletas de Sargento contrasts oddly with the sentiments of 'religious duty', 'self-sacrifice' and 'public welfare' that issue from his mouth in scene 6. The resounding phrase from Doña Simplicia's speech of welcome, '¡Un príncipe de la milicia levanta su espada victoriosa y sus luces inundan los corazones de las madres españolas!', is perhaps a deliberate echo of the description of the General in scene 2 with 'luces alcohólicas en el campanario' (*Anatomía*, p. 289). The presentation of the General preparing 'con heroico alarde' to suffer the verbal onslaught of La Sini for losing all his money in scene 2 is a parody of the man who 'heroically' prepares to take on the enemies of the State in scene 6. The trembling pathetic figure who in scene 3 is terrified of being discovered with the body by the neighbours ('¡Sinibalda, prudencia! Una escena de nervios nos perdería', 'Sería nuestra ruina una escena de nervios', 'Sini, no te desboques, Las paredes son de cartón. Todo se oye fuera') later places himself at the head of a military coup and issues a manifesto to the nation. Just as the currency of honour and patriotic duty is debased by the representatives of the military, the vocabulary of business ethics is devalued by certain members of the civilian population. The characters of the underworld, the fences, crooked lawyers ('acróbatas del código' as they are called in the *dramatis personae*) parade under a cloak of middle-class respectability. They sit behind desks with telephones and typewriters and talk the language of commercial propriety ('El Batuco ha puesto a modo de una agencia. ¡Una oficina en toda regla!'; 'El Batuco vive de esas operaciones y su crédito está en portarse con decencia'; 'Yo siempre le he visto proceder como un caballero'). It is not improbable that, as Valle was a devoted admirer of Cervantes, this ironic contrast of style and content could have been inspired by *Rinconete y Cortadillo* where the device is used to great effect.

Apart from the real self-interest behind the myth of disinterested moral conduct, there is the real contingency and arbitrariness behind the myth of stable institutions. *La hija* is based on an elaborate joke which is summed up in La Sini's last words: '¡Don Joselito de mi vida, le rezaré por el alma! ¡Carajeta, si usted no la diña, la hubiera diñado la Madre Patria!', thus attributing the salvation of Spain to El Pollo's death. A similar pattern is visible in *Farsa y licencia* and also in the novel *Tirano Banderas*: a series of events arising from a trivial incident gathers momentum and ends in the collapse of a government, implying a comment on the stability of the regime in question. In *Los cuernos de don Friolera* the same device is used in reverse in that the accidental killing comes at the end. The basic purpose is the same, however: to portray the hollowness of the social imperatives which achieve only the death of an innocent and irrelevant victim, Friolera's daughter. In *La hija* the exploitation by various groups of an irrelevant crime of passion in which the wrong man is killed is finally enshrined as the 'salvation of the nation's values'. The pompous edifice of 'sacred and inviolable principles and institutions' is erected on a foundation of chance exploited by opportunist self-interest.

The central contrast between myth and reality also finds expression in some of the visual images of the play. At the beginning of scene 3, the General and the Captain, on hearing El Pollo's cry for help, rush out on to the verandah carrying a paraffin lamp. Valle visualizes the scene illuminated by the flickering light of the lamp:

Se ilumina el vestíbulo con rotario aleteo de sombras: la cigüeña disecada, la sombrilla japonesa, las mecedoras de bambú. Sobre un plano de pared, diluidos, fugaces resplandores de un cuadro con todas las condecoraciones del capitán: placas, medallas, cruces. Al movimiento de la luz todo se desbarata. (Beginning of scene 3)

Two things can be observed about this image. One is that it is essentially cinematic in that it involves the isolation of details and the focusing of the spectator's attention on objects in a way that would be difficult to accomplish in the theatre. The other is that it is an image selected not simply for its contribution to 'atmosphere', but for its *thematic* relevance. All the Captain's souvenirs from overseas, all his military decorations briefly illuminated in the unstable light of the paraffin lamp and then suddenly disappearing as the lamp is moved are a visual statement of the theme, debunking the myth of military heroism.

In the final scene, the decor, as Sumner Greenfield has pointed out, plays a significant part (*Anatomía*, p. 286). It is set in the sordid surroundings of a railway station in a *pueblo* outside Madrid. In this scene we see the dual result of El Pollo's demise: the humble triumph of El Golfante and La Sini, with whom it all started, preparing to make good their escape with the loot and the larger-scale triumph of the monarch in connivance with the military establishment. Valle stresses the squalor and the silence of the third-class waiting room in preparation for the contrasting noise and splendour to follow: 'Sala de tercera. Sórdidas mugres. Un diván de gutapercha vomita el pelote del henchido. De un clavo cuelgan el quepis y la chaqueta galoneada de un empleado de la vía. Sórdido silencio turbado por estrépitos de carretillas y silbatadas, martillos y flejes' (p. 228). Then like the drawing aside of a discovery curtain in a Golden Age play, the waiting-room door is opened to reveal, framed in this squalor, a pageant of 'La España oficial'. The alliance of Church and Army is expressed in the image of a colonel 'que viste de gala con guantes blancos, obeso y ramplón' kissing the ring of a bishop. The top hats and frock coats of civil dignitaries mingle with the splendour of martial uniforms: 'Pueblan el andén chisteras y levitas de personajes: muchos mantos, fajines y bandas'. As in the example of the Captain's medals, these elements are selected to reinforce the thematic intention, to highlight the contrast between the squalid reality (station waiting-room of a Spanish *pueblo*) and the mythical pomp of Spain. Even the railway man's uniform with its cap and stripes on the sleeves hanging up in the waiting room is not a gratuitous detail. It was in fact added to the 1930 *Martes de carnaval* version and is evidently intended as a parody of the military uniforms 'outside'. The clatters, whistles and discordant sounds of the railway station are associated with and made a parody of the military band that welcomes the royal train: 'El humo de una locomotora que maniobra en agujas infla todas las figuras alineadas al canto del andén, llena de aire los bélicos metales de figles y trombones, estremece platillos y bombos, despepita cornetines y clarinetes' (p. 229).

If one fails to visualize the contrast between El Golfante and La Sini in their silent and squalid waiting-room and the sudden and violent interruption of the costume parade outside the door, the scene loses much of its point. The humour depends on this contrast and on the fact that, in their nervous state, the two fugitives think that the whole display has been organized for their benefit. Valle has evidently tried to imagine a concluding scene which would bring together the 'initiators' of the farce and its 'beneficiaries' in higher spheres and, at the same time, a scene in which the myth and reality of Spain could be seen side by side.[17]

As I said at the beginning of this chapter, my aim was to link the discussion of the different plays by tracing the evolution of the *esperpento* idea through them. It may now be helpful to abstract the core of the argument from the detailed discussion and recapitulate on the principal changes of emphasis.

In *Luces* the anti-hero figure is to a large extent the creation of society. The central character is given a set of values which are in opposition to (and, by implication, superior to) the standards of an institutionalized society. We see those values made to appear ludicrous and anachronistic by the mere fact of being placed in an alien context. The play focuses on the metamorphosis of the hero's image under the pressure of circumstances and on the reappraisal of himself that Max is compelled to make, because society shows him a reflection that is a distortion of his former self. The main theoretical emphasis of the *esperpento* falls on the distorting agent, the concave mirror, the society.

The situation in *Los cuernos* is somewhat different. The central character has no values of his own and no genuine self-awareness with which to oppose the society and he is shown as manipulated by collective and self-perpetuating myths and traditions which he is powerless to resist. Hence the central image in the play changes from the distorted reflection of a concave mirror to the strings of a puppet theatre. In *Los cuernos* Valle concentrates his attack on the social imperatives that *control* the individual rather than on an unheroic society that degrades and distorts the one-time hero. Don Friolera undergoes no metamorphosis; he is, in himself, inadequate to the role that society demands him to play. He emerges without tragic dignity because he has no self-awareness; he is merely the 'fantoche' who has had the tragic role thrust upon him.

These first two *esperpentos* primarily involve (a) an individual *vis-à-vis* society relationship and (b) a contrast between an anti-heroic protagonist and some kind of heroic literary archetype. Most of the definitions that Valle is known to have given us involve one or other of these points. And it is the second point that he most consistently stresses after the publication of *Los cuernos*, i.e. that contemporary 'protagonists' are lamentably out of place in their roles as tragic heroes, because they are *essentially* inadequate – 'enanos y patizambos que juegan una tragedia'. Now this definition no longer fits *Luces de Bohemia* with any degree of accuracy because, although Max is given a heroic literary archetype to live up to, his failure to do so is because society or history changes him, not because he is an *intrinsically* unheroic figure.

In the later *esperpentos* both these central features begin to disappear and the emphasis moves towards a more general and political satire of the social panorama. The individual–society relationship changes dramatically in *Las galas* and the one-time victim of social pressures becomes a negative kind of rebel who, because he can exist in society only by adopting its methods, ultimately becomes indistinguishable from the context around him. The development is taken a step further in *La hija* in which the victim turns exploiter. The other important feature – the central character as a degeneration of a classic archetype – has only limited relevance to *Las galas* and disappears altogether in *La hija*. The whole question of society or destiny forcing grotesquely unsuitable characters into heroic roles no longer has any clear application to either play. This means that the standard definitions made by Valle in press interviews (some of them, incidentally, after 1926)[18] no longer fit the later *esperpentos* in practice. Rather than on pomposity, pretentiousness or self-deception, the new emphasis is on the portrayal of anti-heroic cynicism and self-interest. There is also a corresponding shift in the characteristic language of the *esperpento*, from humorous bombast and rhetoric to a racy underworld slang or *germanía*, particularly in *La hija del capitán*. The use of this slang is incidentally not in the interests of enhanced realism. Its purpose is to create the impression of a self-sufficient, closed world with its own peculiar values, tone and style, a society uniformly permeated by roguery, corruption, deceit and cynicism.

In stressing the stages of the *esperpento*'s evolution, it has not been my intention to deny the existence of any unifying characteristics. Clearly Valle had his reasons for labelling some of his plays as *esperpentos* and others not. Broadly speaking, the *esperpento* is a vehicle which Valle saw as appropriate for commenting on *contemporary* society – a subject which he had not always regarded as worthy of literary attention. It represents a change in Valle's use and conception of the theatre since its essential purpose is to be subversive. In most of the works of his middle period that purpose had been to 'recoger las voces amplias', that is, to reflect some sort of collective regional or national personality. He was always intrigued by the comic or dramatic possibilities of the clash or interplay of cultures, as between the medieval Provençal and Castilian in *Cuento de abril* or the Castilian and French in *La Marquesa Rosalinda* or between the pagan and the Catholic in *Divinas palabras*. The *esperpento* evidently aims to do more than reflect a collective reality or ironically observe contrasts and contradictions. Its purpose is to demolish myths. To destroy the illusions with which the society deceives itself: the idea of a tragic or heroic destiny, the idea of being the standard-bearer of certain imperishable values, honour, patriotism, heroism, self-sacrifice. The confrontation of these myths with the unheroic reality is perhaps the most consistent unifying feature of the *esperpento*. The only play where the deflation of myth and pompous rhetoric is not *directly* shown is *Las galas del difunto*, but the protagonist's actions are clearly a response to them. Without this opposition of myth and reality, whether explicit or implied, the *esperpento* would lack a specific identity since Valle's vision of Spanish society was of one that feeds on dead myths, a society in which the rhetoric and the facts are always at variance.

9

The hero's return? *Cara de plata*

Originally published in *La Pluma* (July–December 1922), *Cara de plata* was designed as the opening volume of the trilogy of *Comedias bárbaras*. It takes place before the open rift has developed between Montenegro and his sons and before the seduction of his ward, Sabelita – although he is already shown as estranged from his wife. Valle's motives for returning to an earlier source of heroic inspiration at a time when he had just published such anti-heroic works as *Divinas palabras*, *Luces* and *Los cuernos* have been the subject of much critical speculation. It has not always been pointed out that an incomplete version probably existed from the time of the composition of *Aguila* and *Romance*. We have the testimony of C. Rivas Cherif, a close follower of Valle's work, that he had begun *Cara de plata* after the other two volumes, but some twelve years before its eventual publication (*España*, 16 February 1924). Furthermore, in a letter thanking Rivas for his article, Valle himself lets slip the phrase 'al dar remate a *Cara de plata*' which seems to confirm the theory that at least part of the play had been lurking amongst his papers for some time (*España*, 8 March 1924). This does not of course provide a complete explanation for his decision to publish, but given Valle's tendency to make maximum use of his material, one can understand his reluctance to allow a half-finished version to go to waste.

The theory goes some way towards explaining certain apparent inconsistencies of style and attitude to characters in the play. Some of the stage directions in the early scenes seem to belong to the heroic phase of Valle's development,[1] while, as the action proceeds, the more we realize that the aesthetic of the *esperpento* is beginning to dominate the author's view of the characters. The earlier references to age-old tradition and the timeless links between man and nature, possibly left in from a previous version, begin to seem out of place when Valle indulges his new 'esperpentic' style of isolating details to characterize his figures, i.e. Doña Jeromita's 'brazos en aspa' and the lean angular figure of the Abad with horned *bonete*. The delicate suggestive power of the dialogue in act 1, scene 2, with its rhythmic control and lyrical cadences, are reminiscent of the style of *Aguila de blasón*. While drawing exclusively upon the immediate situation, this dialogue subtly and obliquely suggests a whole network of feeling: between Cara de plata and Sabelita, between Sabelita and Montenegro and between Montenegro and his sons. By contrast act III plunges into the deliberately discordant and strident frenzy characteristic of Valle's later aesthetic. This does not imply that *Cara de plata* is therefore confusing or artistically unsatisfactory. Such oversights – if that is what they were – in the process of revision do not destroy the unity of the work and could even be said to fit into the play's dramatic rhythm.

The overall impact of *Cara de plata*, as José Alberich has convincingly shown, is decidedly different from the other parts of the trilogy.[2] Thematically, Alberich argues, there was no need to add a third volume to the series. The early *Comedias* had stressed the heroic aspects of Montenegro as opposed to the unheroic world that was threatening to engulf him. The theme of degeneration had been fully developed. The very qualities of arrogance, pride and energy, which had led the old families to noble enterprises in the past, worked against them once there were no more noble enterprises to be undertaken. Deprived of a social context in which to operate, they had fallen into idleness, lust and crime. But although Montenegro is portrayed as divorced from his savage and rapacious sons and from the values of the contemporary world, his heroic stature does not come from himself alone. He draws his strength from a whole collective tradition behind him, from the semi-feudal system which unites *hidalgo* and *pueblo*, from a traditional landscape and way of life that has shaped the attitudes of master and serfs alike. *Aguila* and *Romance* had stressed that interdependence between hero and chorus, an interdependence which affirms its strength at the end of *Romance* when Montenegro leads an army of the poor and underprivileged against his own degenerate sons, thus recognizing a loyalty higher than that of caste and birth, which is the loyalty to the collective tradition.

Alberich rightly points out that *Cara de plata* contains no trace of this paternalistic loyalty to his dependants. On the contrary, much of the action turns on Montenegro's stubborn refusal to let anyone cross

his land to get to the fair at Viana del Prior. It is not simply the
character of Montenegro that has changed, but the whole context. In
reality there are no dependants any more and so the whole stress on
this relationship and the collective tradition as the source of the
hidalgo's strength has disappeared. Only Don Galán is left and he only
puts in a brief appearance towards the end of the play. Whereas
previously we saw Montenegro surrounded by old retainers, faithful
servants, bastards proud to acknowledge him as their father and
shrewd tenants willing to supply his bed with succulent wives and
daughters, in *Cara de plata* we see only tenant farmers and cattle
dealers loudly asserting their rights and protesting against traditional
privilege. As Alberich says, Montenegro's behaviour and the whole
social context in which we find him are more like those of a
nineteenth-century landowner than the *hidalgo* of the old school.

However, what makes *Cara de plata* so different from its predecessors is not just a change in the social context or Valle's inability
or unwillingness to re-immerse himself in the sort of patriarchal
society for which he no longer had any sympathy. It would, in any
case, have made very little sense if Valle, having chosen to amplify the
pre-history of his *Comedias*, had consciously introduced anachronistic
elements of peasants being assertive and rebellious in the first part of
the trilogy, only to revert to fatalism and submission in the second and
third parts. The real difference is that the social dimension is actually
given less importance. In the early *Comedias*, Montenegro is presented almost nostalgically as the expression of certain traditional
heroic values and type of social structure. In *Cara de plata*, Valle gives
us an asocial caricature of human behaviour under the whiplash of
pride and lust. The play was of course given its definitive form in the
period of the *esperpentos* and probably when he was contemplating the
works of the *Retablo*. It bears the stamp of the *bululú*'s philosophical
detachment as he watches the frenzied antics of his characters from
stellar distances. The contrast with the former heroic nostalgia could
not be more marked. Once the Abbot of Lantañón becomes involved
in the struggle with Montenegro, the social dimension fades into
insignificance. After this, Montenegro becomes the centre of a conflict
of pride and sexual jealousy with the Abbot on one side and his son on
the other. The demonic figure of Fuso Negro – lechery incarnate – flits
in and out of the action like a demented master of ceremonies. This
character is the one who provides us with an adequately cosmic
perspective and prevents us from seeing the action too much in purely
social or psychological terms.

What has disappeared in *Cara de plata* is the artist's implicit belief that transcendence can be perceived in the manifestations of life, that harmony and stillness can be glimpsed beneath the surface of perpetual movement. Faith in the *existence* of that 'still centre of things' has not been destroyed, but the 'enlace místico' which enables the poet to unite the world of time and change to the infinite has been broken. The characters of *Cara de plata*, like those of the *Retablo*, are portrayed as locked in a movement that is as sterile as it is ceaseless. Like Valle's idea of Satan in *La lámpara*, they are sealed into a self-centred vision and ruled by passions of pride and lust which drive them blindly from one action to another.

Los círculos dantescos son la más trágica representación de la soberbia estéril. Satanás, estéril y soberbio, anhela ser presente en el Todo. Satanás gira eternamente en el Horus del Pleroma, con el ansia y la congoja de hacer desaparecer el antes y el después. Consumirse en el vértigo del vuelo sin detenerse nunca, es la terrible sentencia que cumple el Angel Lucifer. (pp. 31–2)

Sumner Greenfield's analysis implies that Valle is ridiculing the Abbot's (and Montenegro's) belief in the 'ocultas fuerzas satánicas' simply because the caricature does not allow us to take the satanism seriously (*Anatomía*, p. 180). However, if we take *La lámpara* as our guide and definition, the caricaturesque behaviour seems perfectly compatible with Valle's idea of Satan. Satan's plight, he considered, was essentially absurd since pride impelled him to aspire to God's stillness and omniscience while being condemned to remain in the dimension of Time and Movement. Man's situation, in so far as he is the victim of his own self-centred pride and the need to gratify his senses, is no less absurd, when viewed from Valle's extra-temporal vantage point. Back in 1907–8 the pride of Montenegro was seen as heroic and magnificent, a bulwark against the rising tide of institutionalized life. In *Cara de plata*, the conflict of pride between Montenegro and the Abbot is grotesque and absurd, a duel of self-imagined titans portrayed as manipulated puppets. The escalation of the conflict between these men and the frenzied activity it provokes is presented with ironic detachment by Valle-Inclán as comic melodrama.

In fact, it should be pointed out, there are three characters in conflict; the other being Cara de plata who, despite being the eponymous hero, comes a poor third to the other two. The dramatic action consists fundamentally in a three-way contest between Montenegro, the Abbot and Cara de plata. The bones of contention between them are Sabelita, the Abbot's niece and Montenegro's ward, and the question of the public right-of-way over Montenegro's land. These, however, turn out to be simply pawns in the battle of wills in which the real issues are personal pride or frustrated sexual desire. The jealousies, minor tensions and confrontations are skilfully engineered by Valle-Inclán in an escalating pattern which culminates in Montenegro's sacrilegious seizing of the Host from the hands of the Abbot and everyone fleeing in horror from the scene. Once it has been appreciated that pride is mainly responsible for pulling the strings, the dramatic action of *Cara de plata* can be seen to proceed with a measure of rigour and inevitability not to be found in the earlier *Comedias*. The characters are trapped into taking up one intransigent posture after another, sometimes being led into contradictory stances, such as when the Abbot appeals for assistance to those very diabolical forces he claims to oppose. The attitudes become more hysterical, the movement more frenetic, the language more grotesque, as the play spirals to its conclusion.

The demon *soberbia* is behind the situation with which the play opens. The tenant farmers of the surrounding area have gone to law to obtain *by right* the right-of-way which had traditionally been granted them as a concession by Montenegro as lord of the manor. To Alberich this action of demanding something they already enjoyed made very little sense, and indeed this is so, unless we see it as a question of pride determined to turn a privilege into a right. Montenegro's reaction to this, having won the lawsuit, is one of pique; he withdraws the concession and closes the estate to all comers. Attention is next concentrated on Cara de plata with clear but unobtrusive hints of his feelings for Sabelita and the sexual jealousy between father and son. In fact this encounter with his father is possibly a contributory cause of Cara de plata's intransigent attitude towards the Viejo de Cures and his followers over the right-of-way especially if we contrast this with his more magnanimous gesture to the *feriantes* at the beginning of act I, scene 2.[3] Because of his commitment to the cattlemen of Cures that there shall be one law for all, he is also obliged to deny the right-of-way to the Abbot of Lantañón who claims to be on his way to administer the last rites to a dying man. Although he regrets his son's action, pride of caste compels Montenegro to uphold the decision. The chain reaction of pride continues with the Abbot's decision to remove his niece, Sabelita, from Montenegro's house as a reprisal. It is noticeable that

Valle avoids a premature confrontation of the two major antagonists – Montenegro and the Abbot – at this stage, by having the Abbot send his sister, Jeromita, and the sacristan, Blas, to fetch Sabelita.

Perhaps surprisingly, the central theme of self-assertive or self-defensive pride can be seen operating even in the scene of the fair at Viana del Prior. It is unobtrusively immersed in a vivid evocation of the physical atmosphere. Nevertheless, it is pride that tempts Cara de plata to challenge the Abbot again by trying to break the bank in the latter's game of *monte*. This action is not only a deliberate provocation to the Abbot, but also a gesture of defiance to his father who, it must be remembered, had warned him against gambling away the proceeds from the sale of his cows. Incidentally, Valle uses the Penitente at the fair to remind us of Cara de plata's suppressed rivalry with his father. The Penitente's public confessions about killing his father merely by threatening him with an axe are to some extent a prophecy of Cara de plata's actions at the end of the play. After the episode in the gambling den, the struggle of pride between Cara de plata and the Abbot turns on the thirty pieces of gold. These had been fraudulently won by the Abbot with a marked card, but snatched back by Cara de plata's brothers at the end of the gambling scene. At this point the comic tone becomes more pronounced as pride leads the two opponents into contradictory positions. Cara de plata insists on returning the money even though he knows the Abbot cheated to win it and the Abbot refuses to accept it because Cara de plata is offering it. The comic tone is heightened by the presence of Doña Jeromita whose ill-disguised avarice threatens to undermine her brother's proud resolve to leave the money unclaimed on the road. By the middle of act II, Cara de plata has become, for the Abbot and his sister, the Devil incarnate who has come to tempt him to accept his ill-gotten gains.

With the fall of night, at exactly the half-way stage in the play (II, 4), the sexual motif asserts itself. Cara de plata is tempted to abduct Sabelita, but stops short of desecrating the sanctity of the church. The mysterious Fuso Negro, having made only two brief appearances in previous scenes, suddenly takes on new significance from this point in the action as a demonic figure and representation of the unfettered sexual instinct.[4] Fuso, proclaiming the rule of Satan in the world, attempts to rape Sabelita, but is frustrated by the arrival of Montenegro who carries her off on his horse. Fuso's role, though partly functional as a purveyor of information and linker of scenes, is principally to suggest a demonic presence which takes possession of the other principal characters. Fuso pops like a lascivious demon from scene to scene in the second half of the play, commenting on and marginally intervening in the main action, trying, unsuccessfully, to satisfy his lust. He is a grotesquely comic rather than sinister figure, because he is consistently frustrated. This no doubt reflected Valle-Inclán's view of Satan himself as a being condemned to pursue what must eternally elude him. Fuso's failure to rape Sabelita, followed by his failure to buy the services first of the sacristan's daughter and later La Pichona, sets the seal of comedy on the remaining scenes in the play, particularly in the last act.

Fuso's satanic influence turns out to be contagious. His sudden appearance at nightfall marks the eruption of Montenegro's dormant and semi-incestuous passion for his ward, Sabelita. We see him, possessed by demonic power and a touch of madness, demanding not merely her body, but her soul. The calculatedly grotesque melodrama of the dialogue is matched by a brilliant visual conception of the scene: a dramatically lit Montenegro with glass raised aloft, backed by a crucifix on the wall, while Sabelita cowers by the door. The Abbot's own pride is so determined to humble that of his antagonist that he too commends himself to Satan's power. In reply to Montenegro's '¡El Diablo te lleve!', the Abbot exits with the splendidly melodramatic line: 'Por castigar tu soberbia soy capaz de encenderle una vela. ¡Tiembla!' He then pledges himself to the Devil in a grotesque ritual and prepares to commit sacrilege by profaning the sacraments in order to humiliate his rival. That pride is the real issue here is indicated by the fact that the Abbot returns to the original insult to his dignity, which was the denial of the right-of-way, apparently renouncing any attempt to recover his niece. He devises a sacrilegious charade in which the sacristan feigns death and the Abbot demands the right-of-way to administer the last rites. We thus return to the situation which had set the whole conflict in motion. The comic function of Fuso Negro is well illustrated when, in response to the Abbot's invocation to the Devil, he suddenly emerges from nowhere with the words: '¡Presente, mi capitán!' Even Cara de plata, in his turn, is infected by Fuso's pervasive influence since he too, on learning of Sabelita's abduction by Montenegro, calls upon the Devil for protection with the cry: '¡Satanás me ampare!'

In the first two acts, most of the explicit action has been concerned with the clash of wills between Cara de plata and the Abbot. In the final scenes both these characters realize that their antagonism has been merely the shadow of the real conflict that exists between each of them and Montenegro. We have long sensed that the real object of the Abbot's rivalry in pride was the authority behind Cara de plata and that the confrontation with the old man was simply a matter of time. The sexual jealousy between Cara de plata and his father had been deliberately kept in a low key to enhance the dramatic effect of its eruption in the penultimate scene. After its intimation in act I, scene 2, we are given only the oblique references of the Penitente in the fair scene and La Pichona's fortune-telling in the cards at the end of act II.[5] Distant rumblings of this approaching conflict are discernible in Cara de plata's boorish ill temper to La Pichona after his failure to persuade Sabelita to go with him. But, although Pichona hints at the situation in her reading of the cards, Cara de plata himself seems to be hardly aware of it. The news of Montenegro's abduction of Sabelita is the factor which brings these hostilities sharply into focus and steps up the rhetoric and hysteria. The Abbot and Cara de plata converge on Montenegro, the one with a view to vanquishing his pride, the other with a view to killing him with an axe. The conflicts of pride and jealousy merge in the spectacular final scene when for the first time the three protagonists are brought together. Cara de plata stands with his executioner's axe at the ready as the Abbot arrives, attended by a torch-lit procession, dressed in the full regalia of his office and holding the ciborium with the holy sacrament. Montenegro plays off one against the other by requesting permission to confess his sins to the Abbot before dying at the hands of his son. Then, in a charade of false humility, he makes a sacrilegiously unrepentant confession for which he demands the Abbot's equally sacrilegious absolution: '¡Dame la absolución, bonete!' He crowns this action by seizing the ciborium from the Abbot's hands, which causes his son, the Abbot and all his followers to flee from him in holy terror. What we have in *Cara de plata* is a caricature of humanity enslaved by self-centred passions which build from one posture to another to this final apocalyptic charade.

Despite its connections with the other parts of the trilogy, *Cara de plata* stands up reasonably well as a self-contained dramatic structure. Even the stylistic differences noted earlier between the gentler, more lyrical early scenes and the increasingly harsh and expressionistic second half of the play are consistent with the dramatic rhythm of mounting frenzy in the passions and movement of the characters.

This rhythm and dynamism is undoubtedly assisted by Valle's decision to create a continuous flow of action in an unbroken time sequence. The author himself draws attention to the 'angostura de tiempo' in the work and points out that the action begins at dawn and ends at midnight. The dramatic impact has nothing to do with our intellectual appreciation of the passage of time, i.e. the concentration of time in *Cara de plata* does not make it more urgent or pressing. On the contrary, its effect – and indeed its conscious purpose – is to make us less aware of chronology, to blur our sense of time, and make us more aware of the intensity of the action. For time passes mainly in visual terms; the action flows from pale early morning light through the blazing midday sun, to the gentle light of evening, to dusk, and finally to the blackness of night. The seventeen scenes of the play are divided between day and night with act II, scene 4 as the twilight hour and pivotal scene in both a chronological and thematic sense. The passage from light to dark is given some thematic significance in the action. It is, as we have noted, no coincidence that the satanic presence of Fuso Negro begins to spread its influence as darkness falls. In very general terms, the passage from light to dark is paralleled by the intensification of benighted passions and the darkening of the human comedy.

Cara de plata could be described as a 'metaphysical cartoon' in which attitudes and passions are mostly stylized in bold and simple forms. This is a technique entirely consistent with the *esperpento* – obsessive concentration on isolated detail, the part as an expression of the whole, the person presented in terms of a single gesture, item of clothing, etc. The distant metaphysical perspective is what produces the cartoon-like quality. It is a perspective that transcends moral judgement because it stands outside human values. Valle has taken up his dispassionate stance amongst the dead to view the comedy of the living and the cool, uninvolved eye appreciates the comic discrepancy between the way the characters see themselves – as unique beings in control of their own destinies – and their objective reality as prisoners of pride and passion.

10

The grotesque as tragedy: *Retablo de la avaricia, la lujuria y la muerte*

La rosa de papel and *La cabeza del Bautista* were originally published in 1924 in the collection *La novela semanal* under the subtitle 'novelas macabras'. This was later changed to 'melodramas para marionetas' in the 1927 edition of the *Retablo* which also included, in addition to *El embrujado*, two new plays, *Ligazón* and *Sacrilegio*, subtitled 'autos para siluetas'. Overshadowed by the more fashionable *esperpento*, these short plays have attracted relatively little critical attention and Sumner Greenfield's book, for reasons not immediately apparent, gives them no more than a page of passing comment (p. 271). Nonetheless, they are a by no means negligible part of Valle's production and two of them (*La cabeza del Bautista* and *Ligazón*), unlike any of the *esperpentos*, were given public performances during the author's lifetime. One possible contributory factor to this neglect of the *Retablo* may be that it tends to confuse the theory supported by many critics that Valle-Inclán's work culminated in a resounding phase of social and historical commitment. For these plays, written at the same time as the later *esperpentos*, take us out of the social and historical sphere and return us once again to a totally ahistorical view of humanity in the clutches of *Mundo*, *Demonio* and *Carne*.

Certainly there is no evidence to suggest that, as he became more socially conscious, Valle abandoned his former mystical outlook as expressed in *La lámpara maravillosa*. In some respects, it revives with greater force, as demonstrated by the change of emphasis given to the world of the *Comedias bárbaras* in *Cara de plata* (1922). In this play the themes of satanic pride, lust and sacrilege involved in the duel between Montenegro and the Abad de Lantañón override any social or historical considerations. Valle is clearly more interested in moral absolutes than social comment. He presents, just as he does in the *Retablo*, a caricature of the mechanisms of human behaviour. It would appear that he saw no essential contradiction between the new social awareness and his mystical conception of the world, for both remained active in his later work. The dichotomy between concern for social and political realities and an ahistorical view of the world lie at the root of novels like *Tirano Banderas* and those of *El ruedo ibérico*. A man who had been converted to an exclusive social–historical view of humanity would not have gone to such pains to devise a novelistic form which tried to eliminate the notion of linear time. The conviction that all art aspired to a condition of stasis remained with Valle until the end of his life. The artistic problem was how to impose a stasis on kinetic material. In the same year as the revised (and very socially orientated) version of *Luces de Bohemia*, he produced *La rosa de papel* and *La cabeza del Bautista*; in the same year as *El terno del difunto*, *Ligazón*; and *Sacrilegio* in the same year as *La hija del capitán*. It could be argued that even behind the political–social surface of the *esperpento* lay the mystic's vision of a humanity imprisoned in the 'whirligig of Time'. While commenting on his *esperpento* in a lecture at the Ateneo in Burgos (1925), Valle used this phrase: 'No sabemos nada de nada, no conocemos nuestras horas. Estamos perdidos en el terrible pecado del mundo' (see p. 123 for full context). And, indeed, the grotesque social picture of the *esperpentos* is one of human beings 'perdidos en el terrible pecado del mundo', i.e. not something that could be put right simply by a change of government. It is ultimately a vision of men locked in a dantesque circle of time and flux, remote from any perception of the essential oneness and unity of the world which Valle identified with God and Truth. Max Estrella himself uses this analogy when he says: 'Nuestra vida es un círculo dantesco' (*Luces*, scene 11). All Valle's theatre written after 1924 shares this common basis, *esperpentos* and *Retablo* plays alike. Whether the subject matter is historical and political or not, life is shown as the sterile agitation of hollow men blown hither and thither by the winds of circumstance and collective passions. Only at certain times, when death intrudes abruptly into the action, is the ceaseless movement momentarily arrested and the stillness beyond fleetingly glimpsed. Such are the moments of suspended animation that Valle introduces on the deaths of El Jándalo in *La cabeza del Bautista*, of Sócrates Galindo in *Las galas del difunto* and of El Pollo de Cartagena in *La hija del capitán*.

It would naturally be foolish to deny the existence of any differences between the *esperpentos* and the *Retablo* plays. The socio-political emphasis and myth-deflating purpose are evidently more characteristic of the former. Yet, with the possible exception of *Luces de Bohemia*, the artistic distance remains constant across the whole range of his later works. The theory in these later works – if not always the practice – is one of detachment rather than commitment. The artistic ideal of seeing life from the standpoint of the dead, totally removed from the agitation of life in time, emotionally neutral, above laughter and tears is hardly a philosophy of commitment, at least in any narrow social or political sense. This viewpoint, formulated in the Prologue to the second *esperpento*, is in fact best realized in the plays of the *Retablo*. This unflattering spectacle of a humanity dominated by a few primary instincts and dehumanized to marionettes or mere two-dimensional shadows is one in which the grotesque inhibits tragedy and a sense of the macabre inhibits comedy. In *Luces* the interaction of pathos and the grotesque is emotive, because we are aware of tension within Max Estrella and are permitted to a limited extent to identify with his world. In *Los cuernos* the spectacle inhibits tears but not laughter. The *Retablo* plays achieve a blend of contrasting elements which is curiously dispassionate, which makes us aware of incongruities without inviting us to struggle between laughter and tears.

The *Retablo* plays do not deflate social myths like the *esperpentos*. They do, however, implicitly deride certain basic human assumptions, such as the idea that human attitudes have some kind of meaning or authenticity. It must be remembered that it was in 1924 (the year in which the 'melodramas para marionetas' appeared) that Valle wrote to Cipriano Rivas Cherif affirming his belief that human activity was conditioned by forces outside man's control and that 'sólo el orgullo del hombre le hace suponer que es un animal pensante' (see p. 45 for full context). The *Retablo* plays and *Cara de plata* seem to have been written with this idea in mind. Man as an 'animal pensante' is ridiculed in various ways. Primarily, he is shown as a creature dominated by instinctive lust and avarice or, more precisely, the victim of a tug-of-war struggle between the two. On a different level he is the puppet of social conditioning and these attitudes are often ironically contrasted with the biological conditioning. This is particularly evident in *La rosa de papel* where we have an incongruous juxtaposition of ritual observances in matters of religion and morality with instinctive avarice and lust. Finally, Valle questions the concept of 'authenticity' in human attitudes by showing, as he does in *Sacrilegio*, external rhetoric influencing thought and feigned attitudes developing into inner convictions. This latter question is evidently one which preoccupied Valle in his later plays. It is crucial to the understanding of *Luces de Bohemia* in which Max's clowning and self-deprecation are defences against the temptation to assume inauthentic postures. Indeed, it is the problem of authenticity or Valle-Inclán's suspicion of its non-existence or unattainability that lies behind his rejection of the tragic hero.

It is difficult to agree with Professor Brooks's view that in the *Retablo* 'the author has returned to the portrayal of people who have control over their own destiny, who can choose the path they will follow' (Brooks, p. 87). More so than in the early *Comedias bárbaras* or in *Divinas palabras*, collective instincts are seen to be in control. The coarse strings that manipulate human behaviour are made aggressively visible and obvious. In fact the *Retablo* draws our attention more to the movement of the strings than to the dangling marionettes. Inevitably critics have been led to speculate on the possible relationship between the themes of lust, greed and death in the *Retablo.* In both *La rosa de papel* and *La cabeza del Bautista* (written at roughly the same time) there seems to be a causal link between the presence of death and the erotic urge which is then able to supplant the passion of greed or avarice. Bermejo has no hesitation in offering the psychoanalytical explanation of necrophilia for the transformations we see taking place in Julepe and La Pepona at the end of these two plays (p. 268). Without wishing to deny the generally accepted link between death and sexual desire – after all, *Sonata de otoño* is evidence enough to show that Valle was aware of such refinements – the explanation seems perhaps a little too clinical. A reference to the connection between *muerte* and *lujuria* in fact crops up in the rather unlikely context of *La media noche* (chapter 33):

Por la guerra es eterna el alma de los pueblos. La lujuria creadora se aviva por ella, como la antorcha en el viento que la quiere apagar. Sólo la amenaza de morir perpetúa las formas terrenales, sólo la muerte hace al mundo divino. Si en las claras entrañas de los cristales no se engendran hijos es por su ilusión de eternidad, y las entrañas de la mujer son fecundas porque son mortales. Los monstruos gigantescos que rugieron ante la caverna del adamita, y fueron amenaza para todos los seres vivos, perecieron porque la lujuria se enfrió en ellos. Como eran llenos de fuerza y de dominio, estaban libres del terror de la muerte, y ninguna voz de la naturaleza pudo advertirles que no eran eternos. La muerte es la divina causalidad del mundo. ¡Y qué mística iniciación de esta verdad tan vieja se desvela en la guerra! Aquella ciega voluntad genesíaca que arrastra a los héroes de la tragedia antigua, ruge en las batallas. (pp. 151–2)

The first point to be made about this passage is its mystical, decidedly unclinical tone, akin to that of *La lámpara maravillosa*, and its tendency to see human behaviour in broad, impressionistic patterns. The second point is that the link between death and the sexual drive is here seen as a natural and necessary phenomenon. *Lujuria* is considered a force for good when associated with the 'idea creadora', when it is a manifestation of the primitive instinct to perpetuate the species in the face of death and destruction. It must be admitted that the description hardly seems appropriate to the *lujuria* of the *Retablo*. Yet it is not without usefulness, for what the *Retablo* shows is the degeneration of the instinct, *lujuria* as a simple enslavement of the senses in which the sensual pleasure has become detached from the 'idea creadora'. This 'lujuria estéril' is described in *La lámpara maravillosa* as one of the 'enigmas del mal': 'La carne es el pecado nefando, aquel goce sensual donde se relaja y profana la Idea Creadora. Es la lujuria estéril que no perpetúa la vida en la entraña de la mujer con el sagrado semen: el Incubo, Sodoma y Onan. Su alegoría es la serpiente enroscada al árbol de la vida: su enigma, el Futuro' (p. 93). What I believe Valle is stressing in the lustful antics of Julepe in *La rosa de papel* and of Pepona in *La cabeza del Bautista* is precisely this element of *sterility* rather than the erotic or necrophilic overtones.

How does the other principal theme of *avaricia* fit into all this? Guerrero Zamora sees this as the element which devalues or debases the tragic potential of the love–death motif, in other words, *avaricia* is the distorting mirror in which the human tragedy appears as a grotesque charade (p. 188). The theory is attractive but one could object that the nature of that 'love' – the 'lujuria estéril' of the characters – is quite sufficient in itself to debase the tragedy. It could hardly be claimed that 'love' is 'contaminated' or 'undermined' by greed in these plays. Sex and greed are shown in conflict, but on the same moral level. 'Love' – such as it is – is not presented as more 'ideal' or 'tragic' – even potentially – than its rival passion. In fact, in both *La rosa de papel* and *La cabeza del Bautista* greed is vanquished by erotic passion, though without any suggestion that this constitutes a moral victory. Rather then greed debasing love, lust and greed jointly debase the tragic potential in life and death. The situation of *La rosa de papel* provides a graphic illustration of this when the Encamada's body is the dramatic focus for all the avarice-inspired frenzy going on around it.

This is perhaps as far as one can – and should – go on the theoretical side. Valle-Inclán's view of the world stands or falls more by its theatrical impact than by its intellectual coherence and, theatrically, the *Retablo* plays contain more interesting features than they have hitherto been given credit for. One point that has been insufficiently stressed is that Valle was experimenting with a different dramatic form. All these short plays are based on a *single* stage image. The action of *La cabeza del Bautista* takes place exclusively in a café, of *La rosa de papel* in a smithy, of *Ligazón* in front of an inn and of *Sacrilegio* in a cave. The multiple-scene principle which Valle continued to use even in the later *esperpentos* has been abandoned. The experimentation with more condensed dramatic forms from about 1924 seems to suggest that Valle was seeking more practical alternatives to the commercial theatre, rather than contenting himself with expression in the printed text alone. The adjustment of the action of a play – even a short play – to a single setting was a considerable concession to practicality in Valle-Inclán, a fact which did not go unnoticed when *La cabeza del Bautista* was produced in Madrid in October, 1924 and in Barcelona later the same year. In his review, Rivas Cherif makes the point that it is a play written with performance in mind and that it is 'un drama breve en el que están rigurosamente observadas las reglas y unidades más estrictas' (*España*, 29 March 1924). The unity of time had never given Valle much trouble. Unity of place, however, was a new departure for one who had always claimed that the essence of drama lay in its dynamic succession of scenes of differing tone and tempo.

In previous work the different settings had provided the tonal variations in dialogue and the rhythmic shape of the piece. Working within the limitations of the unities compelled Valle to find alternative means to achieve these ends. His modified technique in the *Retablo* consists of creating a rhythmic dramatic structure within a static framework. Changes of tone and pace are engineered in *La rosa de papel*, *La cabeza del Bautista* and *Ligazón* by the exit and re-entry of a central character. In *Sacrilegio* there is variation between planes of action, between foreground and background action and different groups of characters. Carefully devised and controlled images are created by the posture or gesture of characters, by the manipulation of stage properties or by effects of light and shade in *Ligazón* and *Sacrilegio*. Essentially, the main emphases on rhythm, tone and visual impact have not changed but, in some ways, the method of achieving these things has become more subtle and complex.

MELODRAMAS PARA MARIONETAS: 'LA ROSA DE
PAPEL' AND 'LA CABEZA DEL BAUTISTA'

It should be remembered that most of the plays after 1920 were probably written with puppet performance in mind. It therefore seems highly probable that the subtitle 'melodrama para marionetas' for *La rosa* and *La cabeza* was intended to be taken literally, although this does not exclude the possibility of performance by actors imitating the antics of marionettes. Their purpose was not primarily to be parodies of bourgeois melodrama, as has sometimes been suggested. The melodrama and the puppet convention, the mechanical gestures and rhetorical expression of emotion, the abrupt transitions from one attitude to another reflect a general vision of humanity as totally manipulated by external stimuli.

Of the two 'melodramas para marionetas', *La rosa de papel* is the more underrated and was not given its first performance until José Luis Alonso's production in 1967. The dramatic ingredients of *La rosa* are similar to those of *Divinas palabras* in that the humour rests on a sense of ironic contrast between what we might term socially conditioned attitudes and instinctive behaviour. This means that although the characters are constantly expressing conventional sentiments or performing certain social rituals, the real motivations are forces of collective instinct. There is no reason to assume that such attitudes are lacking in sincerity or conviction, as David Bary does when he writes: 'llevan a cabo las acciones rituales necesarias para cada momento de la vida, pero lo hacen sin convicción, mecánicamente, un poco como actores ya cansados de sus papeles en una comedia de mucho éxito que lleva meses en las tablas' (p. 223). The rituals are merely ingrained customs which they do not question, carried out with familiarity but without contempt. As in *Divinas palabras*, Valle is not depicting religious or moral 'hypocrisy', since the incongruity between attitudes and basic motive goes totally unperceived by the characters themselves.

The 'social' attitudes I have mentioned do not only refer to matters of religious or moral observance. They also embrace the anti-religious postures of the blacksmith Simeón Julepe who, in his rejection of conventional standards, is not unlike Séptimo Miau in *Divinas palabras*. Julepe is a small-town tavern politician whose devotion to the working-class movement is second only to his love of *aguardiente de anís*. He mouths atheistic philosophy ('¡Solamente existe la nada! No asustarse, vecinos, es el credo moderno') and the formulas of his political church ('El trabajo regenera al hombre'). His church is the local Casa del Pueblo and the choral society, Orfeón Los Amigos, which, he says, will sing the Marseillaise at his wife's funeral.

Julepe's views contrast sharply with those of his wife who lives by the principles and rituals of the Church. As the play opens we see her dying in her bed and calling for the last rites, while a drunken Simeón works with callous indifference at the anvil. In order to prevent him leaving her without the consolation of religion, she reveals a hoard of 7,000 *reales* wrapped up in a bundle of rags. The sight of money causes an abrupt change of gear in Simeón from callous boor to dutiful husband and respecter of religion ('yo conozco mis deberes', '. . . me sobra educación', 'yo respeto todos los fanatismos') and he goes off to fetch the priest. As we shall see, the abrupt switches of attitude are characteristic of the 'melodramas' and Simeón undergoes several transformations in the course of the play. In this way Valle contrasts the insubstantiality of social attitudes with the basic greed that animates him. But this does not only apply to Julepe. His wife (referred to throughout as 'La Encamada') reveals similar incongruities. Peasant avarice is sharply juxtaposed with her need for religious ritual. Her revelation about the hoard is prompted by her desire to persuade Julepe to fetch 'los Divinos', but, having achieved this, she then hides the money to prevent Julepe or anyone else from spending it.

With Julepe out of the way, two neighbourhood gossips, Pepa Mus and Juana Dis, enter and start to discuss La Encamada's state of preparedness for the next world. Their delightfully matter-of-fact dialogue reveals the same duality, a colourful blend of ritual observance and hard economics: 'if you're going to die, don't go wasting your money on doctors' bills; you'd be better off spending a "duro" on a mass to San Blas. On the other hand, if you don't call the doctor, he might refuse to sign the death certificate, in which case you get legal complications and it would work out more expensive in the long run!' After these reflections, Julepe returns, drunker than ever, and instantly suspects the neighbours of stealing the money. The passion of greed now rages in comic and macabre fashion round the death bed as Julepe ransacks the bedclothes and mattress while his wife lies 'in extremis'. Even La Encamada's death causes only a momentary hiatus in the desperate search. The scene could easily have degenerated into simple black farce, but Valle again reminds us of the essential contradiction at the heart of the play. When La Musa realizes that the wife is dead, she raises her hand in a declamatory pose and instructs Julepe to kneel and remove his cap. There is a brief suspension of the frenzied search for the money while the actors compose a suitably solemn tableau, only to continue a moment later with renewed vigour. Even while their lives are being threatened, La Musa and La Disa are still very conscious of the social rituals, exclaiming as they face Julepe's loaded revolver, 'iNo me quites la devoción de rezarle por el alma de la difunta!' or commenting that it is a bad example for the children and that the body should have its nightshirt pulled over its bottom. The situation is resolved by one of the children ('voz de rata') revealing the whereabouts of the money. With greed satisfied, Julepe instantly switches to an attitude of contrite sentimentality and heaps rhetorical praise on to his departed spouse: 'Floriana, angel ejemplar, no tengo lágrimas para llorar tu irreparable pérdida.' And, casting his eyes heavenwards, exits clutching his bundle to arrange the funeral.

The following scene in which more and more neighbours file in to pay their last respects and prepare the corpse for burial is, like the brief dialogue between La Musa and La Disa earlier on, essentially a collective one. It is the kind of scene that Valle does supremely well, in which the sentiments are rooted in the total life of the community rather than in the attitudes of individuals. The dramatic chemistry is provided by the same opposition of social ritual and instinctive avarice. The whole scene is a series of ritual actions in the ceremonial of death: the 'planto', the sprinkling with holy water, the farewell kiss from the children, the laying-out, the washing and dressing of the corpse in its Sunday best, the lighting of candles and prayers for the soul of the departed – all this accompanied by ritualistic phrases such as 'mujer de su casa', 'criaturas no saben el bien que se pierden', etc. Into this pattern are woven the obsessions with money and possessions, the comments on the finery adorning the body and on the hoard of money saved by the deceased, the amount of which becomes exaggerated during the course of the scene from 7,000 reales to 20,000 and finally to 'dos mil pesos'.

The ritual beautifying and decking-out of the corpse also has an important dramatic function since it has the direct result of arousing Julepe's erotic passion in the final scene. What significance did Valle attach to this sexual arousal? David Bary's theory is that the transformation of the body, with all its *mal gusto*, by the neighbours affords Simeón an insight into a dimension of life beyond the senses and

beyond Good and Evil. This he associates with the 'cuarta dimensión' referred to by Bakunín in *Baza de espadas* and with the
'inaccesible categoría estética' alluded to in one of the *acotaciones* of *La
rosa*. Bary appears to refer to a purely aesthetic intuition provoked by
objects or phenomena which have no beauty in themselves. Indeed,
the contrary would seem to be the case, since the examples he gives, in
addition to the tawdry trimmings adorning the Encamada, are the
sentimental letter at the end of *Las galas* and the *romance de ciego* at the
end of *Los cuernos*. (It is difficult to see how Valle concedes any power
of positive aesthetic inspiration to these latter examples, incidentally.) This insight, it is argued, operates a transformation in Julepe. It
gives him a new – though, admittedly, belated – interest in his wife
and a new sincerity of attitude. Bary sums up the play as 'Julepe o lo
que puede la inaccesible categoría estética de Don Ramón del Valle-
Inclán'. There are cases in Valle's later plays where a character is
given a fleeting glimpse into an order of reality beyond the barrier of
the senses, time and space. I have argued that Mari-Gaila in *Divinas
palabras* is an example of this. The 'revelation' afforded to Julepe,
however, is of a different order. What he calls his 'visión celeste' is no
more than an erotic titillation of silk stockings and a paper rose. In no
way does it transcend the limits of time or mere sensuality. He
glimpses no 'beyond'. What he sees is a comic parody of a 'celestial
vision', expressed in terms of a cabaret or music-hall star ('Dispuesta
pareces para salir a un espectáculo', '. . . una cupletista de mérito',
'. . . una estrella de la Perla'). What moves Julepe is a satanic *lujuria*
and what Valle is stressing is the sterility of this passion, symbolized in
the tawdry artificiality of a red paper rose clutched between the
fingers of a dead woman.

Bary bases his theory on the following *acotación*:

La difunta, en el féretro de esterillas doradas, tiene una desolación de figura
de cera, un acento popular y dramático. La pañoleta floreada ceñida al
busto, las cejas atirantadas por el peinado, las manos con la rosa de papel
saliendo de los vuelillos blancos, el terrible charol de las botas, promueven un
desacorde cruel y patético, acaso una inaccesible categoría estética. (p. 68)

His interpretation is that it is the clash between these various
adornments (hands holding paper rose, patent leather boots, etc.)
that produces the 'desacorde cruel y patético' which constitutes the
'inaccesible categoría estética'. If instead we take the 'desacorde' to
exist not in the discordant combination of the items themselves but
between all these things jointly and the 'desolación de figura de cera'

of the body they adorn, then we obtain a different reading of the passage. In this case the 'inaccesible categoría estética' would refer to the incongruous juxtaposition of the stark fact of death and the grotesque indignities to which it is subjected or, to put it in more general terms closely associated with the *esperpento*, the *desajuste* between the tragedy of life and the absurdity of those who act it out. This is why Valle speaks of a 'desacorde' and why it is termed both 'cruel' and 'pathetic'. The discord, in fact, could justifiably be taken to refer to the tension between the constant presence of death in the play and the grotesque charade that surrounds it. Death is in turn profaned, abused, dressed up and finally made an object of erotic desire.

The most debatable point of Bary's argument is the claim that Julepe's language switches from false rhetoric to sincere and spontaneous discourse. It is true that lust supplants avarice, but there seems no good reason to attribute greater or lesser sincerity to one or the other. It is simply the last of a series of changes we observe in Julepe during the course of the play as he goes from callous indifference, to extravagant sentimentality, to violence inspired by frustrated greed and finally to erotic frenzy. There is little to suggest that any one attitude is more 'authentic' or 'sincere' than another. In fact, Valle's purpose is to depict a character going through a series of marionette-like postures as dictated by different external stimuli, revealing in this process the vacuousness of human attitudes.

The distanced viewpoint 'desde la otra ribera' exaggerates the external manifestations of feeling (if one can talk of 'feeling' in this context); it also emphasizes the abruptness of the transitions from one set of stimuli to another. All reactions and emotions are in fact seen as either mechanical responses or as attitudes which the characters strike. Julepe, on seeing the neighbours prying in his house, 'da una zapateta . . . y se arranca los pelos'. The voice of Pepiña de Mus, on discovering that La Encamada has died, is described as 'declamatoria' and she accompanies her command for Julepe to remove his cap and kneel with a histrionic gesture of 'un brazo en el aire, como alón desplumado'. Julepe's reaction to the rediscovery of the cash is expressed in cartoon terms as he races up the stairs and scatters the children like ninepins ('se lanza a la escalera y sube en dos trancos, desbaratando el retablo de monigotes'). His descent is no less precipitated and puppet-like ('Julepe se tira por la escalera con los brazos en aspa y cae a los pies de la difunta'). All Julepe's reactions and vocabulary are made calculatedly melodramatic and rhetorical. He brandishes his pistol like a villain of the silent screen 'con gozo y rabia de peliculero melodramático' and, once greed is appeased, he declaims his wife's praises with 'tremo afectado y patético'. There is no need to go on multiplying examples. Valle-Inclán establishes an unmistakable tone and style of performance which removes all possibility of identifying with the characters and their emotions as befits a 'melodrama for marionettes'.

The result is undoubtedly a comic one. Commentators have been somewhat reticent about the humour of Valle's later plays since, according to the canon of Don Estrafalario, laughter proceeds from emotional involvement and here we are supposed to be in a realm 'above laughter and tears'. Perhaps one should begin by questioning Valle's assertion in the Prologue to *Los cuernos* that we laugh or cry only at the things with which we can identify. While it may be true that pity involves identification, is this equally true of laughter? In his analysis of humour in the Theatre of the Absurd, Martin Esslin appears to lean in two directions at once. On the one hand he argues that the laughter we experience when watching Absurdist drama is the result of non-identification, that is when we laugh at a film of a character slipping on a banana skin we do not identify with the pain of the fall: 'As the incomprehensibility of the motives and the often unexplained and mysterious nature of the characters' actions in the Theatre of the Absurd *effectively prevent identification*, such theatre is a comic theatre in spite of the fact that its subject matter is sombre violent and bitter' (italics mine) (Esslin, p. 401). However, he also declares that laughter comes from recognition of experiences that we associate with our own lives or with our sense of human life in general. The spectator, he claims, is made to recognize his predicament and that 'by seeing his anxieties formulated, he can liberate himself from them'. 'This', he adds 'is the nature of all gallows humour and *humour noir* of world literature of which the Theatre of the Absurd is the latest example' (p. 404). There is no real contradiction here. It is simply that the kind of humour he is describing springs simultaneously from non-identification with the particular characters and actions and from recognition of – and hence a measure of identification with – the general predicament depicted. The case is similar in most of the later Valle-Inclán theatre; we remain detached from the characters themselves but there is an important element of recognition. Despite Valle's remarks in *Los cuernos*, the removal of empathy does tend to stimulate a comic response in *La rosa de papel*. Even in *Los cuernos* itself theory and practice are at variance in that the humour stems largely from the 'mechanization' of behaviour, that is from detachment not involvement. In the *Retablo*, particularly in the 'melodramas', Valle shows human life approximating to a mechanism, but he also intends the audience to feel that mechanism as applicable to themselves. In *La rosa de papel* La Encamada's body serves as a constant reminder of our mortal situation. Its sobering presence at the hub of the action modifies our reactions to the antics that surround it and makes us see the puppet attitudes as a representation of our own.

La cabeza del Bautista appears to have some connection with the *esperpentos* in so far as Valle had a literary model in mind when he wrote the play. The title clearly links it to the story of Herod, Salome and John the Baptist. Yet, unlike other archetypal targets of the *esperpento*, these have nothing to do with Spain or Spanish society, nor do they enshrine any heroic myth of honour or patriotism. The plot of *La cabeza* contains few parallels with either the Bible version or with Oscar Wilde's one-act play *Salomé* (1905), sometimes quoted as inspiration for the work. Don Igi el gachupín is a caricature of an *indiano* who after making his fortune in Mexico, returns to his native village in Galicia together with his mistress, La Pepona. Valle devises a deliberately elaborate and melodramatic plot, evidently a parody of the popular *folletín*. A ghost from Don Igi's past arrives in the form of his son, El Jándalo, who reveals his intention to blackmail the old man for the murder of his former wife. La Pepona and Don Igi plan the murder of El Jándalo. La Pepona pretends to seduce him while Don Igi stabs him in the back. As she feels the young man's lips grow cold on hers, La Pepona's dormant sexuality is aroused and she swears she will be buried with El Jándalo in the garden. Don Igi's final comment is '¡mejor me fuera haberlo transigido con plata!' In the Bible story (and in Wilde's play) it is Herodias who wishes to have John the Baptist killed for declaring her marriage to Herod unlawful. La Pepona, however, (who is an amalgam of Herodias and Salome) is motivated by greed because she sees El Jándalo's blackmail as a threat to her security. Unlike Herod, who has to be trapped into consenting to the execution, Don Igi has obvious motives for wishing to rid himself of El Jándalo. It is possible that the association of death and eroticism in the Wilde play might have attracted Valle's interest. The kiss on the dead man's lips is an element common to both plays which lends some substance to this theory. *Salomé* presents an aesthete's view of the erotic associations of death in terms of the Baptist's ivory-like pallor, his jet-black hair and red mouth. It is possible that Valle's intention was to parody this view, using the passion of avarice (not present in the original) as the element which debases the tragedy. On the whole, however, *La cabeza* is able to stand on its own without any reference to Wilde's 'archetypal' version. The archetypal literary model has no essential function in this play, which can be read as a savage pantomime of lust, avarice and death, based on an aspect of Galician life.

In comparison with *La rosa de papel*, *La cabeza del Bautista* is more anchored to a specific situation with antecedents before the action of the play. Much of the early dialogue therefore is taken up with plot elucidation of such questions as who El Jándalo is and why he has suddenly appeared in a remote Galician town. The play thus lacks the internal tensions and ironies that Valle was able to introduce in the less encumbered dialogue of *La rosa*. Potential for developing the play along these lines existed had Valle wished to do so. One could for example imagine ironic juxtapositions between Don Igi's selfish greed and his patriotic utterances ('Yo en todas partes fanaticé por mi patria') or his pretensions to being a free-thinking liberal and social benefactor (p. 162). But these ironies are not developed. Instead Valle concentrates on the tug-of-war between greed and the sexual instinct operating in each of the principal characters. It would of course be inappropriate to speak of 'psychological conflict', given Valle's expressionistic approach to the question. The oscillation of motive between naked greed and unfettered lust is too blatant and stylized to admit of this interpretation. What interests Valle is the irony of how these passions mutually frustrate one another.

For greed and lust are shown as irreconcilable passions. In La Pepona, around whom the play revolves, greed has replaced sexual attraction as the basis for her relationship with Don Igi. On the appearance of El Jándalo, the sexual instinct begins to revive in her as she fixes him with a sex-hungry gaze while he converses with Don Igi: 'Había sentido el magnetismo de los ojos de la mujerona, fosforecidos bajo el junto entrecejo. La Pepa le sonrió, pasándose la lengua por los labios, y el respondió con un gesto obsceno' (p. 163). Greed takes over once again when it becomes apparent that El Jándalo's blackmail is about to threaten her living standards. It is she in fact who persuades Don Igi to stab El Jándalo in the back while she feigns love to him. In the act of feigning, Pepona's sexual feelings are aroused. Even before

Don Igi strikes the fatal blow it is clear that Pepona's charade is beginning to carry her away and, when El Jándalo dies in her arms, the carnal instinct triumphs over greed. This ironic reversal of Pepona being hoisted by her own petard, of greed and avarice frustrating the satisfaction of lust, constitutes the basic structure of the play.

The same general pattern of attempting – unsuccessfully – to satisfy the demands of conflicting passions is repeated in the other two protagonists. Don Igi's consuming avarice is balanced by his sexual dependence on Pepona. After his fears of losing his money to El Jándalo have been allayed, he begs Pepona for a 'besito' which she playfully denies him. He has all the conflicting interests of a miser with a mistress to keep. As in the case of Pepona the defence of avarice leads to the frustration of lust. It is reported that Don Igi has killed his former wife for her money, with the money he has 'bought' his mistress and then finally loses his mistress through avarice. There is a measure of ironic retribution in Don Igi's last line of '¡mejor me fuera haberlo transigido con plata!' The attempt to combine greed with sex proves in El Jándalo's case to be fatal. The casual seduction he carries out, almost in passing, on his way into the café momentarily distracts him from the serious business of blackmail and results in his downfall. The sexual bait laid by avarice lures him to his death. The two irreconcilable passions are graphically caught in the image of El Jándalo making love to Pepona and simultaneously extracting money from Don Igi. He declares that he will even modify his demands for money as he proposes to take the woman in lieu of cash:

EL JANDALO: Pensaba pedirle a usted mucho más, pero en vista de que me llevo a esta niña, lo dejo en ese pico.
DON IGI: ¿A quién te llevas?
EL JANDALO: A esta morena.
DON IGI: Dale tú la respuesta que merece, Pepita.
LA PEPONA: Siempre se desagera.
EL JANDALO: Don Igi, ándele por la plata y no más se preocupe por esta chinita. Es el trato que yo me la lleve. Una mujer como ésta a usted no le conviene. (p. 181)

This three-cornered dialogue in the scene leading up to El Jándalo's murder ties up the themes of lust, greed and death in a single dramatic knot in much the same way as love, religion and death are brought to their climax in *Sonata de otoño*.

La cabeza del Bautista has a markedly less marionette-like quality than *La rosa de papel*, particularly in the more gradual and motivated transitions from one attitude to another and in the action–reaction pattern of much of the dialogue. The critic Fernández Almagro, who was present at the *estreno*, saw this as a literary virtue, claiming that the characters represent 'mejor que en el otro [*La rosa de papel*] las formas del ser vivo' and that they do not utter a word 'en que no aflore una profunda – y horripilante, por cierto – verdad humana' (p. 203). On the other hand a contemporary producer, José Luis Alonso, remarks in his notes on the 1967 production that the mental processes and reactions of the characters are not sufficiently graded to put the play into a realist convention: 'Creo, así mismo, que de las tres, es la menos interesante. Tal vez por ser la más convencional. Con su anécdota y su argumento cerrado, no tiene, sin embargo, los procesos y las reacciones de los personajes bien graduados. Está llena de baches en que los actores pierden pie a menudo' (p. 28). It is interesting to note that the small step towards conventional realism had constituted a literary virtue for the first critic and a dramatic defect for the second, because it had not gone far enough. *La cabeza del Bautista* is perhaps in danger of falling between the two dramatic conventions of expressionism and psychological realism. By falling short of a whole-hearted use of the puppet convention it fails to exploit its full thematic and theatrical possibilities.

AUTOS PARA SILUETAS: 'SACRILEGIO' AND 'LIGAZÓN'

Guerrero Zamora, in one of the best assessments of Valle-Inclán's theatre, suggests that the *autos para siluetas* are distinguished by two main characteristics: first, that they are concerned with the execution of justice, and secondly, that, like the original *autos sacramentales*, they have a ritualistic form and purpose. It is true that sentence is duly carried out on the bandit in *Sacrilegio* and on the rich Jew in *Ligazón*. However the nature of the 'justice' meted out is problematical to say the least and impugns those who execute it as much as those who receive it. In fact, such concepts as justice and the rights and wrongs of individual cases do not get us very far in the investigation of Valle's moral universe which, as I pointed out earlier, is more concerned with absolutes than with matters of conscience or individual choice. The point that Guerrero Zamora makes about the ritualistic aspects of the *autos*, however, is extremely suggestive. In addition to the earthbound charade of lust and avarice, the *autos* convey a sense of ambient mystery enveloping the purely human level. Both plays, in fact, centre round a ritual act: the confession in *Sacrilegio* and the blood bond in *Ligazón*. In the first case it is a parody of a sacrament carried out by a false priest and, in the second, a satanic rite of witchcraft. The settings of both *autos* are designed to suggest by evocative lighting, reflections in water, etc. a supernatural order of reality above the base comedy of human existence.

Sacrilegio is one of the few Valle-Inclán plays that can be ascribed to a specific source. Harold L. Boudreau has convincingly shown that Valle borrowed the framework of the action and most of the characters from Julián de Zugasti's ten-volume work, *El bandolerismo: estudio social y memorias históricas* (Madrid, 1876–80). The source material is to be found in the final volume in an episode entitled 'La confesión de Lechuga' (pp. 294–311). This episode describes a typical case of revenge or 'ajuste de cuentas' between a group of bandits in Sierra Morena and one of their number who is accused of betrayal. For full details of Zugasti's narrative and the modifications introduced by Valle-Inclán in *Sacrilegio*, I refer the reader to Boudreau's article. Briefly, it may be said that in Zugasti's account, the accused prisoner ('Lechuga') asks for confession before he is killed and, hoping to extract information by this method, the bandits tonsure one of their band to act as priest. Lechuga confesses with such sincerity and emotion, however, that all the bandits who hear him are deeply moved and El Maruso, the leader of the band, resolves to abandon his life of crime. Later, Lechuga is killed by one of the guards not present at the confession and El Maruso is shot down by the Civil Guard. But Zugasti's main point is the moral impact of the confession on the other bandits or, in Boudreau's phrase, 'evil transformed into good through sacrilege'.

Valle-Inclán reduces Zugasti's narrative to a single episode and setting. The moralizing tone and intention of the original is set aside and one of the principal elements of the plot is omitted. This is the suspected involvement of Lechuga in the kidnapping of El Maruso's son, which constitutes the main reason for staging the confession. Valle is deliberately vague on this point. All we know is that the prisoner ('El Sordo de Triana') is accused of having sold information to the authorities. El Sordo makes two last requests: to be allowed to sleep with his wife and confess to a priest. As in the original version, the bandits accede to the second request to extract the information they require and prepare one of the gang, El Padre Veritas, for the role of priest. As the 'confession' is about to take place, the look-out at the mouth of the cave warns the bandits of the approach of three horsemen and the bandits leave. El Padre Veritas, on seeing his priest's image reflected in a deep pool of water, is possessed with religious awe and is appalled by the 'eternal responsibility' of the sacrilegious act he is about to perform. It may be assumed that for El Sordo too the confession is at first a device, in his case a desperate last effort to regain his freedom, as well as the result of some residual religious scruples, since he repeatedly tries to persuade the 'priest' to release his bonds. Gradually, however, the comedy assumes real urgency and the words which Padre Veritas speaks in his role as confessor and those which El Sordo replies in his role as penitent take over and transform the pretence into reality. Padre Veritas tries to fulfil his priestly mission before the other bandits return. When they do, they are astonished to find El Sordo in the full flood of his confession. At first they interject ironic laughter and asides but as the tale of rape and murder unfolds they are gradually drawn into the atmosphere of solemn religious awe and 'la tropa de caballistas, con pasmo, recalca su bulto sobre el espejo de la charca, avanza con inadvertido movimiento sonámbulo'. El Sordo, carried along by the tidal wave of his own words, is no longer thinking of his personal freedom: 'Esos niños están en darme mulé, padre reverendo. Me suena que los grandes arrepentidos, para ser más edificantes, perdonan a sus enemistades.' Padre Veritas is by now so caught up in the power of El Sordo's emotion that he steps out of his assumed character to exclaim: 'Es la veri, Frasquito. ¡En todos los ejemplos de los misioneros!' El Sordo reaches a frenzied climax in his appeal for absolution and forgiveness at the height of which the captain of the band raises his shotgun and shoots him dead with the words 'Si no le sello la boca, nos gana la entraña ese tunante.' The emotive contagion of words, the intuitive communication of anguish and despair through tone, is ironically dispelled in a cloud of gunsmoke.

What attracted Valle-Inclán to this episode? Boudreau suggests that his interest was purely aesthetic and was stimulated by the 'shocking nature' of the material and its 'dramatic vitality'. He adds that he chose to emphasize the sacrilegious aspect of the action 'by stressing the sexual, adding diabolic overtones, excising the moral good resulting from the sacrilege and treating the matter with much greater levity than did Zugasti'. He supports this argument by quoting other works in which sex and religion are juxtaposed, e.g. the

Sonatas and *Flor de santidad*. However, it must be pointed out that sex does not play a vitally important part in *Sacrilegio*. El Sordo's request to 'dormir con la parienta' is quickly dismissed by the bandits and not developed after the first two pages of dialogue. Moreover, the sacrilege does not consist in the association of sex and religion in this case. It consists in the profane ends to which a sacred ritual is employed, in making a charade of a religious sacrament. Of course, it could still be argued that the subject's attraction for Valle was largely an aesthetic one, simply because the theme of sacrilege provided a strong dramatic experience. Boudreau's contention is that Valle took and intensified from his source the contrast of joke and sacrament and that the black comedy resulting from this opposition was as far as his intentions went. This, in my view, does not do justice to the complexity of the work. If we look at a similar example of sacrilege in the last act of *Cara de plata* in which the Abad de Lantañón stages a feigned death and false religious sacraments in order to force a passage through Montenegro's estate and humiliate his rival, we can see that there is a moral intention as well as a dramatic one. In that case the point is to illustrate, in a burlesque epic style, a clash of one obsessive pride against another. The point at issue in *Sacrilegio* may not be one of the 'yo satánico' or of 'soberbia estéril', but the possibility of Valle having some kind of moral interest in the theme merits further investigation.

What Boudreau's analysis neglects to mention is that the joke or charade ends up by convincing those who are taking part in it. The adopted roles begin to take possession of the two characters involved and supplant the original motives for assuming the roles. It is precisely this ambiguous area between acting a part and living it, this capacity of ritual to compel belief and influence men's thoughts, that interested Valle-Inclán in this episode. The whole play turns on this change of attitude in Padre Veritas and El Sordo. The temporary absence of the bandits in fact has little point unless it is seen as a device to allow Padre Veritas and El Sordo to reveal changes in themselves that would not have appeared or would have been interpreted differently if the bandits had been present. At the beginning of the confession scene, El Sordo is playing to the gallery, 'mantenido en el supuesto de que los compadres se hallan en la cueva'. He is immediately told by Padre Veritas that they are alone and that they had better 'despachar antes de que vuelvan esos niños escarrilados'. Consequently, El Sordo has no reason to disguise his desire to escape.

Yet, although he begins by repeating his request to have his hands freed 'so that he can make the sign of the cross', as he warms to his confession he moves from thoughts of escape to concern for his immortal soul. The fact that he knows the bandits are not present obliges us to take seriously what we might otherwise have dismissed as pretence. So how does Valle intend us to respond to El Sordo's confession? The answer is a very odd mixture of cynicism and belief. In one sense, the response to the confession on the part of both characters is a conditioned reflex, a case of the role influencing the actor. On the other hand, El Sordo, Padre Veritas and, to a lesser extent, the other bandits are given a true insight into their lives, a glimpsed vision of themselves as enslaved by their demonic passions against which all human faculties of reason or will are powerless:

¡Un amor ciego de chaval, y para siempre condenado a perderme!. . . . ¡Así es de negra mi estrella! Cuanto mejor quería, peor obraba. ¡Pensé acabar mis días lejos de belenes, con los papeles cambiados, sin trapisondas con la pareja!. . . . ¡Son aire los pensamientos! ¡Menos que aire, con más vueltas que la veleta!

But this glimpse of truth is sterile and offers no hope, since men are irrevocably condemned to be a prey to forces beyond their control. Confirmation for this view can be found in *La lámpara maravillosa*. In chapter 9 of 'El quietismo estético', Valle expresses the view that, this side of the grave, a man can only hope to achieve fleeting glimpses of the 'gesto único' or ultimate truth of his nature. The passing of the hours and the domination of circumstances converts human character into an endless series of masks:

Hay un gesto que es el mío, uno solo, pero en la sucesión humilde de los días, en el vano volar de las horas, se ha diluído hasta borrarse como el perfil de una medalla. Llevo sobre mi rostro cien máscaras de ficción que se suceden bajo el imperio mezquino de una fatalidad sin trascendencia. Acaso mi verdadero gesto no se ha revelado todavía, acaso no pueda revelarse nunca bajo tantos velos acumulados día a día y tejidos por todas mis horas. Yo mismo me desconozco y quizá estoy condenado a desconocerme siempre. (p. 120)

Sacrilegio provides a dramatic *exemplum* of these 'máscaras de ficción', of the power of external factors over internal attitudes and, at the same time, a tantalizing glimpse of the ultimate realities. As his 'confession' rises to its emotional and rhetorical climax and begins to exercise its magnetic influence on the audience of bandits, El Sordo is silenced with grotesque, almost comical, abruptness ('con viraje de cristobeta'). He is shot down before he can formulate a prayer or receive 'absolution'. But the 'fogonazo' from the captain's shotgun does not *prevent* the triumph of good, as Boudreau's analysis implies; it is more an ironic comment on its unattainability.

Further evidence that Valle-Inclán's interest in the episode extended beyond providing the audience with a dramatic shock can be found in the character of Padre Veritas. Though drawn with little detail, the impression is of an ambiguous and enigmatic figure, totally different from the rest of the band. It is Padre Veritas who in fact proposes the sacrilegious ceremony and offers to carry it out. For the other bandits the purpose is clear: 'meter la ganzúa' in Pinto Viroque's picturesque phrase or extract information which will reveal whether or not El Sordo betrayed their secrets to the authorities. As far as they are concerned, the sacrilege is undertaken without awe, partly in jest, partly for practical ends. There are strong suggestions that this is not so with Padre Veritas. Even before he sees his reflection in the pool and begins to take his role seriously, Valle prepares us for this transformation. Both his nickname and his appearance ('barbas capuchinas, muchos escapularios al pecho, sayal de ermitaño') are redolent of an ex-seminarist or renegade priest. The combination of ex-seminarist and bandit recalls the character of Farruquiño in the *Comedias bárbaras*. But whereas Farruquiño is depicted as a character in whom the passionately profane spirit merely coexists with the externals of religion, Valle makes us sense in Padre Veritas a divided personality in whom the power of sacred rituals revives to disrupt the profane surface of his life as a bandit. When the play opens he has been talking to the prisoner and announces El Sordo's last two requests. Unlike the others, he expresses no views on this. His only comment is that 'su pío no sale de lo que autoriza el Sacramento'. All Padre Veritas's observations on the proposed 'confession', though cloaked in thieves' slang, reveal a degree of religious knowledge and a basic seriousness of purpose ('El señor Frasquito pide confesión, y negarle ese pasaporte es contra la ley de Dios'; '. . . en caso de apuro, cualquier hombre o mujer está capacitado para administrar los sacramentos'). Valle's method of depicting Padre Veritas's internal debate could perhaps pass unnoticed in a reading of the play, but would be immediately apparent in performance. It is conveyed by a prolonged *silence*. After his initial remarks, Padre Veritas takes no further part in the dialogue until he suddenly blurts out his proposal to 'darle un bromazo pintándole un padre cura' some seven or eight pages later. The suggestion had in fact been made previously by Carifancho when he said 'un padre cura en un santiamen se ordena, y solamente es menester una navaja para abrirle la corona'. Sensitive direction of the play could bring out this link to suggest that Padre Veritas may have been silently brooding over this remark of Carifancho's.

On seeing his tonsured reflection in the pool of water, Padre Veritas 'sintió cubrírsele el alma de beato temor, frente al reflejo sacrílego de su imagen inmersa, sellada por un cristal, infinitamente distante del mundo en la cláusula azul de la charca, el ojo de la linterna como un lucero sobre la tonsura de San Antoñete'. This presence of the 'charca' (and of the 'dornil' in *Ligazón*) is associated with perceptions beyond the veil of time. It can best be explained in terms of the allusions to mirrors and crystals in *La lámpara maravillosa* which, Valle maintains, provide us with mystical perceptions into a reality hidden from us by time, change and the illusion of the senses (e.g. p. 33). Every action, thought or emotion of human life should be seen not as passing away in the flux of time, but as persisting in the eternity of an all-embracing Present, like circles created by pebbles thrown into a pool. Every human action thus has eternal echoes and repercussions and 'el poeta, como el místico, ha de tener percepciones más allá del límite que marcan los sentidos, para entrever en la ficción del momento, y en el aparente rodar de las horas, la responsabilidad eterna' (p. 34). The awe that Padre Veritas feels is that of seeing an image of himself detached from the immediate world in a dimension beyond time. It is a glimpse of the 'eternal responsibilities' of his action, an interpretation which is reinforced by the next *acotación* when his voice echoes through the cavern: 'Por las cristalinas entrañas del silo, la voz, náufraga y ciega, se dilata con profundos círculos superados de influjo geomántico. Una voz resucitada'. If we take the philosophy of the *Lámpara* at all seriously, this must be interpreted as an instant of revelation, a fleeting glimpse of reality in a world of illusion. It is a split second of stillness occasionally granted to the characters of the later plays when the laws of time and movement are momentarily suspended. The *practical* problems of conveying this symbolism of the *charca* would, of course, be considerable, especially since no reference is made to it in the dialogue. Two allusions in the *acotaciones* might, however, give some assistance to a director. The first is a reference to the bandits being reflected in the pool as they move towards El Sordo, attracted by the magnetic power of his impassioned confession: 'La tropa de caballistas, con pasmo, recalca su bulto sobre el espejo de la charca, avanza con movimiento sonámbulo.' The second comes right at the end when El Sordo is shot. This glimpse of a reality beyond the enslaved senses of the characters is erased and the pool is symbolically clouded over by the smoke from the Captain's shotgun: 'El humo oscurece las figuras atónitas sobre el espejo de la charca.'

To convey the full significance of this extra-temporal dimension via the exclusive use of visual images would tax the ingenuity of even the most skilful director. In other respects, however, *Sacrilegio* is a very theatrical and tautly constructed piece. Like *La rosa de papel*, it has a strong dramatic axis around which to revolve. El Sordo's constant and statuesque presence gives a focal point to the action and to the stage image. Physically, he dominates the scene. Valle refers to his 'magna figura', chained and blindfolded in a niche in the rock like a piece of religious statuary. Apart from this physical and thematic centrality, the dramatic power of El Sordo is enhanced by his isolation within the action. His deafness and the blindfold over his eyes cut him off from his surroundings. Valle skilfully exploits the dramatic potential of El Sordo's inability to hear the bandits discussing his betrayal and the fate in store for him. Certainly, towards the end of the play it is dramatically essential that El Sordo should be unaware of when the bandits return to the cave after their temporary absence. The deafness also serves as a dramatic device for shifting the dialogue from one group to another, using the character of Carifancho as a rather taunting intermediary between El Sordo and the rest of the band. By the end of the play we see this isolation as spiritual as well as physical, as an oppressive confinement from which he tries to escape, begging the 'priest' to shout a prayer in his ear.

The tempo and rhythmic structure of *Sacrilegio* also depend on the character of El Sordo. At the beginning, the bandits are trying to make him talk and succeed in eliciting only obscene monosyllables in reply. Later, after being given some wine and a cigarette by Carifancho, he becomes more communicative though scarcely more cooperative. Finally, in the confession, the words flood out of him in a torrent. The racy, bantering humour of the first half of the play gives way to the mounting urgency and anguish of the second. The basic dramatic shape of *Sacrilegio*, like *La cabeza del Bautista*, is that of an ironic reversal: having started by trying to make El Sordo talk, the bandits eventually shoot him to make him keep silent.

Visually, *Sacrilegio* is a play for shadowy figures and dramatic contrasts of light and shade. Despite the subtitle of 'auto para siluetas', it is not a play for two-dimensional silhouettes as it clearly depends on depth, perspective and colour. Most of the light comes from a flaming torch which illuminates the 'cristalinas arcadas' with 'maravillosos reflejos'. A lantern is carried from one part of the set to another illuminating the local areas that Valle wishes to emphasize. *Ligazón* could conceivably be performed as a shadow play since perspective and colour are by no means so important. Nevertheless, effects of light and shade are vital to its nocturnal, lunar atmosphere. The performance of *Ligazón* in the then new Teatro de Bellas Artes, to mark the inauguration of Valle's short-lived independent theatre company 'El Cántaro Roto' on 19 December 1926, is known to have been directed by the author himself. Contemporary reviews unfortunately give scant details about the staging. However, Díez-Canedo refers to the characters as 'sombras parlantes' and to 'una decoración esquemática, entrevista, como las figuras, a una luz no bien ponderada', which seems to suggest reduced, atmospheric lighting rather than silhouettes against a screen (*El Sol*, 21 December 1926).

There are four characters in *Ligazón* (a fifth, described as 'un bulto jaque de manta y retaco', is assassinated before he can utter a word): an old procuress (La Raposa), an innkeeper and her daughter (La Ventera and La Mozuela) and an itinerant knifegrinder (El Afilador). The mother and procuress scheme jointly to sell the daughter to a rich Jew. Their efforts to appeal to her acquisitive instincts fail and the Mozuela ('virgin'), determined to follow her natural inclination, offers herself to El Afilador who happens to be passing by. The play ends with a mimed sequence in which the girl and the knifegrinder murder the rich Jew who has been admitted by the mother into the girl's bedroom. *Ligazón* is an *auto* 'a lo diabólico' in which greed and lust (which Valle might have generalized into *Mundo* and *Carne*) struggle for possession of the young virgin's soul. As in the other *Retablo* plays these are antagonistic forces and the pressure on the Mozuela to sell herself for gain provokes the opposite reaction: to give herself for nothing.

In the first scene the Mozuela is subjected to the temptation of material possessions, as La Raposa dangles a pearl necklace before her. At this stage it should be noted that the Mozuela is far from being the sensual creature that she later becomes. Dominated by her mother, she is portrayed as naïve and lacking in even the normal female vanities:

LA RAPOSA: Podías ser más orgullosa. ¿Tú no te miras al espejo?
LA MOZUELA: Cuando voy a la fuente.
LA RAPOSA: ¿Y el espejillo de tu alcoba nada te dice cuando de noche te acuestas?
LA MOZUELA: No me veo con el sueño.

Although momentarily tempted by the necklace, she immediately rebels against the idea of selling herself. The knifegrinder's disdain for monetary payment is in sharp contrast to the rapacious greed of La Raposa. He offers to sharpen her scissors for a kiss. The dialogue between the Mozuela and knifegrinder is charged with sensuality and the sharpening of the scissors becomes by implication closely associated with the awakening of the Mozuela's sexual responses. She offers him a drink of *anís* and they both drink from the same glass, clearly foreshadowing the *ligazón* or blood bond of the second meeting when they suck each other's blood. In this first encounter it is the Afilador who is the seducer, though evidently not a Devil in disguise, since his seduction is essentially human and good-natured. He is seen more as the unconscious instrument of awakening the satanic *lujuria* in the Mozuela than the Devil incarnate. The allusions to pacts with the Devil are made in a spirit of light-hearted jest:

LA MOZUELA: Te bebes la copa, tomas soleta y, cuando acabes la vuelta del mundo, te daré respuesta.
EL AFILADOR: Esa rueda que tan deforme te pintas, la corro yo en menos de un credo.
LA MOZUELA: ¡Ni que tuvieras las botas de siete leguas!
EL AFILADOR: Para esos viajes me suspendo del rabo de un amigo.
LA MOZUELA: ¡Buenas amistades tienes!

The sharing of the glass with the Afilador at the end of this scene confirms the sexual awakening of the Mozuela.

Between this scene and the second encounter of the knifegrinder and the Mozuela is sandwiched a dialogue between La Raposa and La Ventera drunkenly celebrating a pact that they have made – based on greed – to sell the Mozuela to the rich Jew. The theme of witchcraft is introduced for the first time into the work as the women vie with each other in claiming demonic powers. The tone of this dialogue is unequivocally comic and constitutes an abrupt – and completely conscious – descent from the sensual to the burlesque. After La Raposa's departure, mother and daughter have a violent quarrel over the latter's refusal to accept the necklace.

In the second meeting of the Mozuela and the Afilador there is a complete change of atmosphere and a reversal of former roles. The seducer becomes the seduced. The Mozuela becomes the embodiment of lust, the siren, the serpent of Genesis, the demon temptress, and the one-time seducer is reduced to a quaking and bemused acceptance of her will. Elements of black magic and the supernatural are introduced. The Mozuela claims to have followed all the Afilador's movements by watching their reflection in the crystal ball of the water-trough and she brings down darkness all around them by magic arts. Once possessed by lust, the virgin is a slave to satanic evil and, in her turn, enslaves the Afilador by means of the satanic ritual of the blood pact and the ritual sacrifice of a victim.

In *Ligazón* Valle is evidently thinking in terms of a ritualistic style of presentation in the sense that certain moments of the action, certain visual impressions, are highlighted and, as it were, 'frozen' to convey an atmosphere of mystery. This is never stated explicitly in the text, but the whole tenor of the play, the concentration on precise silhouetted forms, the dwelling on moonlight effects, etc. dictate a slow, deliberate and ceremonial style of performance which would allow these visual impressions to make their impact. I refer to such moments as the necklace, suspended from La Raposa's claw-like hand, turning and glinting in the moonlight, the silhouetted shape of the scissors or the glint of metal in the dark, the Mozuela silhouetted in the doorway tossing 'una moneda negra', the ritual drinking from the raised glass, the execution of the blood pact and the final sacrifice. *Ligazón* goes further than any other play in Valle-Inclán's output towards achieving his declared intention of communicating meaning through the power of the 'plastic image' alone (see quotation on p. 105). That meaning is by no means easy to analyse or express in rational terms. The images are not intended to have any clearly definable symbolic values; they are there to evoke sensations and responses rather than to make moral or philosophical statements. In this respect, *Ligazón* does not lend itself to the same kind of thematic analysis as *Sacrilegio* does. I believe Guerrero Zamora overstates his case when he attributes a moral loading to Valle's use of the colour black, as in, for example, the 'moneda negra' with which the Mozuela is about to pay the knifegrinder (p. 190). In a silhouette play, black is so predominant that the argument tends to lose its force.

It is a play which stands or falls by the impact of its dominant visual images. The scissors are one of the central images of the work and they provide an important link between the lust and greed motifs. The Mozuela tells La Raposa that she will sleep with her scissors under the pillow to protect herself against the attentions of the unwanted lover. The scissors are the focal point of the Mozuela's first dialogue with the knifegrinder in which, through the pervasive air of sensuality and innuendo, they become a metaphor for the Mozuela's dormant sexuality. They are also associated with the link that is forged between the girl and the knifegrinder when the scissors later become the instrument of the blood bond (the Mozuela drives them into the palm of her hand) and the instrument of death for the rich lover at the end. One could perhaps argue that the scissors also have certain archetypal associations, such as the Fates snipping the threads of life, but the image derives most of its energy from the action itself. Other images, such as the knifegrinder's wheel and the three paths fanning out across the field in front of the inn, are not energized by the dialogue and thus rely exclusively on visual impact. It is therefore impossible to proffer anything more than tentative explanations. Valle is plainly fascinated by the silhouetted form of the knifegrinder's wheel and refers to it in several *acotaciones*. On one occasion he alludes to its 'rueda con rara sugestión de enigmas y azares', which suggests possible associations with such archetypes as the Wheel of Fortune or the spinning wheel of the Fates (hence a cross reference to the scissor image). The shadow of the knifegrinder is linked on two occasions with the 'estrella de senderos' or fan of paths. In one case the silhouette of his wheel covers the intersection of these paths: 'Proyecta la rueda su círculo negro en el cruce barcino de las tres sendas.' The association of the circle and the three paths radiating from a centre have the geometric quality of a magic emblem (the significance of which is unfortunately unknown to the present writer). One is tempted to speculate that the uncertain paths of destiny are being alluded to and possibly the three dimensions of time, past, present and future. Further speculation would, however, be pointless since Valle is interested (and likewise his audience) in the capacity of these images for subliminal, 'magical' evocation in the actual dramatic experience.

Guerrero Zamora's illuminating comparison of the theatre of Valle-Inclán and Michel de Ghelderode rests very largely on their common predilection for the themes of lust, avarice and death so explicitly explored in the *Retablo* (pp. 173–4, 180–1, 188–9). There is, however, one important difference between Valle's treatment of these themes and the attitude of Ghelderode. The latter's plays show a humanity exulting with Dionysian abandon in the life of the senses. The impression one derives from his theatre is similar to the desired impact of the theatrical experience as described by Antonin Artaud in his *The Theatre and its Double*: that is, as a valve which releases the dormant forces in human nature. In his celebrated comparison of the theatre to the Plague, Artaud claims that 'it unravels conflicts, liberates powers, releases potential and if these powers are dark, this is not the fault of the plague or the theatre, but life' (p. 21). This is not generally true of Valle-Inclán's theatre. Even in the early *Comedias* and the trilogy of novels *La guerra carlista*, where one can detect a feeling of aesthetic excitement in the portrayal of full-blooded barbaric behaviour, the work does not come over as an unequivocal apologia for the instinctive life. The characters do not intoxicate themselves with lust and greed, there is no frenzied enjoyment or sense of liberation in the affirmation of the instincts. It is doubtful whether Valle – even at this early stage – would have asserted with Artaud and Ghelderode that our deepest emotions and insights into our nature are released through Dionysian revelry. The later plays certainly do not take such a heroic view of instinctive behaviour and from *Divinas palabras* onwards any idea of fulfilment through indulgence of instinctive passions disappears from his work. Fulfilment and liberation in Valle's later work comes rather from detachment from the senses than from their affirmation. Man's servitude to the senses was seen as inseparable from his enslavement to time. The momentary ex-perience of detachment and release afforded to Mari-Gaila and the villagers is rigorously denied to the characters of the *Retablo*. In the *Retablo* man becomes a tragically hollow creature, remote from love and truth, pulled by confused and contradictory forces of generic passions, the rhetoric of words, ritual attitudes, social myths and imperatives, condemned to wear a succession of 'masks of fiction' imposed by changing circumstances and the passage of time. The grotesquely agitated action and extravagant verbiage betoken a sense of emptiness within. Using the forms and language of the *folletín* and the penny dreadful, Valle evolves a style in which the marionette characterization, truculent melodrama and strident posturing are designed to drain the words of internal force and leave them hollow. Their subtext is man's tragic lack of authenticity.

11

Valle-Inclán and the modern theatre

Since the centenary of Valle-Inclán's birth in 1966, the revival of interest in his theatre has been largely stimulated by what critics and directors have seen as his modern sensibility. His narrative style of drama has been linked with the 'epic' theatre of Brecht, his strongly visual emphasis with the theatre of Ghelderode and the anti-tragic vision of the *esperpento* with that of certain 'Absurdist' playwrights of the 1950s.[1] In many cases these comparisons have been made simply to give Valle some kind of European seal of approval. Almost always they have been made with too few qualifications. In this final chapter I propose to examine some general parallels and differences between the later plays and the two main dramatic trends that emerged in Europe during and after the Second World War: the socially orientated theatre of Brecht and the metaphysically orientated Theatre of the Absurd. Obviously there is no question of tracing influences here. It will be an attempt to establish how far Valle anticipated later trends in the theatre. At the same time it may be helpful in defining his position *vis-à-vis* certain important issues: the question of the historical as opposed to the ahistorical view of man, the categories of the tragic and the comic, the nature and purpose of artistic distance and the influence of the silent cinema on his plays.

Since Brecht struck out on the socio-political path, European theatre has, broadly speaking, polarized itself into the social–historical viewpoint of Marxist-inspired theatre and the ahistorical, metaphysical 'Aristotelian' viewpoint. The debate between those who studied man as a product of changing social structures and those who preferred to regard him as a victim of a static universal condition has existed since the 1920s and reached its climax in the 1950s. The question of Valle-Inclán's degree of social commitment in his works of the 1920s is a complex one. How far is the *esperpento* a theatre of social action and how far is it an image of the human condition? His friend and admirer, C. Rivas Cherif, describes Valle's new style in the following manner:

Esperpento llama a un subgénero de la farsa en que las acciones trágicas aparecen tal y como se muestran en la vida actual española, sin grandeza ni dignidad alguna. Inicia con éste [*Luces de Bohemia*] una serie de estudios dramáticos que pudiéramos decir de los fenómenos sociales precursores de la futura revolución española. ¿Cómo permanecer alejados de estos pre-liminares tragicómicos del día heroico? ¿Cómo no asomarse a esas almas donde se fraguan los atentados? (*La Internacional*, 3 September 1920, p. 4)

A more recent critic claims that one of the constants of the *esperpento* is its 'sentido directo de denuncia específica, de incitación a la repulsa y condena de determinados comportamientos sociales' and compares it with the 'agit prop' genre in Germany between the wars (Hormigón, *La cultura*, p. 380). These critics tend to see the later Valle-Inclán as committed to attacking specific injustices in Spanish political and social life, after abandoning the false gods of mysticism and aesthetics. For them the *esperpento* is a kind of *teatro de urgencia* in which ethics take priority over aesthetics. The Rivas Cherif article clearly states that, in creating the *esperpento*, Valle is creating not art but history. In other words, although he is not renouncing his philosophy of art, he is temporarily suspending artistic activity in order to devote himself to the cause of social justice.[2] If we take Valle at his word here (or Rivas's version of it), we must conclude that the *esperpentos* have no pretensions to the artistic detachment which, for Valle, had always been the hallmark of truth. The viewpoint seems somewhat extreme, since all Valle's comments on the *esperpento* point to a conscious search for an artistic form and idiom that would be appropriate to the historical period, which in itself is an aesthetic preoccupation. Certainly, none of these statements places art at the service of social reform. As I said in a previous chapter, the *esperpento* bears every sign of being controlled by a guiding aesthetic which safeguards objec-tivity and detachment. Furthermore, it must be remembered that the views expressed by Rivas and Hormigón are in part a reflection of their own Marxist ideology.

On the evidence of the *esperpentos* themselves, few would deny that they show social concern and awareness. The objects of Valle's attacks may not be specific injustices and abuses, but the plays could be described as 'subversive' in that they seek to undermine what he saw as the general Spanish tendency to 'mythification' and self-aggrandizement. The real question is not whether he used social or topical material or whether he became socially concerned as a writer – this is not in doubt – but whether this development marks a switch from a static, 'essentialist' view of the world to a *historical* view. In claiming the parallel with Brecht's 'epic' theory of drama, Anthony Zahareas is also claiming that Valle changed his whole philosophy of life and art, that he threw overboard the aesthetic philosophy of *La lámpara*, the quest for transcendent unity, and embraced the once despised *visión cronológica* as the only truth.[3] For Brecht the historical process is the only reality and everything – including human nature itself – is subject to it. His view of the world explicitly denies the notion of 'essentiality', whether in the world, society or human character. As nothing is fixed and permanent, so nothing is inevitable. Historical circumstances are not mysterious external forces, they are the result of human actions and are capable of being changed by human actions.[4] It would be difficult to extract such a philosophical view from the *esperpentos* and there is no evidence to suggest that Valle ever repudiated the philosophy of *La lámpara*. On the contrary, in an interview in 1921, he declared it to be the work which had most satisfied him (Velázquez Bringas, p. 171). Further evidence against the argument that Valle underwent a radical philosophical transformation is provided by the *Retablo* plays which, as we have seen, clearly indicate an ahistorical viewpoint.

Curiously, after arguing very strongly for the concrete historical and social basis of the *esperpento* and for the author's 'commitment to history', Zahareas claims that this serves a basically existentialist and 'absurdist' world view ('the so-called No-Exit, meaningless and alienated condition of man').[5] It is difficult to see how belief in cosmic absurdity can be reconciled with belief in the historical view, since the one is a static concept of the human condition and the other a dynamic, evolutionary one. It is, of course, possible to become socially conscious and aware of historical developments without adopting a Marxist view of history. Valle does not deny or ignore historical change. History has changed the image of the hero. Human attitudes and beliefs can appear heroic or ridiculous according to their historical context. But history for Valle-Inclán was not the only reality, as it was for Brecht. Simultaneously he retained a belief in a static cosmic order, viewed from which time and history appear as limitations on the human perspective. The march of historical events may be a reality to which, apart from occasional liberating insights, man is inevitably chained, but it is not an absolute reality.

If the view of society in the *esperpentos* is not underpinned by a philosophy of historical commitment, is it presented as an image of the Absurd? If we define the Absurd as the basic contradictions of the human condition – the human need for permanence, happiness and meaning in a world that offers death, suffering and non-meaning – then we would have to conclude that neither the *esperpentos* nor the *Retablo* plays reflect such a philosophy. The *esperpentos* do not as a rule lead our imaginations beyond the immediate historical situation towards the metaphysical view, though *Luces* is a possible exception here. They limit us to a social and national frame of reference, while the *Retablo* plays remind us of Valle's extra-terrestrial view of the human species. The main distinction is, however, that Valle does not believe in *universal* absurdity. In the plays of Beckett and Ionesco, the Absurd is identified with total lack of objective meaning or coherence in the world. In Valle's plays the grotesque is a deviation from an implied norm of unity and truth which lies beyond human perception and the veil of time. The human condition is one of exile from truth, of being trapped in time and manipulated by forces of instinct, myth and contingency. It is this fact that divides the 'absurd' from the 'grotesque' and probably brings Valle-Inclán's late plays closer to Expressionism. The Theatre of the Absurd recognizes no absolute order. Beckett and Ionesco focus on what for them are the ultimate realities of the human condition – death, solitude and, above all, non-meaning. Valle-Inclán's primary motifs of pride, lust, greed, may be inescapable facts of the human condition, but they are not ultimate realities in the same sense, since his view is determined by a belief in an order of reality *beyond* the human condition.

Having made this distinction between the different philosophical bases, it must be said that many of Valle-Inclán's intuitions do seem to anticipate later developments in European theatre, particularly with regard to the breakdown of traditional tragic and heroic values. I have tried to show in a previous chapter how the later theatre passes through stages of dynamic tension between tragic and comic elements (*Luces*), triumph of the comic (*Los cuernos*) and the grotesque as expression of the tragic in plays written after about 1924. This is not posited as a strict chronological development because the issue is complicated by the interpolated scenes in *Luces*, four years after its original publication, which materially alter the audience response to this play. Nevertheless, it is clear that Valle recognized the in-adequacy of traditional tragic–heroic values in contemporary circumstances and that he saw the potential of the grotesque as an alternative route to tragedy.

It is remarkable how often the theoretical analyses of Ionesco and Dürrenmatt serve to elucidate intuitively perceived insights by Valle-Inclán. In his now classic essay 'Problems of the Theatre', Dürrenmatt comments perceptively on the relationship between theatre and the general social ethos, a relationship, as his reported statements confirm, which always interested Valle-Inclán. Dürrenmatt argues that traditional tragedy reflects a relatively uniform world, with commonly shared moral assumptions, a world compact and coherent enough to be absorbed by the mind of the spectator. It presupposes common assumptions about the nature of guilt and about the dignity of human suffering. It was a world in which there were clear distinctions between what was deserving of our pity and fear and what was deserving of our laughter. The modern world has become too complex, too anonymous, too paradoxical and irrational for such assumptions to survive and the distinctions between tragic and comic values have become blurred. As far as I know, Valle-Inclán never formulated these sentiments in any of his theoretical comments on the *esperpento*, but *Luces de Bohemia* expresses them clearly enough. An unheroic, institutionalized society of vain or self-interested individuals turns the poet Max Estrella into an absurd anachronism. Values, it is implied, cannot exist in some kind of vacuum; they need the collective corroboration of a social context. There is a striking thematic parallel between *Luces* and Ionesco's *Rhinocéros* in this respect. Outwardly Ionesco's plot of having all his characters gradually change into rhinos is a parable on the contagious power of new cults and fanaticisms, but the play ends by leaving us with an ambiguous picture of Bérenger, the hero and only surviving human being. At the end of the play, Bérenger wavers between envy of the rhinoceroses and defence of his human status. Unobtrusively, the suggestion is being made that, because the norm is to be a rhinoceros, to be human is to be a grotesque monstrosity. The defence of 'human values' has been made into an absurdity by the change of context.

This realization that the collective context was capable of transforming the nature of one-time heroic values, that what had been held in unquestioned esteem could become ludicrous, is at the root of the early *esperpentos* and, in a more indirect way, of some Absurdist theatre. It naturally contributed to a questioning of the nature of all values *per se* and this climate of universal scepticism manifests itself in the repeated technique of using the tragic and the comic in opposition to one another. In his essay 'Expérience du théâtre', Ionesco explains how his drama, far from trying to resolve the paradoxes of experience, deliberately exploits the tensions and contradictions between the tragic and the comic:

Sur un texte insensé, absurde, comique, on peut greffer une mise en scène, une interprétation grave, solennelle, cérémonieuse. Par contre, pour éviter le ridicule des larmes faciles, de la sensiblerie, on peut, sur un texte dramatique, greffer une interprétation clownesque, souligner par la farce, le sens tragique d'une pièce. (p. 13)

Dürrenmatt in 'Dramaturgical Considerations about *The Anabaptists*' proposes a style of comedy in which the action alone has comic implications while the protagonists are treated seriously and even tragically (*Writings*, pp. 137–45). European theatre of the 1950s and 1960s offers abundant examples of such calculated contrasts. In almost all cases, they are a deliberate attempt to jolt the audience out of mental laziness and routine responses, to make them objectify the action and become consciously aware of the essential strangeness and paradoxical nature of the world. The use of tragic and comic elements in calculated conflict is perhaps a consistent feature of only *Luces de Bohemia* (definitive version), though probably not as a conscious audience-alienating device. It begins to disappear as the contrast between protagonist and social context becomes less pronounced in the later *esperpentos*. As the plays lose the contrast between the values and perspective of a *self-aware* protagonist and those of the society, so they lose the capacity to set up conflicting emotions within the audience. The contrasts between the farcical and the macabre in, say, *Divinas palabras* and *La rosa de papel*, are of a different order and leave us less emotionally involved. It is perhaps the measure of identification that Valle allows us with the protagonist of *Luces* that accounts for its distinct tone of ironic pathos, not unlike that of O'Casey's *Juno and the Paycock*.

Max Estrella's assertion that our lives are not a tragedy but an *esperpento* might lead us to conclude that Valle was negating the whole idea of tragedy. If, however, we take *Luces* scene 12 in conjunction with other reported comments on the *esperpento*, it becomes clear that this is not the case (see Appendix 10). What is being denied is the existence or possibility of the tragic hero in the modern world; he unequivocally affirms the continued validity of the tragic in both life and literature. The fundamentals of the human condition, he claims, are unchanging and inherently tragic (a statement Brecht would surely have disapproved of!), only the people change. Modern man is unequal to his tragic role. The parts once played by gods and heroes are handed out to dwarfs and clowns. Valle is not very explicit in any of his statements about what makes modern man so unequal to his role but, once again, Dürrenmatt's lucid analysis of the same question helps us to rationalize Valle's intuitions:

Tragedy presupposes guilt, despair, moderation, lucidity, vision, a sense of responsibility. In the Punch-and-Judy show of our century, in this backsliding of the white race, there are no more guilty and also, no responsible men. It is always 'we couldn't help it' and 'we didn't really want that to happen'. And indeed things happen without anyone in particular being responsible for them. Everything is dragged along and everyone gets caught somewhere in the sweep of events. We are all collectively guilty, collectively bogged down in the sins of our fathers and forefathers. ('Problems', p. 69)

The general drift of this passage echoes Valle's view of men as bad actors caught up in a drama which is beyond their capacity and comprehension. The final sentence recalls some words of his reported in 1925: 'No sabemos nada de nada. No conocemos nuestras horas. Estamos perdidos en el terrible pecado del mundo' (*El Castellano*, 23 October 1925), which to some extent hint at Dürrenmatt's analysis. There can be no heroes because nobody is aware. Man no longer suffers fate, he is blindly manipulated by an over-complex reality which allows him no margin for responsibility except in a collective sense. In Valle's later work manipulation can be seen as the essence of the grotesque and the element which effectively wipes out the possibility of the tragic hero.

Again, *Luces* stands out as an exception, for Max, at least, is lucid and aware. Whether he is a 'responsible' character in the existentialist sense is a more doubtful proposition. Anthony Zahareas writes that Valle-Inclán 'would agree with Sartre that man has his salvation and his authenticity in his own hands as long as he acknowledges that he is responsible' (Introduction, p. 37).[6] If by this he means that, in a world without pre-established values, man has the freedom and the responsibility to forge his own, one would have to admit that neither Valle's theoretical statements nor his other works bear out such a view. Max does not become aware of existential freedom and its responsibilities, he comes to realize his 'manipulated' condition. He is not a man forging his own values 'in a relativistic and alien world' (words applied by Zahareas to Don Friolera's dilemma) (Introduction, p. 50). The world is making him into a clown and he knows it. His voluntary assumption of the tongue-in-cheek role is not the act of a man who, having discovered his existential freedom, decides to use it in this way. It is the act of a man desperately trying to grasp a measure of freedom and authenticity from a world that denies these things to him. Max's situation is not dissimilar to that of Romulus in Dürrenmatt's *Romulus the Great*. Jan Kott sums it up as follows:

> History has made a fool of him. He can either die in a spectacular fashion, or lie in his bed and wait to be butchered. He can surrender, compose speeches or commit suicide. In his position as the last Roman emperor, every one of these solutions is compromising and ridiculous. History has turned Romulus into a clown and yet demands him to treat her seriously. Romulus has only one good move to make: *consciously to accept the part of clown and play it to the end*. He can breed chickens. In this way historical inevitability will have been made a fool of. (p. 107, italics mine)

Max's clowning, as often happens in the Theatre of the Absurd, is a release from a situation and a method of detachment more than a positive assertion of value. In Beckett's *Waiting for Godot* and *All that Fall*, humour springs spontaneously from the heart of suffering as a defensive mechanism. Dürrenmatt defines parody as a way of regaining artistic freedom.[7] And Eugène Ionesco claims that 'humour is the only possibility we possess of detaching ourselves – yet only after we have surmounted, assimilated, taken cognizance of it – from our tragicomic human condition, the malaise of being' (Esslin, p. 187). Humour is the modern catharsis.

Max is still a kind of 'hero' in that he is allowed insight, detachment and hence a modicum of triumph. Later *esperpentos* and *Retablo* plays eliminate these features and give no such hope. The dance of the marionettes takes over and there are no men of feeling and lucidity to cope with it. In these final plays humour turns to grotesquerie and elicits a markedly different response. The nature of the humour becomes less cathartic in that it does not release the emotions to the same extent. Instead, the melodramatic attitudes, strident posturing, abrupt changes and extravagant hyperbole become the representation of universal inauthenticity and tragic emptiness. This final phase of Valle's theatre also finds an echo in the Theatre of the Absurd. Ionesco included the following in a programme note in 1952:

Le monde m'apparaît à certains moments comme vidé de signification, la réalité: irréelle. C'est ce sentiment d'irréalité, la recherche d'une réalité essentielle, oubliée, innomée – hors de laquelle je ne me sens pas être – que j'ai voulu exprimer à travers mes personnages qui errent dans l'incohérent, n'ayant rien en propre en dehors de leurs angoisses, leurs remords, leurs échecs, la vacuité de la vie. Des êtres noyés dans l'absence de sens ne peuvent être que grotesques, leur souffrance ne peut être que dérisoirement tragique. (p. 165)

Valle and the Absurdists thus confronted a common aesthetic problem, which was how to give theatrical expression to non-meaning and emptiness – though, as we have previously observed, the non-meaning is relative in Valle's case. In a letter to the first director of *Les Chaises*, Ionesco explains that the essential theme is 'le non-sens, l'arbitraire, une vacuité de la réalité, du langage, de la pensée humaine' (p. 167). To give tangible form to this theme, he uses agitated movement, grotesque pantomime gestures and the empty chairs which proliferate and encumber the whole acting area. The sensation of unreality, of evanescence in the world, is often expressed in Ionesco's plays by an excess of presence, oppressive accumulation or the accelerating rhythm of a machine gone mad. Valle-Inclán does not share Ionesco's obsession with proliferation of objects, but a number of his later pieces show a tendency towards frenzied see-sawing or spiralling movement and accelerating rhythm (e.g. *Cara de plata*, *La rosa de papel* and *La hija del capitán*), the contemplation of life as if it were a demented mechanism. The 'systematic distortion', which is advocated by Max in *Luces* but does not come into its own until the *Retablo*, is an aesthetic of the grotesque aimed at resolving chaos into artistic order and non-meaning into artistic coherence.

To convey this sensation of vacuity, hollowness and automatism in human values and behaviour, Valle-Inclán makes good use of parody and, particularly, of certain lower art forms such as puppetry, the newspaper *folletín*, the penny dreadful, late-nineteenth-century melo-drama and images of the silent screen. This closely parallels the use by Absurdist playwrights of clichés from diverse popular arts which were wholly transformed by being placed in a different context. The use of music-hall and circus routines in *Waiting for Godot*, Ionesco's allusions to the Marx Brothers, silent film antics in Arrabal and comedians' cross-talk in Pinter, contribute to the impression of a strange, out-of-joint world in constant and purposeless movement (Esslin, pp. 324–7).[8] Valle's allusions to the puppet show in the abrupt appearances of Doña Tadea at her window and the shooting of Friolera's daughter, to the silent screen in the grotesquely expressive collapse of Sócrates Galindo or Julepe's gleeful brandishing of the villain's pistol, to the clichés of sentimental melodrama in Pachequín's abduction of Doña Loreta and of satanic melodrama in Montenegro's abduction of Sabelita, are all part of a comparable intention: to present the world as travesty when viewed from the serene detachment of infinity.

However, it is on the question of viewpoint that we come up against an important distinction between Absurdist drama and Valle-Inclán. In the former, the sensation of absurdity is usually presented as experienced by the individual, an aspect which Martin Esslin stresses when he says it communicates 'one poet's most intimate and personal intuition, his own sense of being, his individual vision of the world' (p. 392). Absurdist theatre thus tends to be written from the individual's anguished apprehension of reality and directed towards re-creating that anguish in the audience. The late plays of Valle-Inclán do not generally communicate a sense of anguish (again with the possible exception of *Luces*) because the author situates himself outside the individual's personal experience of reality and looks at the world from stellar distances. The detachment afforded by art was Valle's refuge from the insanity of the world.

Some critics have tried to link this artistic detachment with the much-discussed 'alienation effect' of Brecht and the rather less discussed equivalent in the Absurdist drama. As a result aesthetic intentions have been attributed to Valle which do not square either with the evidence of his reported statements or with the works themselves. Both Absurdist and Brechtian theatre incorporate 'alienation effects' in that they depart from representational realism in order to jerk the spectator out of mental lethargy or routine acceptance and persuade him to adopt a different perspective. Absurdists try to convince him that the world he accepts as basically rational and 'normal' is, in reality, strange, irrational and absurd. Brecht tries to persuade him that the world he resignedly accepts as unchangeable can be altered by the application of man's rational and critical faculties. In both types of theatre, the aim – more conscious though not necessarily more successful in Brecht – is to inhibit the audience's tendency to identify with the characters in order to break their habitual frame of reference, the mould of familiarity, either by puzzling and disconcerting the spectator or sharpening his critical awareness (see Esslin, pp. 400–2). Valle-Inclán's theory of artistic distance (expressed mainly in the Prologue to *Los cuernos*) is concerned more with the author's relationship to his work than with the play's effect upon the audience. What he stresses is the importance of the author's own emotional detachment from his creations in order to reflect a more objective and comprehensive truth. The kind of response he wished to elicit from an audience is not directly mentioned and is largely a matter for speculation. The important thing for him, as for James Joyce, was to establish the right attitude to the material, which was that the artist should remain outside his handiwork 'invisible, refined out of existence, indifferent, paring his fingernails' (p. 245). Lest it be imagined that Valle had outgrown such a philosophy by the 1920s, we should refer to an interview he gave during his visit to Mexico in 1921: 'El alma creadora está fuera del tiempo. Esto se logra, aislándose del paisaje para no mirarlo como si se estuviese dentro de él, sino contemplarlo desde la altura, como si el ojo estuviera colocado en la punta de un cono' (Velázquez Bringas, p. 171).

It is surprising that Zahareas is able to conclude from such statements of aesthetic philosophy that Valle 'had at his disposal the same technique of artistic distance which Brecht later called *Verfremdung*' (Introduction, p. 30).[9] Valle considered identification and empathy undesirable, not because they made the spectator irrational or clouded his critical judgement, but because they limited the field of vision. Nor is it true that Valle saw 'spectacle' and the visual emphasis in his theatre as a means of keeping the audience 'sober and critical' (p. 31). This was, of course, the constantly reiterated purpose of Brecht: to free the audience from empathy in order to stimulate a spirit of rational enquiry and provoke social awareness. But Valle-Inclán's advocacy of visual communication was founded on reasons quite contrary to this. In fact, he regarded the 'plastic' approach to theatre as particularly suited to Spanish audiences precisely because it was non-rational, because, as he says, 'nos mueve la plástica antes que el concepto' (Appendix 2 and Madrid, p. 117). Although he generally avoided any kind of emotional empathy with characters in his plays, Valle was clearly not opposed to the idea of influencing an audience by emotive means. A glance at the relevant passages in the Appendix should provide evidence for this. The example of the bullfight that he gives in the Prologue to *Los cuernos* does not imply that those sentimental souls who identify with the disembowelled nags thereby lose their *rational* perspective on the *fiesta* (see Zahareas,

Introduction, p. 43). What Valle says is that they are incapable of feeling the 'emoción estética' of the contest. What they lose, therefore, is the ability to respond emotionally to the whole by identifying with the part.

Valle-Inclán's narrative and episodic approach to drama has often called forth rather loose comparisons with Brecht's 'epic' theatre. These comparisons are usually based on purely external features of dramatic structure and, more often than not, on a mistaken association of the terms 'epic' and 'narrative'. Brecht's style of construction is a distillation of a social and political as well as theatrical philosophy and cannot be reduced to a simple 'story-telling' definition. 'Epic' theatre was conceived in contrast to the dramatic or 'Aristotelian' theatre and, in fact, Brecht later preferred the term 'non-Aristotelian' to 'epic'. It rejects certain notions associated with Aristotle's thinking on tragedy, such as the idea of tragic inevitability and that of 'eternal' or 'essential' characteristics in human nature. The basic premise of 'epic' drama is that, since history forms people and people create history, both people and history are amenable to change by the application of reason. 'Epic' drama also rejects mimesis and illusionism. It claims to present life for critical judgement rather than to imitate it, a process which involves the use of various anti-illusionist devices to create distance. Finally, Brecht's theory has no place for the Aristotelian idea of catharsis, which invites identification with the protagonist's emotions and suffering. The spectator, says Brecht, should remain uninvolved and able to assess the situation portrayed with critical detachment. These, in very general terms, were the convictions which lay behind and shaped Brecht's constructional method.[10] The substitution of separate, self-contained scenes for a continuous cause-and-effect development was intended to prevent the spectator from being carried away and to allow him to interpose his judgement as the action proceeded. Each incident or scene is generalized to a certain extent and often given a label or title, in order to remove us from the immediate emotions in play and to clarify the general principles involved.

Valle's method of constructing plays in a series of visually conceived scenes has little to do with the ideas that underpin Brecht's 'epic' theatre. The rationale behind his technique is aesthetic rather than ideological. Like Brecht's, however, his theory appears to be conceived in reaction to a prevailing trend. In Valle's case this was the theatre of ideas and the Neoclassical inheritance (see Appendix 1). The *pièce à thèse*, usually encased in three acts, three unities and, at the most, three bourgeois interior sets, was for Valle both a denial of drama and an alien growth on Spain's dramatic tradition. The multiple-scene principle came very largely out of the conviction that intellectually orientated drama and its concomitant impoverishment of sensual appeal was leading Spanish theatre into an impasse. Valle, as was stressed in the first chapter, saw drama as inseparable from the physical atmosphere that gave it life. Though by no means exclusively visual, his method is to a large extent based on a belief in the expressive power of images in sequence, in dynamic rhythm or dramatic juxtaposition.

The question naturally arises: to what extent was he influenced by the cinema in this?[11] It is not clear at what stage he became conscious of this new artistic medium. What cannot be doubted is that he took it seriously as an art form, that the cinema served to confirm many of his artistic theories and that his later work shows certain specific influences. Many of these cinematic images would not be realizable on the stage. The example of the opening *acotación* to scene 3 of *La hija del capitán* has already been mentioned (see p. 147). C. B. Morris, in his book *This Loving Darkness*, quotes a number of examples of cinematic influence: effects of light and shade, silhouetted forms, close-ups and the mute eloquence of physical objects (pp. 34–7). Let us take the example of the death of Sócrates Galindo in *Las galas del difunto*:

El desconcierto de la gambeta y el visaje que le sacude la cara, revierten la vida a una sensación de espejo convexo. La palabra se intuye por el gesto, el golpe de los pies por los ángulos de la zapateta. Es un instante donde todas las cosas se proyectan colmadas de mudez. Se explican plenamente con una angustiosa evidencia visual. (p. 26)

Surely nothing but the silent cinema could have inspired this image. It tries to illustrate the point Valle often made in his theoretical comments: that the visual image can be self-sufficient, i.e. render the other senses unnecessary. The cry is suggested by the facial expression; the thud of the fall by the grotesque movement of the body. But the image conveys more than a cinematic cliché of the period. The sudden silence concentrates the mind and powerfully suggests the shock of a rupture in life's rhythm, the sensation of time standing still. It is as if Valle had discovered the cinematic technique of the frozen frame or the silent slow-motion sequence.

The character of the visual image undergoes a number of changes throughout Valle's career. From the faded romantic *estampas* of *El Marqués de Bradomín*, he goes to the archetypal heroic poses of the *Comedias*, until he arrives at the cartoon-like stylization of the *esperpento*. The post-1920 period is characterized by an interest in the expressive power of the isolated feature or detail, such as Teniente Rovirosa's unstable glass eye (*Los cuernos*) or the Abbot's horn-shaped biretta in *Cara de plata*. Such use of reiterated detail or movement to typify a character was probably cinematic in origin. Such close-ups as the letter in *Las galas* 'que, con rara sugestión, acusa su cuadrilátero encima del mostrador' were almost certainly suggested by early *montage* techniques. An effect such as this last one is obviously impossible to achieve on the stage since the dramatist cannot dictate the audience's angle of vision to the same extent. But from this sort of evidence we can appreciate how Valle's imagination was moving away from evocative pictorial effects, background landscapes, etc., towards images in which the part expresses the whole. An interesting insight into this development is provided by an ex-pupil of his at the Escuela Superior de Bellas Artes who recalls a conversation with Don Ramón while walking up the Carrera de San Jerónimo:

Durante el camino, Don Ramón me habló de teatro y de escenografía . . . Me describió perfectamente los escenarios sintéticos y la escenografía estilizada hasta lo inverosímil . . . Me describió una escena (no recuerdo para qué obra) en la que él sólo precisaba una ventana al fondo, aislada sobre cortinas; una cuerda que atravesase la escena con la ropa tendida de los personajes y dos pares de zapatos, que, 'solos', darían la impresión de quienes los calzaban. (V. Durán, *La Voz*, 20 January 1936)

The idea of using two pairs of shoes, visible below a row of clothes on a line, to express character and situation is a startlingly modern one. It reveals a Valle-Inclán interested not merely in the gawky, angular and the grotesque, but in the expressive capacity of small, precise and detailed movement, not unlike those which Beckett envisaged for *Happy Days*.

Valle's belief in the near self-sufficiency of the visual image made him a devotee of the cinema which many of his contemporaries dismissed as an ephemeral novelty. He recognized the potential of the medium when it concentrated on the plasticity that was proper to it and did not encumber itself with literary plots, which, as he said in an article, was rather like adapting the materials to the blueprint (*El Bufón*, 15 February 1924). In the same article he sketches out a rough scenario for a Holy Week procession in Seville. It is interesting to see how his eye gives meaning and tension to the images by picking out the contrasts between Catholic and pagan elements. He juxtaposes images of the religious procession with the 'ronda pagana de las noches tibias' of the lovers, and cuts between shots of mitres, cowls and the figure of El Cristo de los Poderes and images of flashing eyes 'que rasgan el ambiente como ráfagas eléctricas' and of Pastora Imperio 'descalza, penitente y provocativa' singing a *saeta*. As far as the theatre was concerned, he saw the cinema as a challenge. It was, on the one hand, a possible source of inspiration, but, should the challenge be ignored, it constituted a threat to the theatre's survival. The great lesson to be learned from the cinema's example was its quality of dynamism. This did not mean a slavish – and indeed pointless – attempt to reproduce the cinema's mobility in a purely pictorial sense by means of a series of elaborate and detailed sets. His letter to Rivas Cherif makes it clear that he was concerned with the 'furia dinámica' of the total conception – dialogue, rhythm, tone, dramatic impetus – products of the dramatic, not just the pictorial, imagination (see Appendix 3). Dramatists should respond to the challenge by incorporating the gestural, dynamic and sensually immediate qualities of cinema into the *literary* techniques of writing for the theatre. The technical improvements of composite sets and more sophisticated lighting would follow; the challenge must first be answered in the playwright's imagination.

Appendix

Valle-Inclán never wrote a systematic treatise on the subject of drama. Most of the evidence we have comes from newspaper or magazine interviews, press reports of lectures and, occasionally, letters. The main source is Francisco Madrid, *La vida altiva de Valle-Inclán*, which consists largely of Valle-Inclán's own comments on a variety of topics gleaned from the press. Unfortunately, Madrid rarely gives his sources or dates the passage he quotes. In this selection of comments on dramatic theory and the *esperpento*, I have quoted original sources wherever possible. In the case of press interviews, the questions and comments of the interviewer have been omitted when they are not essential to the sense of the passage as a whole.

1. 'Don Ramón habla de teatro a sus contertulios', interview

Cuatro indocumentados sin imaginación forjaron esa patraña del teatro de tesis. De mala tesis casi siempre. No sabían que aunque ellos hubieran traído una magnífica doctrina que enseñar no lo hubieran podido hacer en el teatro, ni en ningún sitio, con argumentos. La multitud no sabe más que conmoverse o regocijarse. Y lo que conmueve es el tono, no la razón. San Bernardo fue a Alemania, en misión de apostolado, sin saber una palabra de alemán. Pero se encaramó en pedestalillos de plazas y calles y habló a los teutones, que no le entendían. Tampoco hizo falta, porque el tono obró el milagro. San Bernardo levantó una cruzada de millares de alemanes, que partieron henchidos de fe, a reconquistar Tierra Santa. Si en el teatro algo ha de levantar con palanca de emoción el alma de las multitudes, sólo el tono obrará el prodigio . . . El teatro dramático ha de ser un teatro de tono o no ha de ser, y resulta difícil de escribir e interpretar. Se dice que no hay intérpretes, y tienen razón. 'Vengo de pasear por la Castellana' se puede decir de muchas maneras y en todos los tonos. Eso cualquiera lo dice. Pero el '¡Demasiado tarde!' de *Hamlet*, es muy difícil de lanzar. Se necesita un gran actor . . .

Por otra parte, la técnica francesa ha echado a perder nuestro teatro. Este absurdo decadente de querer encerrar la acción dramática en tres lugares – gabinete elegantemente amueblado, patio andaluz o salón de fiestas – ha hecho de nuestro teatro, antes frágil y expresivo, un teatro cansino y desvaído . . . Nuestro teatro fue siempre un teatro de escenarios, de muchos escenarios. Porque se parte de un error fundamental, y es éste: el creer que la situación crea el escenario. Eso es una falacia, porque, al contrario, es el escenario el que crea la situación. Por eso el mejor autor teatral será siempre el mejor arquitecto. Ahí está nuestro teatro clásico, teatro nacional, donde los autores no hacen más que eso: llevar la acción sin relatos a través de muchos escenarios . . . Shakespeare empezó a escribir *Hamlet*, y de pronto se encontró con que Ofelia se le había muerto. 'A esta mujer hay que enterrarla', se dijo, sin duda. '¿Dónde la enterraremos? En un cementerio romántico, que puede ser, mejor que ningún otro, el cementerio de una aldea.' Allí llevó Shakespeare la acción de uno de los cuadros, sin ocurrírsele contar el entierro, como hubiera hecho cualquier autor de nuestros días. Una vez en el cementerio, Shakespeare se dijo: 'Aquí tiene que salir un sepulturero. Pero como un sepulturero solo se va a hacer pesado, lo mejor es que aparezcan dos sepultureros. Estos sepultureros tienen que hablar de algo mientras cavan la fosa de Ofelia. Al cavar la fosa lo natural es que encuentren algún hueso humano, y ya que han encontrado un hueso hagamos que éste sea el más noble: el cráneo.' Y de ahí surgió la admirable situación de *Hamlet*. Como lo son las admiraciones de los corifeos . . .

. . . Por esto nuestro género chico constituyó un teatro nacional cuando la tradición casticista se había borrado del teatro, desde que Moratín, a espaldas de nuestros clásicos, importó a España la técnica francesa con sus tres célebres unidades . . .

. . . Es un disparate decir que el teatro se ha de hacer sin literatura. En el teatro todo es literatura. Lo que ocurre es que a veces esa literatura es buena y otras es mala. Ejemplo: 'Tú me tragas a mí como se traga ese río el tiburonazo del mar.' Este párrafo es literatura. Y dice lo mismo que aquel otro de: 'Yo voy a ti como va sorbido al mar ese río.' Lo que ocurre es que el segundo es literatura buena y el otro es literatura mala. En el teatro todo es literatura, desde Calderón de la Barca hasta Muñoz Seca . . . Tal vez el teatro de Muñoz Seca es el que tiene mayor cantidad de literatura . . .

. . . El teatro ha de conmover a los hombres o divertirles; es igual. Pero si se trata de crear un teatro dramático español, hay que esperar a que esos intérpretes, viciados por un teatro de camilla casera, se acaben. Y entonces habrá que hacer un teatro sin relatos, ni únicos decorados; que siga el ejemplo del cine actual, que, sin palabras y sin tono, únicamente valiéndose del dinamismo y la variedad de imágenes, de escenarios, ha sabido triunfar en todo el mundo. (*Luz*, 23 November 1933, reproduced by Madrid, pp. 340–2)

2. 'Valle-Inclán y el teatro nuevo', interview with Luis Emilio Soto

El teatro es lo menos universal que existe. Cada país tiene el suyo. Cuanto más típico es un medio cuyo desarrollo le permite esa expresión de arte, mayor impedimento también para ser llevada a otra latitud. Así resulta cándido querer trasplantar el teatro brumoso del Norte al Mediodía. Allá impera la niebla, aquí el sol se recorta con sacabocados sobre Castilla. Además, el teatro antes que nada exige un público, incluso antes que el propio autor. Y la condición específica de este público es estar ligado por un sentimiento común, lo cual es privativo de un solo ambiente. Esta imprescindible cohesión se perfecciona y encarece hasta convertirse en fondo religioso (re-ligari), íntima y suprema comunidad hacia donde debe converger el haz de incitaciones estéticas. Y no crean que esta aptitud de conmover al que oye o al que ve, calando en su ser inefable, reclama siempre la comprensión ni es virtud tampoco del idioma . . . En Santiago de Compostela he visto a un fraile italiano que abrazándose al leño santo y gritando 'Dios' y el 'infierno' comunicaba más fervor a las almas que la más bella pieza oratoria sagrada. Radica este milagro por lo que al español toca, en que nos mueve la plástica antes que el concepto . . .

. . . El aficionado [taurino] que desde el tendido sigue con emoción las escenas del ruedo, se apasiona por los ojos al punto de llegar a extremos de delirio. Parejo espectáculo se desarrolla en el Frontón con el deporte éuskaro. Y bien, ambos no los concibo sino donde surgieron, como no puedo imaginar que haya regatas en el Manzanares.

. . . Otra prueba de la preponderancia que ejerce la plástica sobre el español la hallamos en la liturgia. La Pasión representada no tiene sentido para nuestra gente sino a través del espectáculo. Este elemento prestigia asimismo otros oficios religiosos. Así fué cómo San Ignacio sufrió siete procesos por practicar el culto a oscuras. En cuanto al latín, acá lo que menos interesa a nadie es entenderlo o no. Para juzgar la importancia de esto basta recordar que varios países, sin contar a Gran Bretaña, aprovechando la descomposición de la lengua del Lacio, adoptaron la propia con respecto al culto. Dentro de la Iglesia este acontecimiento es correlativo al cisma que originó la Vulgata. No ocurrió así en España, donde el mantenimiento del latín perdura todavía inalterable. Sintetizando, deducimos que el gran problema del dramaturgo español consiste en crear escenarios, combinar nuevas formas de espectáculo para regalo y solaz de los ojos. Remontándonos a *La Celestina*, hallamos esa variedad de cuadros que hoy convendría para ciertas obras con asistencia de decorados sintéticos. Pero esto no es todo. La salvación del teatro en España depende además de otro factor no menos importante . . .

El espíritu de la lengua es otro aspecto que el dramaturgo debe tener presente. Todo idioma que cuenta con muchas vocales es de medio tono como el francés (Francia es por antonomasia el país del medio tono). Justamente la obra de Rubén y del modernismo ha sido adaptar esa modalidad a la aspereza de nuestra habla, cuya falta de matices se compensa por la copia de acentos finales. El matiz, que es patrimonio de mentes ejercitadas, explica por qué son las clases cultas las que hablan mejor en Francia. La especial aptitud de ese idioma para sugerir, para traducir la ligereza, la reticencia y todos los grados sutiles de la expresión, no se revela si no es al servicio de espíritus finamente sensibles. Por eso, cuando conversan los franceses encantan, debido al juego de intenciones que consiente la flexibilidad de su idioma. Incluso en la comedia de bulevar más desamparada de gracia, destácase por lo común el diálogo pleno de *esprit*. Carece por completo de esta disposición para la frivolidad el recto romance de Castilla, lengua de labriegos, de clérigos y de jueces. Sucede aquí al revés de lo que pasa en Francia; su riqueza y su perfección hay que ir a sorprenderla entre el pueblo cuyos estados de alma van de extremo a extremo. Es el genio de nuestro idioma el que impone esas formas totales y definitivas: la sentencia, la imprecación, el denuesto, el grito. A causa de ese registro máximo que singulariza al español, antes que atraer, fatiga cuando se le oye. Es fácil comprobarlo. Dos cómicos tan pronto se encuentran, hablan a gritos por natural impulso. Por analogía recuerdo también que uno de los más altos momentos en *La noche del sábado* se suscita cuando entran en escena varias personas a todo gritar. Es éste, pues, otro de los términos capitales a cuyo régimen debe someterse en nuestro teatro toda creación genuina que aspire a tocar el alma del pueblo. A la importancia que asume el escenario, antes referida, es preciso ahora añadir la del grito. Ambas exigencias entroncan con nuestra tradición más legítima y son hoy más imperiosas que nunca, si es que madura el esfuerzo renovador entre nosotros. Concretemos la fórmula que tiene por delante el dramaturgo español: escenarios y gritos . . . (*La Nación*, 3 March 1929, quoted by Madrid, pp. 347–50)

3. Letter to C. Rivas Cherif, dated 12 December 1922

Querido Cipri: Tiempo hace que estoy para escribirle, y responderle al tema del teatro que me propone en una de sus cartas. Bueno es todo cuanto se haga por adecentar el concepto literario del teatro, y estimo así la voluntad de usted – Comedias arquetípicas o simplemente discretas, sea cualquiera su estructura y concepto escénico. Mis deseos acerca de un teatro futuro son otra cosa algo diversa. Dentro de mi concepto caben comedias malas y buenas – casi es lo mismo – lo inflexible es el concepto escénico. Advenir las tres unidades de los preceptistas en furia dinámica; sucesión de lugares para sugerir una superior unidad de ambiente; volumen en el tiempo; y tono lírico del motivo total sobre el tono del héroe. Todo esto acentuado por la representación, cuyas posibilidades emotivas de forma, luz y color – unidas en la prosodia – deben estar en la mente del buen autor de comedias. Hay que luchar contra el cine – Esa lucha es el teatro moderno. Tanto transformación en la mecánica de candilejas como en la técnica literaria.

Yo soy siempre un joven revolucionario, y poniéndome a decir la verdad, quisiera que toda reforma en el teatro comenzara por el fusilamiento de los Quintero. Seriamente, creo que la vergüenza del teatro es una consecuencia del desastre total de un pueblo, históricamente. El teatro no es un arte individual, todavía guarda algo de la efusión religiosa que levantó las catedrales. Es una consecuencia de la liturgia y arquitectura de la Edad Media. Sin un gran pueblo, imbuído de comunes ideas o dolores no puede haber teatro. Podrá haber líricos, filósofos, críticos, novelistas y pintores. Pero no dramaturgos ni arquitectos. Son artes colectivas. Primero los Faraones y las Pirámides después. Primero el honor caballeresco, después Don Pedro Calderón. El sentimiento de los espectadores crea la comedia, y aborta al autor dramático. ¿Quiénes son espectadores de las comedias? Padres honrados y tenderos, niñas idiotas, viejas con postizos, algún pollo majadero, y un forastero. Por eso los autores de comedias – desde Moratín hasta Benavente – parecen nacidos bajo una mesa-camilla. Son fetos abortados en una tertulia casera. En sus comedias están todas las lágrimas de la baja y burguesa sensibilidad madrileña.

Son los hijos de una sensibilidad y de un ingenio, que se estremece como ante un enigma alejandrino, cuando el bizarro capitán que agita la bolsa de lotería canta guiñando un ojo: los dos patitos. En fin, cuente conmigo, si algo puedo hacer en pro de ese intento. (Reproduced by Caamaño Bournacell)

4. 'El teatro futuro según las actuales generaciones', interview with T. Ortega

Yo creo que mi teatro es perfectamente representable. Más aún: que al actor español le va bien. Porque nuestros actores tienen, más que nada, el sentido de lo popular, de lo desgarrado ... Déles usted un párrafo literario o una tirada de versos, y la generalidad está perdida. En cambio, el tipo callejero o el tipo rural lo hace como nadie. Yo creo que mis 'esperpentos', por lo mismo que tienen una cosa de farsa popular entre lo trágico y lo grotesco, lo harían a perfección nuestros actores . . . Yo me imagino a Bonafé, por ejemplo, representando *Luces de bohemia* . . . Lo que caracteriza de una manera rotunda la tradición estética de nuestro teatro es el grito y la diversidad, la magnificencia de los escenarios. El grito le dan la luz y el idioma. Nuestro teatro no puede negar que nace en Castilla. Dos actores franceses se sientan frente a frente y empiezan a hablar. Cuando venimos a ver están hablando casi en voz baja. Dos actores españoles cruzan cuatro frases y ya están gritando. Es el idioma. El castellano es para gritar. ¿No se ha fijado usted cómo en el *Tenorio*, aquel monólogo, aquella reflexión – porque es una reflexión – que hace don Juan, después de matar a don Luis y al Comendador ('Llamé al cielo, y no me oyó . . .'), la dicen a gritos los actores? Sólo en castellano se puede meditar a gritos . . . Nuestro teatro necesita el grito y la decoración. Por eso me indigna ver adaptados a nuestros clásicos y románticos a la estética francesa: la reducción, la simplificación de escenarios. ¿Por qué le quitan a *El alcalde de Zalamea* los fondos magníficos en que lo imaginó Calderón? ¿Por qué le meten poco menos que en una 'sala decentemente amueblada'? ¡No! Calderón necesita todo su aparato escénico. Imagine usted a Pedro Crespo con su paisaje al fondo, el campo en uno de esos crepúsculos maravillosos de Castilla; imaginemos lo que podrían ser bien compuestas aquellas escenas de los labradores, los soldados, la gran escolta del rey que llega, las cajas que redoblan . . .

¡El campo! ¡La Naturaleza! Ahí está el caso de la adaptación escénica de la novela de Unamuno, *Nada menos que todo un hombre* . . . El personaje se ahoga, se empequeñece encerrado en aquellas paredes en que se desarrolla el último acto. ¡Qué no sería aquel hombre fuera de aquel gabinete burgués! ¡Qué no se podría hacer, si tuviera un fondo de plena Naturaleza, con aquella escena en que el hombre quiere defender a su mujer de la muerte, a puñetazos, a dentelladas, dando su sangre por ella, enfrentándose con Dios, con el Destino! Necesitamos los escenarios. Ibsen, lo he dicho en otras ocasiones, no puede prosperar en España.

Mi teoría tiene pruebas concluyentes. Ahí está Shakespeare. El diálogo de los enterradores, la calvera de Yorik, la escena de Laertes y Hamlet . . . todo aquello lo da, naturalmente, el lugar. No se puede, ni se debe eludir la diversidad de escenarios. Los clásicos y los románticos no escamotean ningún fondo. Ese es el camino del futuro teatro . (Reproduced by Madrid, pp. 351–3, from *La Gaceta literaria*, 15 October 1930)

5. Comments on a performance of Benavente's *Señora Ama*

A mí no me gusta un teatro de esa manera. Con los recursos de presencia que el teatro tiene, nos echa a la cara trozos de realidad. El arte no existe sino cuando ha superado sus modelos vivos mediante una elaboración ideal. Las cosas no son como las vemos sino como las recordamos. La palabra, en la creación literaria, necesita siempre ser trasladada a ese plano en que el mundo y la vida humana se idealizan. No hay poesía sin esa elaboración . . . (Madrid, p. 344)

6. Interview with Francisco Navas

—Al cinematógrafo sí va usted. Y hasta a algún salón de Varietés. Yo le vi, cierta solemnísima noche, en Maravillas, con Cipriano Rivas Cherif.

—Ciertamente; trabajaba Tórtola Valencia. ¿Y cómo no ir yo? Y a los cinematógrafos, ya lo creo que voy. Ese es el Teatro nuevo, moderno. La visualidad. Más de los sentidos corporales; pero es arte. Un nuevo Arte. El nuevo arte plástico. Belleza viva. Y algún día se unirán y completarán el Cinematógrafo y el Teatro por antonomasia, los dos Teatros en un solo Teatro. Y entonces se podrá concurrir, perder el tiempo en el Teatro.

España, tan racialmente teatral y plástica, es más calderoniana y echegarayesca que otra cosa. Y no penetra en el verdadero sentido de la realidad teatral. Y no tenemos ese teatro de universo. Estamos localizados – dígase así –. Nos falta el diálogo. Aunque poseamos el retoricismo vivido y hablado del denuesto, la imprecación, el apóstrofe. Pero nos falta el diálogo, que es el alma, que es el sentido medular; que en el diálogo está la médula vital del verdadero teatro, que no necesita de la representación escénica para ser teatro. Yo escribo todas mis obras en diálogo porque así salen de mi alma; y porque mi sentido de la vida así me lo ordena.

El diálogo, pues, es el signo de la perfección en el hombre y en el artista y en los pueblos. Francia es madre creadora del diálogo. Que es el matiz encantador y sugestivo, y que requiere además unos artistas excepcionales. Pero nos falta aquel, del mismo modo o por la misma razón que nos faltan artistas excepcionales – hay alguno como Ernesto Vilches –; y por la misma razón psicológica que en nuestra literatura de todos los tiempos no existen otros géneros literarios que se corresponden con la progenie que acusa la existencia del diálogo, como son las 'Memorias', los 'Epistolarios', las 'Grandes vidas' o 'Biografías', etc. Lo que supone, ya la dije a usted, artistas dignos de toda esta creación espiritual. Y aquel modo creador, modo de decir, de crear en escena, sólo con dos versos, que arrancan el entusiasmo, la admiración a la obra y al artista. Tal era Coquelin, haciéndose aclamar sólo en dos versos de Racine. Era el modo de decirlos. Y en otro que no fuese él pasaban inadvertidos.

—Y ahora comprendo. Usted, sin un Coquelin que interpretase su obra, usted pasaría inadvertido.

—No sé..., no sé... Eludamos. Es enojoso. Le repito que ignoro ese mundillo de bastidores, etc. Y le insisto en que nos falta ese verdadero Teatro que en Francia y en Italia, y sobre todo en Francia, ha producido los grandes creadores de grandes obras de diálogo, que es doble vida: que al fin ése es el Teatro, diálogo: sencillez y trascendencia. Lemas del diálogo. (Quoted by Alfaya, pp. 32–3, from Francisco Navas, *Las esfinges de Talía o encuesta sobre la crisis del teatro*, Imprenta del Real Monasterio de El Escorial, 1928)

7. 'Hablando con Valle-Inclán', interview with Gregorio Martínez Sierra

Comenzaré por decirle a usted que creo que hay tres modos de ver el mundo, artística o estéticamente: de rodillas, en pie o levantado en el aire.

Cuando se mira de rodillas – y ésta es la posición más antigua en literatura – se da a los personajes, a los héroes, una condición superior a la condición humana, cuando menos a la condición del narrador o del poeta. Así Homero atribuyó a sus héroes condiciones que en modo alguno tienen los hombres. Se crean, por decirlo así, seres superiores a la naturaleza humana: dioses, semidioses y héroes.

Hay una segunda manera, que es mirar a los protagonistas novelescos como de nuestra propia naturaleza, como si fuesen nuestros hermanos, como si fuesen ellos nosotros mismos, como si fuera el personaje un desdoblamiento de nuestro 'yo', con nuestras mismas virtudes y nuestros mismos defectos. Esta es, indudablemente la manera que más próspera. Esto es Shakespeare, todo Shakespeare. Los celos de Otelo, son los celos que podría haber sufrido el autor, y las dudas de Hamlet, las dudas que podría haber sentido el autor. Los personajes, en este caso, son de la misma naturaleza humana, ni más ni menos que el que los crea: son una realidad, la máxima verdad.

Y hay otra tercera manera, que es mirar el mundo desde un plano superior, y considerar a los personajes de la trama como seres inferiores al autor, con un punto de ironía. Los dioses se convierten en personajes de sainete. Esta es una manera muy española, manera de demiurgo, que no se cree en modo alguno hecho del mismo barro que sus muñecos. Quevedo tiene esta manera. Cervantes, también. A pesar de la grandeza de don Quijote, Cervantes se cree más cabal y más cuerdo que él, y jamás se emociona con él.

Esta manera es ya definitiva en Goya. Y esta consideración es la que me movió a dar un cambio en mi literatura y a escribir los 'esperpentos'... El mundo de los 'esperpentos' – explica uno de los personajes en *Luces de Bohemia* – es como si los héroes antiguos se hubiesen deformado en los espejos cóncavos de la calle, con un transporte grotesco, pero rigurosamente geométrico. Y estos seres deformados son los héroes llamados a representar una fábula no deformada. Son enanos y patizambos que juegan una tragedia. Y con este sentido los he llevado a *Tirano Banderas* y a *El Ruedo Ibérico*.

Vienen a ser estas dos novelas esperpentos acrecidos y trabajados con elementos que no podían darse en la forma dramática de *Luces de Bohemia* y *Los cuernos de don Friolera*. (*ABC*, 7 December 1928)

8. Extract from an interview with Esperanza Velázquez Bringas

Estoy haciendo algo distinto a mis obras anteriores. Ahora escribo teatro para muñecos. Es algo que he creado y que titulo 'Esperpentos'. Este teatro no es representable para actores, sino para muñecos, a la manera del teatro 'di Piccoli' en Italia.

De este género he publicado *Luces de Bohemia* que apareció en la revista *España* y *Los cuernos de don Friolera* que se publicó en *La Pluma*.

Esta modalidad consiste en buscar el lado cómico de lo trágico de la vida misma. ¿Imagina usted a un marido que riñera con su mujer, diciéndole parlamentos por el estilo de los del teatro de Echegaray? Porque hay que apropiar la literatura a ellos. ¿Supone usted esta escena? Pues bien, para ellos sería una escena dolorosa, acaso brutal . . . Para el espectador una sencilla farsa grotesca. Esto es algo que no existe en la literatura española. Sólo Cervantes vislumbró un poco de esto. Porque en el *Quijote* lo vemos continuamente. Don Quijote no reacciona nunca como un hombre, sino como un muñeco; por eso provoca la hilaridad de los demás, aun cuando él esté en momentos de pena.

En las figuras de Goya hay también rasgos del que observa el lado trágico-cómico. (Reprinted in *Repertorio Americano*, III, 13, 1921)

9. Comments on literary heroes

Los autores franceses se colocan siempre en éxtasis ante las peripecias del drama y las voces de los personajes. Divinizan sus héroes. Engendran dioses. Es el autor, en Francia, el primer vasallo de su prole. Exalta al protagonista y su drama por sobre lo más alto de los contornos humanos. Sirve a los héroes en el bien y en el mal como a divinidades extraordinarias. Los ingleses, obreros de corrección y sociabilidad, practican una literatura de club. El personaje de su obra se mueve dentro del círculo de sus amistades, sujeto a los derechos y a los deberes de los hombres de mundo. Al héroe lo inscribe en un círculo, le da la carta de ciudadanía y le concede voto en los comicios electorales. A la hora de las exaltaciones, respetuoso de los intereses de clase, le otorga un título de par. El autor y el personaje viven el mismo protocolo de humanidad. El drama es un simple suceso social, apenas digno de una referencia en 'The Times'. Otelo es un individuo de la familia que comete la incorrección de mostrarse exageradamente celoso. Los españoles nos colocamos siempre por encima del drama y de los intérpretes. Nos sabemos siempre moviendo a capricho los hilos de la farsa. Cervantes se siente superior a Don Quijote. Se burla un poco de él, se compadece, a veces, de sus dolores y locuras, le perdona sus arrebatos, y hasta le concede la gracia de una hora postrera de cordura para conducirlo, generoso, a las puertas del cielo. Los autores españoles, juvenilmente endiosados, gustamos de salpicar con un poco de dolor la existencia que creamos. Tenemos áspera la paternidad. Por capricho y por fuerza. Porque nos asiste la indignación de lo que vemos ocurrir fatalmente a nuestros pies. España es un vasto escenario elegido por la tragedia. Siempre hay una hora dramática en España; un drama superior a las facultades de los intérpretes. Estos, monigotes de cartón, sin idealidad y sin coraje, nos parecen ridículos en sus arreos de héroes. Gesticulan con torpeza de cómicos de la legua las situaciones más sublimemente trágicas. Don Quijote ha de encarnarse en un Quijote cualquiera. Los médicos diagnostican de fisiología ambigua los arrestos dramáticos de Don Juan. Todo nuestro censo de población no vale lo que una pandilla de comiquillos empecinados en representar el drama genial de la vida española. El resultado, naturalmente, es un esperpento . . . (Madrid, pp. 344–6)

10. Extract from an interview with José Montero Alonso

La vida – sus hechos, sus tristezas, sus amores – es siempre la misma, fatalmente. Lo que cambia son los personajes, los protagonistas de esa vida. Antes esos papeles los desempeñaban dioses y héroes. Hoy . . . bueno, ¿para qué vamos a hablar? Antes, el destino cargaba sobre los hombros – altivez y dolor – de Edipo o de Medea. Hoy, ese destino es el mismo, la misma su fatalidad, la misma su grandeza, el mismo su dolor . . . Pero los hombres que lo sostienen han cambiado. Las acciones, las inquietudes, las coronas, son las de ayer y las de siempre. Los hombros son distintos, minúsculos para sostener ese gran peso. De ahí nace el contraste, la desproporción, lo ridículo. En *Los cuernos de don Friolera*, el dolor de éste es el mismo de Otelo, y, sin embargo, no tiene su grandeza. La ceguera es bella y noble en Homero. Pero, en *Luces de Bohemia*, esa misma ceguera es triste y lamentable porque se trata de un poeta bohemio, de Máximo Estrella. (Quoted by Madrid, p. 114, from Prologue to Valle-Inclán, *Vísperas de la Gloriosa, La Novela de Hoy,* 16 May 1930)

Valle-Inclán's theatre: dates of first performances during the author's lifetime

Cenizas: by the 'Teatro Artístico' in Teatro Lara.	7 December 1899
El Marqués de Bradomín: by the F. García Ortega company in Teatro de la Princesa.	25 January 1906
La cabeza del dragón: by 'Teatro de los niños' in Teatro de la Comedia.	5 March 1910
Cuento de abril: by the Matilde Moreno company in Teatro de la Comedia.	19 March 1910
Voces de gesta: by the Guerrero–Mendoza company in Barcelona.	18 June 1911
(Madrid opening in Teatro de la Princesa, 26 May 1912)	
La Marquesa Rosalinda: by the Guerrero–Mendoza company in Teatro de la Princesa.	5 March 1912
La cabeza del Bautista: by Enrique López Alarcón in Teatro del Centro.	17 October 1924
(later in Teatro Goya, Barcelona, on 20 March 1925)	
Ligazón: in 'El Mirlo Blanco'.	8 May 1926
(by 'El Cántaro Roto' in Teatro de Bellas Artes, 19 December 1926)*	
Farsa y licencia de la reina castiza: by the López Heredia company in Teatro Muñoz Seca.	3 June 1931
El embrujado: by the López Heredia company in Teatro Muñoz Seca.*	11 November 1931
Divinas palabras: by Margarita Xirgu company in Teatro Español.	16 November 1933

* Directed by Valle-Inclán.

Notes

Full details of all works quoted or referred to in the text are given in the Bibliography. Author, short title (if necessary) and page number appear in the text.

Introduction

1. For a general survey of the Spanish theatre of this period consult Francisco Ruiz Ramón, *Historia del teatro español*. A reasonably full account in English is provided by Gwynne Edwards, *Lorca: The Theatre Beneath the Sand* (London: Calder & Boyars, 1980).
2. In March 1905 Valle composed a note of protest, which was signed by most of the younger writers and intellectuals of his day, against the proposal to organize an *homenaje* to celebrate Echegaray's Nobel prize. See Melchor Fernández Almagro, *Vida y literatura de Valle-Inclán*, pp. 94–5.
3. The most important of these productions were: *Divinas palabras* (1961); *Aguila de blasón* (1966); *La cabeza del Bautista*, *Farsa italiana de la enamorada del rey*, *La rosa de papel* (1967); *Cara de plata* (1968) and *Luces de Bohemia* (1971).
4. Not in Valencia as Rubia Barcia implies, p. 15. See *El Mercantil Valenciano*, 19 June 1911.
5. See Madrid, p. 350 and pp. 353–4 and interview in *ABC*, 23 June 1927.
6. Referring to his plays, he writes: 'Pero observe usted que las he publicado siempre con acotaciones que bastasen a explicarlas por la lectura, sin intervención de histriones. Si alguna de estas obras ha sido representada, yo he dado tan poca importancia, que en ningún momento he creído que debía hacer memoria del lamentable accidente, recordando en la edición el reparto de personajes y la fecha de la ejecución.' (Letter to Enrique Fajardo, 5 May 1927, quoted by Madrid, pp. 350–1.)
7. C. Rivas Cherif, 'Divulgación a la luz de las candilejas', *La Pluma*, August 1920. See Fernández Almagro, p. 210. For further information on Valle's connections with the theatre of the Escuela Nueva, consult Juan Antonio Hormigón, *Estudios Escénicos*, 16 (1972), 10–21.
8. In an interview with 'El Caballero Audaz', *La Esfera*, 6 March 1915, Valle mentioned that he was about to start work on a 'tragedy' for Margarita Xirgu which would be called 'Pan divino'. This could well have been the work that later became *Divinas palabras*.

1. Valle-Inclán and Symbolist aesthetics

1. Amongst those who have examined *Modernismo* and the Generation of '98 in the context of a common spiritual crisis embracing the whole of Europe are: José

María Aguirre, *Antonio Machado: poeta simbolista* (Madrid: Taurus, 1973); D. L. Shaw, *The Generation of 1898 in Spain* (London: Benn, 1975) and '*Modernismo*, idealism and the intellectual crisis in Spain: 1895–1910', *Renaissance and Modern Studies*, 25 (1981), 24–39; H. Ramsden, *The 1898 Movement in Spain* (Manchester University Press, 1974); R. Cardwell, *Juan Ramón Jiménez: the Modernist Apprenticeship 1895–1900* (Berlin: Colloquium Verlag, 1977). Many of the essays contained in Roland Grass and William Risley (eds), *Waiting for Pegasus: Studies of the Presence of Symbolism and Decadence in Hispanic Letters* (University of Illinois, 1979), also take this view. E. González López in *El arte dramático de Valle-Inclán* acknowledges the European climate of ideas behind Valle's work and traces his development through three phases of Decadence, Symbolism and Expressionism. Unfortunately, he tends to over-categorize and, rather than explaining the ideological content, indulges in constant repetition of the terminology.

2. Mallarmé's theories were eventually collected together and published in his *Divagations* (Paris: Fasquelle, 1896).

3. In his article 'Más cosas de don Ramón' (*La Pluma*, January 1923), Rivas Cherif writes: 'Conoce vagamente el italiano y no muy bien el francés' and claims to have seen a copy of D'Annunzio's *I laudi* constantly open at the same page on Valle's desk.

4. See G. Martínez Sierra (ed), *Un teatro de arte en España: 1917–1926*. This is a limited edition with reproductions of sets and costume designs.

5. See M. Maeterlinck, Preface to *Théâtre*, vol. 1, pp. xi–xii. He writes for example: 'Mais le poète dramatique ne peut se borner à ces généralités. Il est obligé de faire descendre dans la vie réelle, dans la vie de tous les jours, l'idée qu'il se fait de l'inconnu. Il faut qu'il nous montre de quelle façon, sous quelle forme, dans quelles conditions, d'après quelles lois, à quelle fin, agissent sur nos destinées, les puissances supérieures, les influences inintelligibles, les principes infinis, dont, en tant que poète, il est persuadé que l'univers est plein.'

6. See *Lámpara*, pp. 88–9 and p. 114; Yeats, *Plays and Controversies*, p. 103 and p. 159.

7. Similar ideas are expressed by Nietzsche in *The Birth of Tragedy*, pp. 40–2.

8. 'Yo no soy escritor. Yo soy militar. Es decir que, por una parte, contemplo las cosas panorámicamente, "a ojo de águila", como contempla el guerrero su campo de combate; y por otra, acometo siempre las obras por rapto de audacia, a lo militar.' (Quoted by Alfonso Reyes in 'La parodia trágica', *España*, 10 July 1920.) See also Madrid, p. 108 and p. 195.

9. 'I hated and still hate with an ever-growing hatred the literature of the point of view. I wanted, if my ignorance permitted, to get back to Homer, to those who fed at his table' (Yeats, *Essays*, p. 511).

10. 'La canzone popolare è quasi una revelazione musicale del mondo. In ogni canzone popolare (vera, terrestra, nata di popolo) è una imagine di sogno che interpreta l'Apparenza. La melodia primordiale, che si manifesta nelle canzoni popolari ed è modulata in diversi modi dall'istinto del popolo, mi sembra la più profonda parola su l'Essenza del mondo' (G. D'Annunzio, *Poesie, Teatro, Prose*, p. 470).

11. Cf. Valle's remarks on the stories told by the blind old woman in *Lámpara*, p. 123.

12. 'En arte, cuando no se es un genio, lo mejor es imitar al pueblo. Éste es el guía y el maestro más certero. Yo me he valido de él siempre y no me ha ido mal' (Madrid, p. 26).

13. 'I would have Ireland recreate the ancient arts as they were understood in Judea, in India, in Scandinavia, in Greece and Rome, in every ancient land; as they were understood when they moved a whole people and not a few people who have grown up in a leisured class and made this understanding their

business' (*Essays*, p. 206). See also 'The Galway Plains', *Essays*, p. 213, in which he maintains that great drama requires above all a people to respond to it and a culture to contain it.

14. 'La suprema belleza de las palabras sólo se revela, perdido el significado con que nacen, en el goce de su esencia musical, cuando la voz humana, por virtud del tono, vuelve a infundirles toda su ideología' (*Lámpara*, p. 60).

15. Examples of scenes with a marked rhythmical structure: *Aguila de blasón* (II, 2) and *Divinas palabras* (II, 5).

16. Much of what follows is reproduced from my article 'Valle-Inclán and the Art of the Theatre'.

17. In this respect, the Belgian playwright Michel de Ghelderode offers an interesting parallel with Valle-Inclán: 'Pour moi, l'oeuvre théâtrale n'existe pas sans la sensualité propre aux arts plastiques, ou alors n'existe que dans la forme d'un dialogue qui peut se lire et n'appelle pas la mise en scène' (M. de Ghelderode, *Les Entretiens d'Ostende*, p. 62). For further comments on this parallel see Juan Guerrero Zamora, *Historia del teatro contemporáneo*, vol. 1, pp. 151–206.

18. Gordon Craig also comments on the scenic and gestural qualities of Shakespeare's dialogue (Craig, pp. 149–55). See Valle's reported comments on the sofa scene in Zorrilla's *Don Juan Tenorio* in R. Gómez de la Serna, *Don Ramón María del Valle-Inclán*, p. 107. One example among many of a dialogue stemming from the physical properties of a scene in Valle's own theatre is *Divinas palabras* (II, 3) in which the detail of Séptimo's eye-patch is used in the arrangement of an assignation between Mari-Gaila and Séptimo Miau.

19. *La cabeza del Bautista* and *La hija del capitán* are the only plays which involve explanations of a situation pre-existent to the action.

20. In an interview in *ABC*, 23 June 1927, he declared: 'Y me gusta, claro es, el teatro, y he hecho teatro, procurando vencer todas las dificultades inherentes al género. He hecho teatro tomando como maestro a Shakespeare.'

2. The early theatre

1. For an account of the incident with Manuel Bueno, see the interview with 'El Caballero Audaz' (*La Esfera*, 6 March 1915) reproduced in José Esteban (ed.), *Valle-Inclán visto por . . .*, pp. 301–10.

2. *El arte dramático de Valle-Inclán*, p. 33. The attribution of a 'decadent' philosophy to Maeterlinck might cause a few critical eyebrows to be raised. González López invalidates his argument by selecting examples mainly from the *acotaciones* added to the revised version of 1908 in which the influence of Maeterlinck is visible in the style and presentation, if not in the content.

3. The story first appeared in *Femeninas* (Pontevedra: Imprenta de Andrés Landín, 1895).

4. This linking of nature and emotion is seen not only in the *acotaciones* (e.g. pp. 144, 146) but also in the dialogue (e.g. pp. 125–6).

5. Bradomín is clearly not representative in the same sense as Padre Rojas and Doña Soledad are representative in *Cenizas*, since his character is not subordinated to an ideological conflict.

3. The hero and his chorus

1. These dates refer to the publication in book form. *Aguila* was published in Barcelona in 1907 and *Romance* (originally in a five-act version) in Madrid in January 1908. Fragments of *Aguila* had previously appeared in the newspaper *El*

Imparcial on 28 May 1905, 2 June 1906 and 11 March 1907. I was unable to discover an item entitled 'Comedia bárbara' in the issue of 18 July 1906 listed by Robert Lima in his bibliography. *Romance de lobos* was serialized in the Madrid newspaper *El Mundo* between 21 October and 26 December 1907.

2. *Cara de plata* will be discussed in a separate chapter in the context of Valle's later development. Alfredo Matilla Rivas in *Las 'Comedias bárbaras': historicismo y expresionismo dramático* puts the case for considering *Cara de plata* as an integral part of the trilogy.

3. I refer principally to the generation of T. S. Eliot, Jean Cocteau and García Lorca who, following the lead of the Symbolists, consciously tried to broaden and universalize the scope of European drama, still dominated by naturalism, by introducing a poetic conception of theatre which did not rely simply on 'poetic' language. The chorus or its equivalent was seen as an essential part of that 'broadening' process which made the audience see beyond the action in itself to its wider significance.

4. *La Mort de Tintagiles* is based on the image of a succession of doors culminating in a final scene of 'une grande porte de fer sous des voûtes très sombres'.

5. Montenegro's 'conversion' thus involves no change of social ideology in that his attitude remains resolutely paternalistic. There is no suggestion that the poor shall inherit the structures of power. See José Antonio Gómez Marín, *La idea de la sociedad en Valle-Inclán*, esp. pp. 31–46.

6. Montenegro refers to him as 'Job' on one occasion (*Romance*, p. 62).

7. It is interesting that Lorca himself failed to see the hinterland of unseen forces and archetypes in Valle's presentation of Galicia. In an interview given in 1933, he dismisses Valle's vision of his native province as 'algo tan falso y tan malo como los Quintero en Andalucía. Si te fijas, toda la Galicia de Valle-Inclán, como toda la Andalucía de los Quintero, es una Galicia de primeros términos: la niebla . . . el aullido del lobo . . .' (*La Mañana* (León), August 1933. Quoted by Antonio Buero Vallejo, *Tres maestros ante el público*, p. 121.)

8. From the reported version of a lecture by Valle-Inclán on 'Concepto de la vida y del arte' in *El Mercantil Valenciano*, 31 May 1911.

9. *España*, 8 March 1924. This is in fact a letter to Rivas Cherif thanking him for an article on the *Comedias bárbaras* published on 16 February in the same periodical.

10. Report of a public lecture by Valle-Inclán delivered in the Teatro Principal and published in *El Castellano* (Burgos), 23 October 1925.

4. Culmination of the collective heroic theatre

1. Fernández Almagro, pp. 144–5. The date of the original interview seems to have been in November or December 1910, but I have been unable to consult this.

2. Ayala refers to *Cuento de abril* as 'un pequeño canon del drama poético'.

3. *Diario de Navarra*, 28 June, 7 and 9 July 1911. Allowance should be made for the political bias of this commentator.

5. The transitional phase

1. These articles were originally published in *Los Lunes de El Imparcial* on 11, 14, 17, 23, 30 October; 13, 23 November and 4, 18 December 1916. A second part, 'En la luz del día' was published in the same newspaper on 8, 22 January and 5, 26 February 1917. Both parts appear in the Espasa Calpe edition of *Flor de santidad* and *La media noche* (Madrid, 1970).

2. Consult Robert Lima, 'The Commedia dell'Arte and *La Marquesa Rosalinda*' in

Zahareas (ed.), *Appraisal*, pp. 368–415. See Greenfield, *Anatomía*, pp. 114–33, for echoes of Darío in the play, esp. pp. 116 and 118.

6. Two late farces

1. Although the landscape in *La enamorada* may not be charged with historical significance, there can be no doubt about Valle's view on Spain's historical destiny. In *La lámpara* (pp. 52–4) he sets out what is more or less the orthodox '98 position. Spain's overseas adventures of conquest and exploration during the reign of the Catholic monarchs had been a historical blunder, contrary to the essential character of the race, which had induced illusions of grandeur and had spawned four centuries of 'literatura jactanciosa y vana'. This split between an external and an 'intra-historic' tradition was, for Valle, encapsulated in the language, in the contrast between the hollow, latinized vocabulary of the 'prosa castiza' and the 'romance castellano' which came from an essentially rural tradition. In this section of the *Lámpara* Valle comes very close to defining the essence of the *esperpento* when he contrasts the present degenerate state of the nation with the grandiose, sacrosanct attitudes that are enshrined in the rhetorical dead wood of the language: 'Ya no somos una raza de conquistadores y de teólogos, y en el romance alienta siempre esa ficción. Ya no es nuestro el camino de las Indias, ni son españoles los Papas, y en el romance perdura la hipérbole barroca, imitado del viejo latín cuando era soberano del mundo. Ha desaparecido aquella fuerza hispana donde latían como tres corazones la fortuna en la guerra, la fe católica y el ansia de aventuras, pero en la blanda cadena de los ecos sigue volando el engaño de su latido, semejante a la luz de la estrella que se apagó hace mil años . . .'
2. Rivas Cherif also includes the play in the list of *esperpentos* ('Más cosas de don Ramón', *La Pluma*, January 1923).

7. The dynamic tension

1. E.g. *El pintor de su deshonra (auto)* and *El veneno y la triaca*. Umpierre suggests that these works may well have inspired *Divinas palabras*, which, like the *autos*, he sees as a play about the sin and redemption of humanity (p. 21).
2. Valle stresses the impossible nature of this ambition, since the Devil's knowledge is inevitably limited to the present. See *Lámpara*, p. 31.
3. 'Ante todo, hay que recordar que en éstas [sus obras dramáticas] los hechos suelen ser la expresión simbólica de ciertas ideas fundamentales a la visión particular del autor sobre el hombre y la realidad. El principio rector de su estética es, generalmente, de analogía y correspondencia; éste se manifiesta por medio de un intrincado sistema de símbolos y alusiones con los cuales Valle-Inclán acentúa el carácter arquetípico, mítico y eterno de su creación literaria' (Umpierre, '*Divinas palabras*', p. 10).
4. These are contradictions inherent in the nature of this subject matter, not, as was the case in much of the early work, artistically contrived juxtapositions to produce interesting aesthetic chemistry.

8. The metamorphoses of the *esperpento*

1. E. Díez-Canedo's review in *El Sol*, 18 October 1924, refers to the performance of the actors and comments adversely on the Argentine accent of one of them.
2. For an excellent summary of these historical events see Gerald Brenan, *The Spanish Labyrinth*, particularly chapters 2 and 4.

3. A similar expression of opinion may be found on p. 151.
4. It appeared in successive issues from 31 July to 23 October 1920. What follows on the question of the two versions is substantially the text of my 'Note on the Two Versions of *Luces de Bohemia*'.
5. A complete list of variants is given in Zamora Vicente, *La realidad esperpéntica*.
6. The only textual clue as to when the revisions were made is an allusion to a 'Sargento Basallo' in scene 4 of the definitive version, substituted for 'Don Torcuato el Aceitero' in the original. Sergeant Basallo was a prisoner of war in Spanish Morocco from July 1921 to January 1923 after the defeat of the Spanish army at Anual. His reputation as a national hero, however, dates from his return to Spain in January 1923 and from the publication of his *Memorias del cautiverio* later that year. It is unlikely therefore that the revisions, assuming they were all carried out at the same period, could have been made before the latter half of 1923. For a full account of Sergeant Basallo, see Zamora Vicente, pp. 108–12.
7. I naturally refer to Valle-Inclán's view of 'Calderonian' values. See Prologue to *Los cuernos*.
8. Elsewhere Cardona claims that 'a través de toda esta obra, camina sobre la cuerda floja entre lo auténticamente trágico y lo radicalmente ridículo' (p. 160).
9. The question of aesthetic distance in Valle's later plays will be discussed in the final chapter.
10. Francisco Madrid notes the following comments by Valle-Inclán without quoting source or date: 'Muñoz Seca sigue acaparando los carteles. Se le desdeña y no con razón, porque Muñoz Seca puede ser la cuna de un gran teatro. Diversas etapas tiene la dramática. Todos los teatros nacen en la plazuela, que es el primer estrato. Y el último es llegar a Molière. Muñoz Seca está en la plazuela. Lo malo no es el teatro cuando está fuera de la literatura como en Muñoz Seca; lo malo es el teatro cuando significa literatura mal digerida y llega a lo cursi' (Madrid, p. 343).
11. I refer of course to Valle-Inclán's well-known and much-quoted remarks on the three ways of looking at the world, artistically speaking – 'de rodillas, de pie, o levantado en el aire'. See Appendix 7.
12. *Las galas* and *La hija* were originally published in *La Novela Mundial* on 20 May 1926 and 28 July 1927 respectively (nos 10 and 72).
13. The original version, published under the title *El terno del difunto*, contains none of the more outspoken political criticisms.
14. Sumner Greenfield acutely observes the significance of this action in his short but very penetrating chapter on *Las galas* (*Anatomía*, pp. 271–7).
15. This seems to be the innuendo behind Juanito's request for 'una soga', followed by the carrying of the Boticaria to the bed and the final stage direction of 'se apaga la luz oportunamente'.
16. For the historical background to *La hija del capitán* I am indebted to Cardona and Zahareas, *Visión del esperpento*, pp. 202–10, whose detailed account I summarize here.
17. Antonio Risco in *La estética de Valle-Inclán* (pp. 116–18) quotes this scene as an example of the impracticability of Valle-Inclán's theatre and his essentially cinematic imagination. I believe that the capabilities of modern stage techniques and the wide range of conventions which contemporary audiences are now prepared to accept should give the lie to this opinion. In the past many critics have tended to take Valle's *acotaciones* as literal instructions to the director rather than as descriptive passages which convey the tone and atmosphere of a scene. If a real train cannot be got on stage then lighting and sound effects can do the job. The essential element in this scene is the contrast of pomp and squalor and what

makes it theatrical is that this visual contrast underlines and reinforces the theme.

18. For example, the Martínez Sierra interview, quoted in Appendix 7.

9. The hero's return?

1. E.g. 'Las voces de los chalanes y el ladrido de los perros prolongan un épico verso en los cristales matinales' (p. 10).

2. There can of course be no doubt that Valle's intention was to incorporate *Cara de plata* into the total structure of the trilogy. The remarks in his 'Autocrítica' and the evidence of a letter to Manuel Azaña, director of *La Pluma*, (see Leda Schiavo, 'Cartas inéditas de Valle-Inclán', *Insula*, 398 (1980), p. 1) point to a conscious attempt to balance the end of *Cara de plata* with the opening scene of *Romance de lobos* by echoing the motif of the nocturnal torch-light procession. His purpose was evidently to create a contrast between the burlesque irreverence, the charade of death, sacrilege and confession that concludes *Cara de plata* and the more solemn treatment of *Romance* as the realities of retribution, repentence and death make themselves felt. The contrast certainly exists; the question is whether it worked as Valle intended. My contention is that the burlesque elements are so steeped in the later anti-tragic aesthetic that they fail to blend with the heroic style of fourteen years earlier.

3. When he allows the *feriantes* to pass with the cry of '¡Pasad con mil demonios!'

4. See Professor Greenfield's chapter on *Cara de plata* for an illuminating analysis of Fuso Negro's 'odyssey' and the hours of light and darkness in the play.

5. *Cara de plata* (II, 7). E.g. 'Este caballo de oros es un enamorado. Si no eres tú, otro no veo. Esta sota de espadas cabeza para abajo es una llorosa Madalena: ¡Tal se me representa! Y este cinco de copas es licencia, y pecado con este rey del palo de bastos, que vino encima de todas las cartas. Hay aquí tres ases, que son poderes y luego tres caballos contrapuestos' (p. 106).

11. Valle-Inclán and the modern theatre

1. By far the most important – and responsible – criticism on this aspect of Valle's theatre is contained in the essays of Anthony N. Zaharreas and Juan Guerrero Zamora's chapter on Valle-Inclán in his *Historia del teatro contemporáneo*, vol. 1.

2. 'No debemos hacer arte ahora, porque jugar en los tiempos que corren es inmoral, es una canallada. Hay que lograr primero una justicia social. Así Don Ramón no quiere hacer arte puro; pretende hacer historia solamente.' 'Valle-Inclán no reniega del Arte; suspende la actividad artística y se lanza a la pelea' (*La Internacional*, 3 September 1920). This article does not appear in *El Sol* as recorded by many critics.

3. See Valle-Inclán, *Luces de Bohemia*, ed. A. Zaharreas, Introduction, pp. 30–1. All future references to this work will appear as 'Introduction'.

4. See *Brecht on Theatre*, pp. 79, 87, 101, 190. All statements on Brechtian theory are derived from this work.

5. Zaharreas, Introduction to *Luces*, p. 36. For Zaharreas's full argument that the *esperpento* combines the Absurdist philosophy with a historical view, see *Appraisal*, p. 627, *Visión*, p. 98, and his article 'The Esperpento and the Aesthetics of Commitment'. Certainly the 'historical view' as defined by Brecht would deny the *a priori* metaphysical assumptions of the Absurdists.

6. See also Zaharreas's article 'The Absurd, the Grotesque and the Esperpento' in *Appraisal*, pp. 78–108, esp. pp. 101–4.

7. 'Therefore the artist must reduce the subjects he finds and runs into everywhere if he wants to turn them into real materials, hoping always that he will succeed. He parodies his materials, contrasts them consciously with what they have actually been turned into. By this means, by this act of parody, the artist regains his freedom and hence his material; and this material is no longer found but invented. In laughter man's freedom becomes manifest, in crying his necessity' ('Problems', p. 73).

8. Ghelderode also refers to the influence of expressionist cinema, the circus and the music hall on his theatre (*Les Entretiens d'Ostende*, p. 77).

9. See also R. Cardona, '*Los cuernos de don Friolera*: estructura y sentido', *Appraisal*, p. 671, n. 32.

10. The most reliable summary of Brecht's theories is perhaps his 'Short Organum for the Theatre' in *Brecht on Theatre*, pp. 179–205. See in particular sections 63–7.

11. Since handing over the completed manuscript, two very illuminating articles by Rafael Osuna on cinematic influence in the theatre of Valle-Inclán have come to my attention – too late, unfortunately, to incorporate their insights and conclusions into this chapter. They are: 'La figura humana en *Las galas del difunto* de Valle-Inclán', *Journal of Spanish Studies: XXth Century*, 8 (1980), 103–16, and 'Un "guión cinematográfico" de Valle-Inclán: *Luces de Bohemia*', *Bulletin of Hispanic Studies*, 59 (1982), 120–8.

Bibliography

The most complete bibliography of works by and on Valle-Inclán up to 1972 is Robert Lima, *An Annotated Bibliography of Ramón del Valle-Inclán* (Pennsylvania State University Libraries, 1972).

Editions of works by Valle-Inclán quoted in the text

Aguila de blasón, Buenos Aires: Espasa Calpe, 1950
Cara de plata, Buenos Aires: Espasa Calpe, 1946
Cenizas, Madrid: Bernardo Rodríguez y Perma, 1899
Divinas palabras, Madrid: Espasa Calpe, 1961
La lámpara maravillosa, Buenos Aires: Espasa Calpe, 1948
Luces de Bohemia, Madrid: Espasa Calpe, 1961
Luces de Bohemia. Trans. A. N. Zahareas and G. Gillespie. Ed. A. M. Zahareas. Edinburgh: Edinburgh Bilingual Library, 1976
El Marqués de Bradomín, Madrid: Espasa Calpe, 1961 (with *Flor de santidad*)
La Marquesa Rosalinda, Madrid: Espasa Calpe, 1961
Martes de carnaval (*Las galas del difunto, Los cuernos de don Friolera, La hija del capitán*), Madrid: Espasa Calpe, 1964
La media noche, Madrid: Espasa Calpe, 1970 (with *Flor de Santidad*)
Retablo de la avaricia, la lujuria y la muerte (*Ligazón, La rosa de papel, El embrujado, La cabeza del Bautista, Sacrilegio*), Madrid: Espasa Calpe, 1961
Romance de lobos, Buenos Aires: Espasa Calpe, 1947
Tablado de marionetas (*La enamorada del rey, La cabeza del dragón, Farsa y licencia de la reina castiza*), Madrid: Espasa Calpe, 1961
Voces de gesta. Cuento de abril, Madrid: Espasa Calpe, 1960
El yermo de las almas, Madrid: Alianza, 1970

Articles and reports of lectures

'Autocrítica', *España*, 8 March 1924
'Concepto de la vida y del arte', lecture reported in *El Mercantil Valenciano*, 31 May 1911
'La literatura nacional española', lecture reported in *El Castellano* (Burgos), 23 October 1925
'Valle-Inclán y su opinión sobre el "cine"', *El Bufón* (Barcelona), 15 February 1924

Other works consulted or cited in the text

Alberich, José. '*Cara de plata*, fuera de serie', *Bulletin of Hispanic Studies*, 45 (1968), 299–308

Alfaya, Javier. *Valle-Inclán viviente*, Colección los Suplementos, 26, Editorial Cuadernos para el Diálogo, 1971

Alonso, José Luis. 'Mi cuaderno de dirección de tres obras de Valle', *Primer Acto*, 82 (1967), 28–31

Amor y Vázquez, José. 'Valle-Inclán y las musas: Terpsícore', in *Homenaje al profesor William L. Fichter*. Ed. D. Kossof and J. Amor y Vázquez, Madrid: Editorial Castalia, 1971, pp. 11–31

Artaud, Antonin. *The Theatre and its Double*. Trans. Victor Corti. London: Calder & Boyars, 1970

Avalle-Arce, J. B. 'La esperpentización de don Juan Tenorio', *Hispanófila*, 7 (1959), 29–39

'*Voces de gesta*: tragedia pastoril', in A. N. Zahareas, ed., *Appraisal*, pp. 361–73

Bary, David. 'La "inaccesible categoría estética" de Valle-Inclán', *Papeles de Son Armadans*, 52 (1969), 221–38

Benítez Claros, Rafael. 'Metricismos en las *Comedias bárbaras*', *Revista de Literatura*, 5 (1953), 247–91

Bermejo Marcos, Manuel. *Valle-Inclán. Introducción a su obra*, Salamanca: Anaya, 1971

Blanquat, Josette. 'Symbolisme et esperpento dans *Divinas palabras*', in *Mélanges à la mémoire de Jean Sarrailh*, I, Paris: Centre de Recherches de l'Institut d'Etudes Hispaniques, 1966, pp. 145–65

Borel, Jean-Paul. *Théâtre de l'impossible*, Neuchâtel: Editions de la Baconnière, 1963, pp. 115–52

Boudreau, Harold L. 'The creation of Valle-Inclán's *Sacrilegio*', *Symposium* (Syracuse), 22 (1968), 16–24

Brecht, B. *Brecht on Theatre*. Ed. and trans. John Willett, London: Eyre Methuen, 1978

Brenan, Gerald. *The Spanish Labyrinth*, Cambridge University Press, 1943

Brooks, J. L. 'Valle-Inclán's *Retablo de la avaricia, la lujuria y la muerte*', in *Hispanic Studies in Honour of I. González Llubera*. Ed. Frank Pierce, Oxford: Dolphin, 1959, pp. 87–104

Brunetière, Ferdinand. 'Le Symbolisme contemporain', *Revue des Deux Mondes*, 104 (1891), 681–92

Buero Vallejo, Antonio. *Tres maestros ante el público*, Madrid: Alianza, 1973. (Article on Valle-Inclán 'De rodillas, en pie, en el aire', originally published in *Revista de Occidente*, 44–5 (1966), 132–45)

Bugliani, A. *La presenza di D'Annunzio in Valle-Inclán*, Milan: Cisalpino–La Goliardica, 1976

Caamaño Bournacell, J. 'Valle-Inclán y el concepto del teatro', in *Mélanges à la mémoire d'A. Joncha-Ruau*, Provence U.P., 1978, pp. 501–15

Caballero Audaz, El. Interview with Valle-Inclán, *La Esfera*, 6 March 1915. (Reproduced in J. Esteban, ed., *Valle-Inclán visto por . . .*, pp. 301–10)

Campos, Gregorio. Interview with Valle-Inclán, *El Correo Español*, 4 December 1911

Cardona, Rodolfo and Zahareas, Anthony N. *Visión del esperpento. Teoría y práctica en los esperpentos de Valle-Inclán*, Madrid: Editorial Castalia, 1970

Cardona, R. '*Los cuernos de don Friolera*: estructura y sentido', in A. N. Zahareas, ed., *Appraisal*, pp. 636–71

Casalduero, Joaquín. 'Sentido y forma de *Martes de carnaval*', in A. N. Zahareas, ed., *Appraisal*, pp. 686–94

Cepeda Adán, José. 'El fondo histórico-social de *Luces de bohemia*', *Cuadernos Hispanoamericanos*, 199–200 (1966), 227–46

Craig, E. Gordon. *On the Art of the Theatre*, London: Mercury Books, 1962

D'Annunzio, G. *Poesie, teatro, prose*. Ed. Mario Praz and Ferdinando Gerra. Milan: Riccardo Ricciardi Editore, 1966

Díaz Ortiz, Pedro. 'Valle-Inclán y el teatro contemporáneo', *Cuadernos Hispano-americanos*, 199–200 (1966), 445–50

Díaz Plaja, G. *Las estéticas de Valle-Inclán*, Madrid: Gredos, 1965

Díez-Canedo, E. *Artículos de crítica teatral. El teatro español de 1914 a 1936*, Mexico D.F.: Joaquín Mortiz, 1968

'Ensayos de teatro dirigidos por Valle-Inclán', *El Sol*, 21 December 1926

El teatro y sus enemigos, La Casa de España en Mexico, 1939

Domenech, Ricardo. 'Para una visión actual del teatro de los esperpentos', *Cuadernos Hispanoamericanos*, 199–200 (1966), 455–66

Duende de la Colegiata, El. Interview with Valle-Inclán, *El Heraldo de Madrid*, 4 March 1912

Durán, M. '*Los cuernos de don Friolera* y la estética de Valle-Inclán', *Insula*, 236–7 (1966), 5, 28

'Valle-Inclán y el sentido de lo grotesco', *Papeles de Son Armadans*, 127 (1966), 109–31

Durán, V. 'Escenografia y vestuario: Valle-Inclán con sus acotaciones en verso', *La Voz*, 20 January 1936

Dürrenmatt, F. 'Problems of the theatre', reprinted in *Theatre in the Twentieth Century*, Ed. Robert W. Corrigan, New York: Grove Press, 1963, pp. 49–76

Writings on Theatre and Drama. Trans. H. M. Waidson. London: Jonathan Cape, 1976

Esslin, M. *The Theatre of the Absurd*, London: Penguin Books, 1968

Esteban, J., ed. *Valle-Inclán visto por . . .*, Madrid: Ediciones de El Espejo, 1973

Fernández Almagro, M. *Vida y literatura de Valle-Inclán*, 2nd edn, Madrid: Taurus, 1966

García Pavón, F. '*Cenizas* (primer drama de Valle-Inclán)', *Insula*, 236–7 (1966), 10

Gardiner, P. *Schopenhauer*, London: Penguin Books, 1963

Ghelderode, M. de. *Les Entretiens d'Ostende*, Paris: Arche, 1956

Gómez Marín, J. A. *La idea de la sociedad en Valle-Inclán*, Madrid: Taurus, 1967

'Valle: estética y compromiso', *Cuadernos Hispanoamericanos*, 199–200 (1966), 175–203

Gómez de la Serna, R. *Don Ramón María del Valle-Inclán*, Buenos Aires: Espasa Calpe, 1944

González López, E. *El arte dramático de Valle-Inclán*, New York: Las Américas, 1967

Greenfield, Sumner M. '*Cuento de abril*: Literary reminiscences and commonplaces', in A. N. Zahareas, ed., *Appraisal*, pp. 353–60

'Stylization and deformation in Valle-Inclán's *La reina castiza*', *Bulletin of Hispanic Studies*, 39 (1962), 78–89

Valle-Inclán: anatomía de un teatro problemático, Madrid: Editorial Fundamentos, 1972

Guerrero Zamora, J. *Historia del teatro contemporáneo*, vol. I, Barcelona: Juan Flors, 1961

Herrero, J. 'La sátira del honor en los esperpentos', in A. N. Zahareas, ed., *Appraisal*, pp. 672–85

Herrero, P. 'Valle-Inclán dramaturge', *Théâtre Populaire*, 24 (1955), 24–30

Hormigón, J. A. *Ramón del Valle-Inclán: la cultura, la política, el realismo y el pueblo*, Madrid: Comunicación Serie B, 1972

'Valle-Inclán y el teatro de la Escuela Nueva', *Estudios Escénicos*, 16 (1972), 10–21

Huret, J. *Enquête sur l'évolution littéraire*, Vanves: Les éditions THOT, 1982. (Reprint of 1892 Charpentier edn)

Ilie, P. 'The Grotesque in Valle-Inclán', in A. N. Zahareas, ed., *Appraisal*, pp. 493–539

Ionesco, E. *Notes et contrenotes*, Paris: Gallimard, 1962

Joyce, James. *A Portrait of the Artist as a Young Man*, London: Jonathan Cape, 1954

Kirkpatrick, Susan, 'From *Octavia Santino* to *El yermo de las almas*', *Revista Hispánica Moderna*, 37 (1972–3), 56–72

Knight, G. Wilson. *Shakespearean Production*, London: Faber, 1936

Kott, Jan. *Shakespeare, Our Contemporary*, London: Methuen, 1965

Landín Carrasco, R. 'El teatro de Valle-Inclán o la profecía de don Ramón', *ABC*, 27 February 1962

Lima, R. 'The Commedia dell'Arte and *La Marquesa Rosalinda*', in A. N. Zahareas, ed., *Appraisal*, pp. 386–415

Ling, D. 'Valle-Inclán's compromise with the Spanish stage. A comparative study of *El Marqués de Bradomín* and its source, the *Sonatas*', *Revue des Langues Vivantes*, 39 (1973), 46–58

López Núñez, J. Interview with Valle-Inclán, *Por esos mundos*, 1 January 1915

Losada, B. 'Valle-Inclán entre Galicia y Brecht', *Estudios Escénicos*, 13 (1969), 61–80

Lyon, J.E. '*La media noche*: Valle-Inclán at the crossroads', *Bulletin of Hispanic Studies*, 52 (1975), 135–42

'Note on the two versions of *Luces de Bohemia*', *Bulletin of Hispanic Studies*, 47 (1970), 52–6

'Valle-Inclán and the art of the theatre', *Bulletin of Hispanic Studies*, 46 (1969), 132–52

Madrid, F. *La vida altiva de Valle-Inclán*, Buenos Aires: Poseidón, 1943

Maeterlinck, M. *Théâtre*, 3 vols, Brussels: Lacomblez, 1911

Le Trésor des humbles, Paris: Mercure de France, 1898

Maravall, J. A. 'La imagen de la sociedad arcaica en Valle-Inclán', *Revista de Occidente*, 44–5 (1966), 225–56

Mariano, E., ed. *Atti del convegno su D'Annunzio e il simbolismo europeo*, Milan: Il Saggiatore, 1976

Marrast, Robert. 'Quelques clés pour *Divines paroles*', *Cahiers de la Compagnie Madeleine Renaud – Jean-Louis Barrault*, 43 (1963), 18–35

Marsillach, A. '*Aguila de blasón*', *Primer Acto*, 82 (1967), 22–8

Martínez Sierra, G. Interview with Valle-Inclán, *ABC*, 7 December 1928

ed. *Un teatro de arte en España: 1917–1926*, Madrid: Ediciones de la Esfinge, 1926

Martínez Torner, E. *Ensayos sobre estilística literaria española*, Oxford: Dolphin, 1953, pp. 110–13

Matilla Rivas, A. *Las 'Comedias bárbaras': historicismo y expresionismo dramático*, New York: Anaya, 1972

Miller, Liam. *The Noble Drama of W. B. Yeats*, Dublin: Dolmen Press, 1977

Montesinos, J. F. 'Modernismo, esperpentismo o las dos evasiones', *Revista de Occidente*, 44–5 (1966), 146–65

Morris, C. B. *This Loving Darkness: the Cinema and Spanish Writers – 1920–1936*, Oxford: OUP for University of Hull, 1980

Nietzsche, F. *The Birth of Tragedy* and *The Genealogy of Morals*. Trans. F. Golffing. New York: Doubleday Anchor Books, 1956

Thus Spake Zarathustra, London: Penguin Books, 1964

Nuez, S. de la and Schraibman, J., eds. *Cartas del archivo de Pérez Galdós*, Madrid: Taurus, 1967

Pérez, María Esther. *Valle-Inclán: su ambigüedad modernista*, Madrid: Colección Nova Scholar, 1977

Pérez de Ayala, R. 'Valle-Inclán, dramaturgo', in *Las máscaras*, Buenos Aires: Espasa Calpe, 1948, pp. 138–46
Pérez Minik, D. 'Valle-Inclán o la restauración del bululú', in *Debates sobre el teatro español contemporáneo*, Santa Cruz de Tenerife: Goya Ediciones, 1953, pp. 121–40
Quinto, J. Ma. de. 'Un teatro desconocido: el de Valle-Inclán', *Insula*, 236–7 (1966), 23–4
Reyes, A. 'La parodia trágica', *España*, 10 July 1920. Reprinted in *Simpatías y diferencias*, 2nd series, Madrid: Imprenta de E. Teodoro, 1921, pp. 19–33
Rhodes, A. *The Poet as Superman: D'Annunzio*, London: Weidenfeld & Nicolson, 1959
Risco, A. *La estética de Valle-Inclán en los esperpentos y en 'El ruedo ibérico'*, Madrid: Gredos, 1966
Rivas Cherif, C. 'Apunte de crítica literaria: La comedia bárbara de Valle-Inclán', *España*, 16 February 1924. Reprinted in J. Esteban, ed., *Valle-Inclán visto por. . .*, pp. 101–6
'Divulgación a luz de las candilejas', *La Pluma* (August 1920)
'Hombres, letras, ideas', *La Internacional*, 46 (3 September 1920), 4
'Más cosas de don Ramón', *La Pluma* (January 1923)
'Teatros', *España*, 29 March 1924
Rogerio Sánchez, J. *El teatro poético: Valle-Inclán, Marquina. Estudio crítico*, Madrid: Sucesores de Hernando, 1914
Rubia Barcia, J. *A Biobibliography and Iconography of Valle-Inclán 1866–1936*, Berkeley and Los Angeles: University of California Press, 1960
Ruiz Ramón, F. *Historia del teatro español*, 2 vols, Madrid: Alianza, 1971
Saillard, Simone. 'De D'Annunzio à Valle-Inclán ou la naissance d'un auteur dramatique', *Cahiers de la Compagnie Madeleine Renaud – Jean-Louis Barrault*, 43 (1963), 36–44
Sainz de Medrano Arce, Luis. 'Valle-Inclán en *La reina castiza*', *Cuadernos Hispanoamericanos*, 242 (1970), 395–406; 245 (1970) 442–60
Salper de Tortella, Roberta. 'Don Juan Manuel Montenegro: The fall of a king', in A. N. Zahareas, ed., *Appraisal*, pp. 317–33
Sánchez, R. 'Gordon Craig y Valle-Inclán', *Revista de Occidente*, 4 (1976), 27–37
Sansone, M. 'Conclusione del convegno' in *Atti del convegno su D'Annunzio e il simbolismo europeo*. Ed. E. Mariano, Milan: Il Saggiatore, 1976, pp. 415–22
Sastre, Alfonso. 'Tragedia y esperpento', *Primer Acto*, 28 (1961), 12–16
Saz Sánchez, A. del. *El teatro de Valle-Inclán*, Barcelona: Gráfica, 1950
Schiavo, Leda. 'Cartas inéditas de Valle-Inclán', *Insula*, 398 (1980)
'Tradición literaria y nuevo sentido en *La Marquesa Rosalinda*', *Filología* (Buenos Aires), 15 (1971–2), 291–7
Segura Covarsi, E. 'Cara de plata', *Revista de Literatura*, 9–10 (1954), 267–79
Sender, R. *Valle-Inclán y la dificultad de la tragedia*, Madrid: Gredos, 1965
Simonson, Lee. *The Stage is Set*, New York: Harcourt, Brace & Co., 1932
Smith, Verity. *Ramón María del Valle-Inclán*, New York: Twayne, 1973
Sobejano, G. 'Luces de bohemia, elegía y sátira', *Papeles de Son Armadans*, 127 (1966), 86–106
Nietzsche en España, Madrid: Gredos, 1967
'Valle-Inclán frente al realismo español', in A. N. Zahareas, ed., *Appraisal*, pp. 159–71
Soriano, Ignacio. '*La lámpara maravillosa*, clave de los esperpentos', *La Torre*, 62 (1968), 144–50
Soto, Luis Emilio. 'Valle-Inclán y el teatro nuevo: en cama con gripe y 40 grados de temperatura crítica', *La Nación*, 3 March 1929

Speratti-Piñero, E. S. 'La farsa de *La cabeza del dragón*, pre-esperpento', in *De 'Sonata de otoño' al esperpento*, London: Támesis, 1968, pp. 35–45. Also in A. N. Zahareas, ed., *Appraisal*, pp. 374–85

Stein, J. M. *Richard Wagner and the Synthesis of the Arts*, Detroit: Wayne State University Press, 1960

Symons, A. *The Symbolist Movement in Literature*, London: Heinemann, 1899

Tomás, M. Interview in the Prologue to *Zacarías el cruzado o Agüero nigromántico*, *La Novela de Hoy*, 225 (1926)

Torre, G. de. *La difícil universalidad española*, Madrid: Gredos, 1965

Tosi, G. 'D'Annunzio et le symbolisme français', in *Atti del convegno su D'Annunzio e il simbolismo europeo*, Ed. E. Mariano, Milan: Il Saggiatore, 1976, pp. 223–82

Umpierre, G. '*Divinas palabras': alusión y alegoría*, Chapel Hill: University of North Carolina: Estudios de Hispanófila 18, 1971

'Muerte y transfiguración de don Juan Manuel Montenegro', *Bulletin of Hispanic Studies*, 50 (1973), 270–77

Velázquez Bringas, E. Interview with Valle-Inclán, *Repertorio Americano*, III, 13 (1921), 171

Wagner, R. *Prose Works*, Trans. W. Ashton Ellis, 5 vols, London: Kegan Paul, Trench, Trübner, 1895.

Weber, F. W. '*Luces de bohemia* and the impossibility of art', *Modern Language Notes*, 82 (1967), 575–89

Wilson, E. *Axel's Castle*, London: Collins, 1961

Yeats, W. B. *Essays and Introductions*, London: Macmillan, 1961

Plays and Controversies, London: Macmillan, 1927

Zahareas, A. N. 'The Absurd, the Grotesque and the Esperpento', in A. N. Zahareas, ed., *Appraisal*, pp. 78–108

'La desvaloración del sentido trágico en el esperpento de Valle-Inclán', *Insula*, 203 (1963), 1, 15

'La elaboración de la historia en *Luces de Bohemia*', in A. N. Zahareas, ed., *Appraisal*, pp. 622–9

'The esperpento and the aesthetics of commitment', *Modern Language Notes*, 81 (1966), 159–73

'Friolera: el héroe visto con "la perspectiva de la otra ribera"', in A. N. Zahareas, ed., *Appraisal*, pp. 630–35

ed. *Luces de Bohemia*. Trans. A. N. Zahareas and G. Gillespie. Edinburgh: Edinburgh Bilingual Library, 1976

ed. *Ramón del Valle-Inclán. An Appraisal of his Life and Works*, New York: Las Américas, 1968

Zamora Vicente, A. *La realidad esperpéntica: aproximación a 'Luces de bohemia'*, Madrid: Gredos, 1969

Index